# IDEA MAN

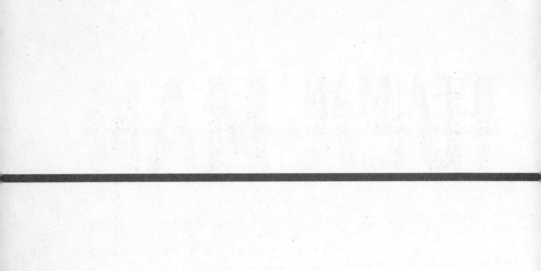

# IDEA MAN

A MEMOIR BY THE
COFOUNDER OF MICROSOFT

## PAUL ALLEN

PORTFOLIO/PENGUIN

PORTFOLIO / PENGUIN
Published by the Penguin Group
Penguin Group (USA) Inc., 375 Hudson Street,
New York, New York 10014, U.S.A.
Penguin Group (Canada), 90 Eglinton Avenue East, Suite 700,
Toronto, Ontario, Canada M4P 2Y3
(a division of Pearson Penguin Canada Inc.)
Penguin Books Ltd, 80 Strand, London WC2R 0RL, England
Penguin Ireland, 25 St. Stephen's Green, Dublin 2, Ireland
(a division of Penguin Books Ltd)
Penguin Books Australia Ltd, 250 Camberwell Road, Camberwell,
Victoria 3124, Australia
(a division of Pearson Australia Group Pty Ltd)
Penguin Books India Pvt Ltd, 11 Community Centre, Panchsheel Park,
New Delhi – 110 017, India
Penguin Group (NZ), 67 Apollo Drive, Rosedale, Auckland 0632,
New Zealand (a division of Pearson New Zealand Ltd)
Penguin Books (South Africa) (Pty) Ltd, 24 Sturdee Avenue,
Rosebank, Johannesburg 2196, South Africa

Penguin Books Ltd, Registered Offices:
80 Strand, London WC2R 0RL, England

First published in 2011 by Portfolio / Penguin,
a member of Penguin Group (USA) Inc.

10  9  8  7  6  5  4  3  2  1

Grateful acknowledgment is made for permission to reprint an excerpt from "Purple Haze," written by Jimi Hendrix, published by Experience Hendrix, L.L.C. Used by permission. All rights reserved.

LIBRARY OF CONGRESS CATALOGING IN PUBLICATION DATA
Allen, Paul, 1953–
    Idea man : a memoir by the cofounder of Microsoft / Paul Allen.
       p. cm.
    Includes index.
    ISBN 978-1-59184-382-5
    1. Allen, Paul, 1953–   2. Businesspeople—United States—Biography. I. Title.
    HC102.5.A49A3 2011
    338.7'610053092—dc22
    [B]
    2010043588

Printed in the United States of America
Set in Sabon Lt Std
Designed by Jaime Putorti

_Penguin is committed to publishing works of quality and integrity._
_In that spirit, we are proud to offer this book to our readers;_
_however, the story, the experiences, and the words_
_are the author's alone._

FOR MY PARENTS

# CONTENTS

# IDEA MAN

# CHAPTER 1

# OPPORTUNITY

As I walked toward Harvard Square on a December weekend afternoon in 1974, I had no inkling that my life was about to change. The weather was snowy and cold, and I was twenty-one years old and at loose ends. My girlfriend had left a few weeks earlier to return to our hometown of Seattle three thousand miles away. I was three semesters shy of graduation at Washington State University, where I'd taken two breaks in the last two years. I had a dead-end job at Honeywell, a crummy apartment, and a '64 Chrysler New Yorker that was burning oil. Unless something came along by summer, I'd be going back myself to finish my degree.

The one constant in my life those days was a Harvard undergraduate named Bill Gates, my partner in crime since we'd met at Lakeside School when he was in eighth grade and I was in tenth. Bill and I learned how to dissect computer code together. We'd started one failed business and worked side by side on professional programming jobs while still in our teens. It was Bill who had coaxed me to move to Massachusetts with a plan to quit school and join him at a tech firm. Then he reversed field to return to college. Like me, he seemed restless and ready to try something new.

Bill and I kept casting about for a commercial project. We figured that we'd eventually write some software, where we knew we had some talent. Over grinders or a pepperoni pie at the Harvard

House of Pizza, we fantasized about our entrepreneurial future. One time I asked Bill, "If everything went right, how big do you think our company could be?"

He said, "I think we could get it up to thirty-five programmers." That sounded really ambitious to me.

Since the dawn of integrated-circuit technology in the 1950s, forward thinkers had envisioned ever more powerful and economical computers. In 1965, in a journal called *Electronics,* a young research physicist named Gordon Moore made that prediction specific. He asserted that the maximum number of transistors in an integrated circuit would double each year without raising the chip's cost. After cofounding Intel in 1968, Moore amended the rate of doubling to once every two years—still dramatic. Similar trends soon emerged in computer processing speed and disk storage capacity. It was a simple but profound observation that holds true to this day. Because of continual advances in chip technology, computers will keep getting markedly faster and cheaper.

The momentum of Moore's law became more evident in 1969, a few months after I'd met Bill. (I was sixteen then, just learning to program on a mainframe computer.) A Japanese company called Busicom asked Intel to design chips for a cheap handheld calculator that could undercut the competition. Busicom assumed that the new machine would require twelve integrated-circuit chips. But Ted Hoff, one of Intel's electrical engineers, had a bold idea: to shave costs by consolidating the components of a fully functioning computer onto a single chip, what came to be called a microprocessor.

Before these new chips arrived on the scene, it took dozens or hundreds of integrated circuits to perform one narrow function, from traffic lights to gas pumps to printer terminals. Microwave-oven-size minicomputers, the machines that bridged mainframes and the microcomputers yet to come, followed the same formula: one chip, one purpose. But Hoff's invention was far more versatile. As Gordon Moore noted, "Now we can make a single chip and sell it for several thousand different applications." In November 1971,

Moore and Robert Noyce, the co-inventor of the integrated circuit, introduced the Intel 4004 microchip at a price of $200. The launch advertisement in *Electronic News* proclaimed "a new era of integrated electronics."

Few people took notice of the 4004 early on, but I was a college freshman that year and had time to read every magazine and journal around. It was a fertile period for computers, with new models coming out almost monthly. When I first came across the 4004, I reacted like an engineer: What cool things could you do with this?

At first glance, Intel's new chip looked like the core of a really nice calculator. But as I read on, I could see that it had all the digital circuitry of a true central processing unit, or CPU, the brains of any computing machine. The 4004 was no toy. Unlike application-specific integrated circuits, it could execute a program from external memory. Within the limits of its architecture, the world's first microprocessor was more or less a computer on a chip, just as the ads said. It was the first harbinger of the day when computers would be affordable for everyone.

Four months later, as I continued to "follow the chips," I came across the inevitable next step. In March 1972, *Electronics* announced the Intel 8008. Its 8-bit architecture could handle far more complex problems than the 4004, and it addressed up to sixteen thousand (16K) bytes of memory, enough for a fair-size program. The business world saw the 8008 as a low-budget controller for stoplights or conveyor belts. (In that vein, Bill and I would later use it in our fledgling enterprise in traffic flow analysis.) But I knew that this second-generation microchip could do much more, given the chance.

My really big ideas have all begun with a stage-setting development—in this case, the evolution of Intel's early microprocessor chips. Then I ask a few basic questions: Where is the leading edge of discovery headed? What *should* exist but doesn't yet? How can I create something to help meet the need, and who might be enlisted to join the crusade?

Whenever I've had a moment of insight, it has come from combining two or more elements to galvanize a new technology and bring breakthrough applications to a potentially vast audience. A few months after the 8008 was announced, one of those brain waves came to me. *What if a microprocessor could run a high-level language, the essential tool for programming a general-purpose computer?*

It was plain to me from the outset that we'd use BASIC (Beginner's All-Purpose Symbolic Instruction Code), the relatively simple language that Bill and I learned back at Lakeside in our first computer experience. The latest minicomputer from Digital Equipment Corporation, the PDP-11, already ran the more complex FORTRAN on as little as 16K of memory. While an 8008 machine would be quite a bit slower, I thought it should be able to perform most of the same functions at a fraction of the PDP-11's cost. Ordinary people would be able to buy computers for their offices, even their homes, for the very first time. An 8008 BASIC could swing open the gate to an array of applications for a limitless clientele.

And so I asked Bill, "Why don't we do a BASIC for the 8008?"

He looked at me quizzically and said, "Because it would be dogslow and pathetic. And BASIC by itself would take up almost all the memory. There's just not enough horsepower—it would be a waste of time." After a moment's reflection, I knew he was probably right. Then he said, "When they come out with a faster chip, let me know."

Bill and I had already found a groove together. I was the idea man, the one who'd conceive of things out of whole cloth. Bill listened and challenged me, and then homed in on my best ideas to help make them a reality. Our collaboration had a natural tension, but mostly it worked productively and well.

Long before coming to Massachusetts, I'd been speculating about the next-generation chip, which had to be coming soon. I was sure someone would build a computer around it—something like a minicomputer, but so inexpensive that it would recast the market. Writing to Intel to find a local 8008 vendor for our traffic machine, I asked about their future plans. On July 10, 1972, a manager named Hank Smith responded:

*We do not intend to introduce any chips in the future which will obsolete the 8008. Our strategy will be to introduce a new family of devices which will cover the upper end of the market (the point where the 8008 leaves off, up through mini computers). . . . The introduction for the new family of devices is targeted for mid 1974.*

I had no way of knowing that Federico Faggin, the great chip designer, was already pushing Intel management to start work on the Intel 8080, to be heralded by *Electronics* in the spring of 1974. The newest microprocessor could address four times as much memory as its predecessor. It was three times as powerful and much easier to program. Hank Smith was wrong; the 8008 would soon be obsolete. As Faggin would say, "The 8080 really created the microprocessor market. The 4004 and 8008 suggested it, but the 8080 made it real."

One thing seemed certain: The 8080 met the criteria for a BASIC-ready microprocessor. As soon as I read the news, I said to Bill, "This is the chip we talked about." I regaled him with the 8080's virtues, not least its bargain price of $360. Bill agreed that the 8080 was capable and the price was right. But writing a new BASIC from scratch was a big job, something we'd never done, and the fact remained that no computer existed to run it on. Which meant there was no market. "You're right, it's a good idea," he said. "Come back and tell me when there's a machine for it."

I kept prodding Bill to reconsider, to help me develop an 8080 BASIC before someone beat us. "Let's start a company," I'd say. "It'll be too late if we wait—we'll miss it!" In my journal entry dated October 23, 1974, I wrote: "Saw Bill Monday night and we may end up writing Basic Compiler/Operating System for 8080." But that was wishful thinking. Bill wasn't ready, and I couldn't forge ahead without him. The whole point of my moving to Boston had been for us to do something special as a team.

We both knew that big changes were coming. But we didn't know what shape they'd take until that chilly December day in Harvard Square.

OUT OF TOWN NEWS sat in the middle of the square. It was near the Harvard Coop, where I occasionally nosed around for books, and across the street from Brigham's Ice Cream, where Bill and I went for chocolate shakes. I'd stop by the stand each month to check on periodicals like *Radio Electronics* and *Popular Science*. I'd purchase any that caught my eye, passing over the covers that hyped build-your-own ham radio transmitters.

Like most magazines, *Popular Electronics* was postdated by a week or two. I was hunting for its new January issue—which stopped me in my tracks. The cover headline looked like this:

PROJECT BREAKTHROUGH!
World's First Minicomputer Kit
to Rival Commercial Models . . .
"ALTAIR 8800" SAVE OVER $1000

Beneath the large-font type was a gray box with rows of lights and binary switches on its front panel, just the sort of thing I'd been imagining.* Given the magazine's frugal, do-it-yourself readership, I knew there had to be a single microprocessor inside; hordes of conventional chips would have cost too much. One question remained: Was that microprocessor the limited Intel 8008 or the turbocharged 8080? I suspected—I hoped—for the 8080.

---

*Little did I know that the "machine" on the cover was in fact a hollow mock-up, subbed in at the last minute after the genuine Altair prototype was delayed in shipping by a Railway Express strike.

I plucked a copy from the rack and riffled through it, my anticipation rising. I found the story on page 33, with another photo of the Altair and a harder-sell headline:

ALTAIR 8800
The most powerful minicomputer
project ever presented—can be built
for under $400.

The first sentence of the text, by H. Edward Roberts and William Yates of MITS, the machine's manufacturer, was the stuff of Allen-Gates dreams: "The era of the computer in every home—a favorite topic among science-fiction writers—has arrived!" The Altair represented "a full-blown computer that can hold its own against sophisticated minicomputers now on the market," but "in a color TV receiver's price class."

The next paragraph clinched it: "In many ways, [the Altair] represents a revolutionary development in electronic design and thinking. . . . Its central processing unit is a new LSI [large-scale integration] chip that is many times more powerful than previous IC processors." That CPU was the 8080. *Bill's got his answer now!* I thought.

I slapped down seventy-five cents and trotted the half-dozen slushy blocks to Bill's room in Harvard's Currier House. I burst in on him cramming for finals; it was that time of year. "You remember what you told me?" I said, feeling vindicated and a little breathless. "To let you know when somebody came out with a machine based on the 8080?"

"Yeah, I remember."

"Well, here it is," I said, holding out the magazine with a flourish. "Check it out!"

As Bill read the story, he began rocking back and forth in his chair, a sign that he was deep in concentration. I could tell he was impressed. "It's expandable, just like a minicomputer," he murmured. Priced at $397 in kit form, scarcely more than a retail 8080 chip alone, the base Altair came with only 256 bytes of memory, just enough to program its lights to blink. But more could be added with plug-in memory cards. Throw in an input/output board and an I/O audiocassette recorder* or a rented Teletype, and you'd have a working machine for under two thousand dollars. Affordability would change everything—not just for hobbyists, but for scientists and businesspeople. And it seemed likely that the Altair could run an interactive language like BASIC, the idea dancing in my head for the past three years.

We were looking at the first commercial personal computer.

Bill set the magazine down, and we planned our next move. The good news was that our train was leaving the station at last. The bad: We had no idea if we'd be in time to board. Though the article made vague references to BASIC and FORTRAN, it wasn't clear whether MITS already had 8080-based languages available or in development. In either case, we'd be sunk.

Hoping for the best, we sent a letter to the company's president on our old traffic-machine business stationery, implying that we had a BASIC ready to roll out. When we didn't hear back, we followed up with a phone call. "You should talk to them. You're older," Bill said.

"No, you should do it, you're better at this kind of thing," I said. We compromised: Bill would make the call but would say he was me. When it came time to meet with MITS face-to-face, our thinking went, I'd be the one to make the trip. I had my beard going and at least looked like an adult, while Bill—who'd routinely get carded into his thirties—still could pass for a high school sophomore.

"Ed Roberts."

---

*Between the paper tape era and the popularization of floppy disks, audiocassettes had a brief run in the midseventies as a leading storage device for microcomputers.

"This is Paul Allen in Boston," Bill said. "We've got a BASIC for the Altair that's just about finished, and we'd like to come out and show it to you." I admired Bill's bravado but worried that he'd gone too far, since we'd yet to write the first line of code.

Roberts was interested, but he was getting ten calls a day from people with similar claims. He told Bill what he'd told everyone else: The first person to walk through his door in Albuquerque with a BASIC that worked would get a contract for the Altair. (As Ed later retold the story in his inimitable style, he'd settled on BASIC because you "could teach any idiot how to use [it] in no time at all.") There was nothing we could do for the moment, he said. MITS was still debugging its in-house memory cards, which they'd need to run a BASIC demo on the Altair. They'd be ready for us in a month.

The whole conversation took five minutes. When it was over, Bill and I looked at each other. It was one thing to talk about writing a language for a microprocessor and another to get the job done. Later I'd discover that MITS's own engineers doubted that an 8080 BASIC was possible.

If we'd been older or known better, Bill and I might have been put off by the task in front of us. But we were young and green enough to believe that we just might pull it off.

# CHAPTER 2

# ROOTS

In the 1940 *Darkonian,* two quarter-page portraits mark the top student honors at Anadarko High School in central Oklahoma. "All-Around Boy" Kenneth Allen, his blond hair slicked back, meets the camera with a square jaw and a confident smile. Edna Faye Gardner, "All-Around Girl," has her hair curled above a heart-shaped face. Even in black and white, her eyes shine.

I know that look well. My mother is eighty-eight now, and not what she was, but you can still feel the positive energy in those eyes.

My parents grew up in hard times and came of age as the world went to war; they had smarts and ambition, but little was given to them. In Anadarko (population 5,579), a small county seat seventy miles southwest of Oklahoma City, they moved in different spheres. Bubbly and petite, a star student who sang in all the music groups, my mother worked nights in the local library, a job tailored to her teenage goal: to read at least one novel from every great author in the world. "Sam" Allen, the student-council president, played center on the varsity football team and excelled at track. (His nickname came from a famous high hurdler of the day, "Sailing Sam.") He moved with the popular crowd, at least until he began showing up at the library. My father liked adventure stories and Westerns, but his interests weren't strictly literary. One day he came to my mother's front door, aiming to ask her to the senior prom.

He never got the chance. As he stood there, turning his hat in his big hands, my mother chatted about the latest book she'd enjoyed. She had grown up with four older brothers and wasn't shy around boys. It just never occurred to her to ask why my father might have come to call. Flustered and red-faced, he left and stalked home. He should have known better.

None the wiser, my mother went to the prom with her friends, without a date. She had a wonderful time.

Three years later, my parents were engaged.

THE FIRST TIME I visited my relatives in Anadarko, I was startled by their accents. My parents were in their late twenties before they left Oklahoma for good, yet I'd never heard a trace of a twang or drawl from either one of them. As my mother told me, "We just decided we were going to speak good English, and that's what we did." When they joined the postwar exodus and made their way to California and then to Seattle, they were leaving their old lives behind. I think they wanted something more, something bigger for themselves and their children to come.

After I was born, in 1953, my mother went back to teaching fourth grade at Ravenna School in north Seattle. Curious and friendly, with an easy laugh, Faye Allen was the kind of teacher whose former students stopped her in the street ten years later for a hug. She read aloud with perfect diction, pausing dramatically at points of maximum suspense to leave the children panting for the next day's installment. I'd feel the same way at bedtime, when I'd beg for one more chapter of *The Swiss Family Robinson*. My mother stopped working after my sister, Jody, was born, five years after me, and I think it was hard for her. "I loved teaching," she'd say. "It's not like work. It's like *living*."

MY FATHER BOUGHT a house on a GI loan and we moved to Wedgwood, a newly developed area north of the University of

Washington. It was a typical Seattle neighborhood: hilly and green, with mature cherry trees and wood-frame homes on quarter-acre lots. There wasn't much traffic, and fathers and sons could toss a football in the street after dinner. Our neighbors included a truck driver and a French couple who owned a restaurant. Our two-story, three-bedroom house had dark gray shingles, a peaked roof, a small front lawn, and a fair-size backyard.

We also had a basement that said a lot about us. On one side sat the laundry machines; on another, when I got older, my chemistry lab; along a third, my dad's workshop, with tools hung on a pegboard. My mother's mountains of literature were stacked two volumes deep on surplus university bookshelves and spilled onto the floor alongside piles of the *New Yorker*. It got worse after she volunteered to price books at the Wise Penny thrift shop and came home each time with a share of the inventory.

My mother read everything, from the classics to the latest novels: Bellow and Balzac, Jane Austen and Chinua Achebe, Nadine Gordimer and Lin Yü-t'ang. That basement jumble was the exception to her otherwise thorough housekeeping. She kept promising to straighten it up but couldn't bear to throw away so much as a *National Geographic*. My father did win one concession, however. After my mother woke him one night because she was too scared to head to the bathroom by herself, he laid down the law: no more ghost stories.

I was reading on my own well before kindergarten. I can remember leafing through some illustrated primer when the page clicked into focus and the words suddenly made sense. Not long after that, for Christmas, I was given an oversize picture book with everything a four-year-old could want to know about steam shovels, tractors, backhoes, and fire engines. I read that book every day. Seeing my interest, my mother had a friend give me a tutorial on steam engines. It wasn't very technical, but I got my first inkling about the gears and belts and all the other hidden things that make a machine come alive.

That book opened a new world to me. Soon I was pleading for one on gasoline engines. Later I progressed to steam turbines and eventually to atomic power plants and rocket engines. I'd pore over each volume, not getting all the details but grasping enough to satisfy me. On some elemental level, the magical became logical. I began to understand how these things worked.

AT AGE THREE, I went to Mrs. Perkins's musical preschool down the hill and made her life miserable. I detested standing in line. If I found a good picture book, I would not eat my soup when it was time to eat soup. I moved on to Ravenna School as a self-taught child who was stubbornly unregimented. In kindergarten, according to my progress report, I needed "greater effort" in observing school rules and complying with the fire drills. In first grade, a few other boys and I found a big metal ring in the cloakroom. We had no idea what it was for, and we dared each other to turn it, a little further each day. One morning I said, "What the heck," and turned it all the way.

That was a dark day for Ravenna School. The sinks wouldn't work; the toilets didn't flush; drinking fountains ran dry. Dishes piled up in the cafeteria, unwashed. I had shut off the building's main water valve, and no one could find the plan for the circa-1920 plumbing. They had to let school out early.

The next morning the assistant principal came to my classroom and said, "Who turned off the valve in the coatroom?"

I slowly raised my hand and said, "I did it." I think he was surprised that anyone would confess.

Sometimes I could get absentminded. One afternoon I set a book down before a dodgeball match and then straggled home without it. The principal summoned me the next day and asked, "Paul, why did you set your math book on fire?" It wasn't me, of course; it was another kid who'd found the book and probably hated long division. Despite my denials, the principal insisted on calling my mother.

She came in with a stern look and declared, "In our family we love books. My son would never burn one." Case closed. I knew that I could always count on my mother's support. Each morning she would send me into the world with a paraphrase of the Spartan mothers' farewell to their sons marching off to war: "Go forth bearing your shield!" I walked out the door a little straighter when I heard that.

MY FATHER WAS like a John Wayne character: big and strong at six foot three, a man of few words but with a huge heart and a strict code of honor. He was serious, direct, and deliberate, with a reason for everything he did. "A gentle bear of a man for all his gruffness," I'd write in a high-school-era journal. "He believes in a good solid purpose in life." He could surprise us, though. One Halloween, as my sister and I came home from trick-or-treating, a menacing figure in a white sheet and an African mask jumped out at us with a terrible yell. We ran into the house shrieking, totally petrified. I was stunned two days later when my mother told me who it was.

In a portrait in crayon, at age eight, I drew my father with a wrench in one hand and a screwdriver in his shirt pocket: a doer, not a talker. When you live with someone who doesn't say much, you come to rely on intuition and body language. I could always tell when my father was displeased about something.

We had dinner together at six sharp. For a while, we brought books to the table, but then they were banned because three of us would read while my father sat silently with his steak. (After growing up in the Depression, he loved having sirloin at least twice a week.) Generally soft-spoken, he'd resolve any issue in what I called his "command voice." He wasn't flexible or tolerant of easy excuses; if you'd agreed to be home by a certain hour, there was no grace period. He quietly held us to high standards, to treat people honorably and stand by our word.

My father never spanked us. He motioned to take off his belt once or twice, but I'd escape with a fervent promise to do better.

It could be different with my mother, a softhearted but more emotional soul. One evening I asked her to make popcorn, and she agreed on the condition that I'd clean my messy room, an oft-broken promise of mine. The next morning, the room still in disarray, she burst in with an open can of Jolly Time Pop Corn, flung the raw kernels at me, and cried, "These are your broken words!" Which made me feel terrible, though I didn't much improve in the cleaning department.

Another time, when I came home two hours after my curfew, she was furious. I was small enough that she could yank me up by the legs and dangle me upside down: "Don't you ever stay out without telling us where you are!" I can still see the nickels and pennies falling from my pockets and past my head to the floor.

My mother was a naturally gregarious woman who could strike up a ten-minute conversation with the grocery checkout lady. But she had a husband who didn't like to socialize, and I can count on my fingers the number of times my parents had other couples to our house. I remember one party, and a second one, and then they tailed off. My mother made the best of it by inviting women friends for afternoon tea and leading a book club, when she could listen and talk to her heart's content.

IN 1960, my father became associate director of the University of Washington's library complex, the number-two job in the largest system in the Northwest. When it came time to name a new director, the UW search committee passed him over for someone from the University of Texas with more degrees. When he got home at 5:30 and I'd ask about his day, his answer never varied: "Fine."

Then he was off to his garden; he was a great relaxer. He seemed happiest amid his bonsai pines and rhododendrons and the live Christmas tree he'd transplanted, which today stands sixty feet high. He'd begun gardening in the backyard and progressed to the front, until there was hardly a patch of lawn left to mow—a happy development for me, as I was allergic to grass pollen. Sunday mornings he'd take me to the nursery, and we'd return with yet another Japanese maple and a fresh-baked apple pie.

Our closest connection came when we fished together. On one Pacific Coast trip, my father had to hold me on board after I hooked a twenty-five-pound king salmon. Every summer the family went for a week to Twin Lakes Resort, where my job was to clean the trout before it hit the pan on the wood-burning stove. Then we'd all play pinochle into the night.

My father was selectively eclectic; he delved deeply into half a dozen pastimes over the course of his life, but no more. He introduced me to Stan Getz and Andrés Segovia, and to Indian art at the Burke Museum. He befriended a local modern artist, and his favorite living room chair sat under a framed Rouault print of a king holding a flower. In midlife he became a connoisseur of Japanese prints and Chinese celadon pottery. You'd see him linger in a store, turning some delicate vase over and over and murmuring, "That's really beautiful." He'd give it back to the proprietor and return six months later to buy it if it wasn't too expensive.

While my mother zipped through five books at once from four different continents, my father took months to digest *The Rise and Fall of the Third Reich* or *The Guns of August*. He kept reading about World War II as though trying to puzzle it out. He'd been in the thick of it as a lieutenant with the 501st Quartermaster Railhead Company in France and Germany, and it still tore at him. He'd been a lot livelier and more talkative, my mother said, before he came back from overseas with a Bronze Star and memories of a dead friend.

I was still young when my father first asked me what I wanted to do with my life. It was his way of imparting his laconic wisdom: "When you grow up and have a job, do something you love. Whatever you do, you should love it." He'd repeat this to me over the years with conviction. Later I'd figure out what he meant: Do as I say, not as I've done. Much later, my mother told me that my father had wrestled with his career choice. He suspected he might be happier coaching football than managing libraries, but he finally chose the safe and practical route, a nine-to-five life under fluorescent lights. Lots of men from his generation did the same.

But he wanted me to choose better.

THE OFFICIAL GOAL of the 1962 Seattle World's Fair was to inspire young people to pursue careers in science. The unofficial goal was to show that the United States had caught up to the Soviet Union in technology and the space race. But for me, a nine-year-old who'd just discovered science fiction, the Century 21 Exposition (as it was officially titled) revolved around my favorite thing: the future. It was like waking up to find my most outlandish ideas made real, just four miles from my house.

As I watched the fairgrounds take shape, the anticipation felt like Christmas squared. I beheld the transportation of the future, the gleaming white monorail gliding along its mile-long track. And the architecture of the future, the Space Needle, then the highest building west of the Mississippi, with a rotating restaurant on top that looked just like a flying saucer. Soon after the fair opened, my mother took Jody and me for our first visit. There's a picture of me that day in my beloved synthetic rubber hat with earflaps, the one I wore for two years until it melted on a radiator. I look as though I'm jumping out of my skin with excitement.

We were there from nine to nine, plenty of time for my mother and sister to roam the sprawling grounds. But I wouldn't budge from the science pavilion. I ran around like a kid on a sugar high—what to see next? After the Spacearium took me through the Milky Way, I found NASA's Project Mercury capsule, the one that had carried Alan Shepard, the first American in space. I watched up close as a Tesla coil threw off twenty-foot-long purple sparks. Before a crowd of thousands, a jet-belted "astronaut" took off with a loud hissing noise and flew forty feet high for what had to be a hundred yards, like a character out of Robert Heinlein. The line between present and future felt very permeable that day. It was only a matter of when.

My mother finally came back for me and took us to the World of Tomorrow and the Bubbleator, a transparent, spherical elevator. (I loved the Bubbleator, just the idea of the Bubbleator.) At the Food Circus, I tried tempura prawns, basically shrimp on a stick with a tangy sauce, plus my first Belgian waffle, which seemed like the most exotic and delicious thing I'd ever eaten. You can catch a close-up of that waffle in an Elvis Presley movie called *It Happened at the World's Fair:* an oversize, crispy square slathered with whipped cream and topped with sliced strawberries and powdered sugar. I've been to Belgium more than once since then, but I've never again had one so good.

On our way out that night, with me wide-awake and starry-eyed, we had more excitement in the parking lot. A Volkswagen had parked behind our Buick, hemming us in. My mother was getting flustered when two hulking lumberjacks materialized to come to her aid with some nineteenth-century manpower. They picked up the little Bug and slid it aside, and we drove home.

LOOKING BACK, I had remarkable exposure to science when I was young. I could go to weekend open houses at the university's labs, where professors and students showed off their latest experiments. On a family visit to UCLA, where my aunt worked, I learned how they made synthetic diamonds and how seismometers recorded earthquakes. Willard Libby, the inventor of carbon dating, poured liquid nitrogen over my hand. I didn't get frost-burned, Libby explained, because a thin layer of vaporized gas cushioned each drop on my skin.

For a time, around fourth grade, chemistry became my number-one hobby. At St. Vincent de Paul, a thrift-shop gold mine, I picked up secondhand sets for fifty cents apiece. Soon the shelves of my basement lab were chockablock with beakers and test tubes and containers of brightly colored chemicals. It was all good, educational fun. Until, that is, I nearly killed the family pet.

Jett Black Allen was a frisky Manchester terrier, a prince of dogs: intelligent, sensitive, eager to please. My father couldn't resist sharing dinner from the table, carefully cutting steak into bite-size pieces. Bred as rat catchers back in England, Manchesters are highly athletic; once my father stopped feeding him, Jett would leap into the air to beg for more. At first it was funny to see his head bobbing up above the tabletop, but after a while it got tiresome, and Jett was exiled to the basement at mealtimes.

One day I'd been working on a chlorine gas generator, using Clorox bleach, when I got called up to dinner. Midway through the meal, we heard a strange noise, somewhere between a wheeze and a choking rasp. What was that? Back to our food and talk, we heard it again, louder this time, clearly coming from downstairs. I trailed behind Dad, who pushed open the basement door. There was Jett, quivering at the top of the stairs. At the bottom it looked like a foggy morning on the Okefenokee, with two feet of yellow-green chlorine gas blanketing the floor. Jett had made the smart move to get as far as possible from the toxic fumes.

As my father raised the basement windows to clear out the gas, he said, "You've got to be more careful with your experiments, Paul."

But I also heard what he didn't say: He never told me to stop. In the Allen household, children were treated like grown-ups. Our parents encouraged us at whatever we tried, and exposed us to Bach and jazz and flamenco, but it was more than that. They respected us as individuals who needed to find our own place in the world.

SOON I WAS buying books on how to build small circuits: amplifiers, radio receivers, blinkers. I'd cart around a shoebox with batteries and lights and switches, the bits and pieces of my half-completed projects. In fifth grade, I read every science book I could find, along with bound issues of *Popular Mechanics* that were hauled home from the university library, to be devoured ten or twelve at a gulp. The magazines commonly had futuristic cars or robots on the cover. The whole culture back then was charged with schemes and speculation about technology, some of which wound up coming true.

By sixth grade, I'd taken up electronics, which became even more fun when I found my first real partner. Doug Fullmer was a classmate who wore heavy horn-rimmed glasses and lived a block and a half up the hill. We were the kind of boys who could talk for hours about physics or astronomy. Living at the cusp between the analog world around us and the digital age about to engulf it, we couldn't learn enough about either one.

Later an electrical engineer at Raytheon, Doug shared my excitement when my dad bought me a Van de Graaff generator kit. It had a belt-driven motor that built up static electricity on an aluminum ball, enough for a two-inch spark. Or you could put your hand over it to make your hair stand on end. I suffered through my share of trial and error; once I nearly electrocuted myself when I grabbed both leads of a transformer at the same time. My muscles clamped up for ten interminable seconds before I could let go, my first near-death experience. But I liked electronics because its applications were open-ended, and you didn't need an instruction book to create something new. Soon my jars of chemicals were collecting dust.

I was the top boy in my class, but I couldn't keep up with Stephanie Hazle because I got B's in phys ed and spelling, and she got straight A's. I was third-chair violin and Stephanie was first chair, and she was smug about it. She was smart and superconfident, but I just thought she was mean.

One day I came to school with a jerry-rigged step-up transformer. The whole class lined up to hold the bare wire contacts, and kids giggled when they felt the tingle of electricity. But when Stephanie's turn came, I moved a wire that raised the voltage from one battery to five. I knew it was harmless, because the current would last only a split second. But it was strong enough to make Stephanie scream and get reprimanded by the teacher. All the other kids had liked it, after all. Why was she making such a fuss?

Almost instantly, my guilt overwhelmed my sense of satisfaction and lasted a lot longer. I still cringe when I think about it.

THE FORCE OF nature always intrigued me. I was spellbound when my mother told us about the time she and my father outran a cluster of tornados at the University of Oklahoma, where my father got his undergraduate degree after the war. My mother wanted him to park beside a ditch under a big tree, but my father gunned the car and kept driving until he got to Anadarko. Later they went back to the university, and that big tree was just *gone*.

One day in sixth grade, I was sitting in a temporary classroom for orchestra practice when I noticed something odd. The nested rings of light fixtures, hung by cables from the ceiling, were swaying like pendulums. Our teacher stayed focused on the score until she finally looked up and shouted, "Everybody out of the portable!" I ran onto the playground, my violin still in my hands, and found the asphalt rippling like waves in the ocean. *That's really strange,* I thought. Later I heard that the earthquake measured over 6.5 on the Richter scale. Rumor had it that the top of the Space Needle swung more than fifteen feet side to side, far enough for water to slosh out of the restaurant's toilets.

I have a copy of the Sears Christmas catalog from 1960, when I was about to turn eight. It's filled with items to quicken a boy's pulse: a set of bongo drums; a student microscope to "reveal the invisible world"; a seven-unit Lionel electric train, complete with "guided missile" for blowing up the boxcar. For $17.98, you could purchase a kit for the Brainiac K-30, a "mechanical brain" that "computes, reasons, does arithmetical and logical problems . . . solves puzzles . . . plays games . . . works out codes—and more."

I knew from science fiction about big machines called computers that did wondrous things. But it was all vague until I turned eleven, when my mother took me for an after-the-dentist treat, a trip to the university bookstore. Passing the adventure section, where I'd already polished off the likes of *Tom Swift and His*

*Flying Lab,* I chose a beginner's volume about computers. In the simplest terms, it explained the fundamental bi-stable circuit, with an illustration of a flip-flop toggling between two transistors. In analog technology, boosting the input amplified output, much like increasing the flow of water from a faucet. But as a true digital device, the flip-flop circuit's state was either one or zero, on or off. That book stripped the haze from computers and began to teach me how they really worked.

Years later, I went with Doug to a science workshop at the Seattle Center, the former site of the world's fair, and helped him build a light-activated robot on wheels that we called the Electronic Paramecium. Long before *Star Wars,* it resembled a scaled-down R2-D2. Although the robot never quite came together, the *idea* that we might do something so sophisticated was almost more exciting than the work itself. It was one more exercise that expanded my sense of the possible.

BACK AT ST. VINCENT DE PAUL, Doug and I trolled for perfectly good televisions with blown vacuum tubes. We'd extract the tubes one by one and plug in spares that we'd bought for a dollar. When a set was beyond repair, I used a soldering iron to cannibalize the parts. (The work could be hazardous. One time I heard a sizzling sound, looked down, and found a glob of solder drilling a hole into my knee.) We also got some toaster-size tube radio sets up and running, and I'd tune into local stations for rock 'n' roll or R & B. Those late-forties radios became my gateway into popular music.

For Christmas in 1964, my parents gave me a three-transistor Sony, my first solid-state device—impossibly small, no larger than a pack of cigarettes. I was the kind of kid who liked to take things apart to see how they worked. When I removed the radio's back panel to install the battery, I stared at those tiny resistors and capacitors, and I thought, *Wow, I need to learn about this.* There was mystery inside there; I felt as though I'd embarked on a quest. If I could just get enough of the details, I was sure I could figure it out.

Sometime after that, Doug introduced me to integrated circuits, where transistors were embedded in the chip. I'd read about the new semiconductor industry, and how Jack Kilby of Texas Instruments had demonstrated the first working integrated circuit in 1958. Even so, it was something to hold one in your hand, all that electronic capacity encased in one miniaturized container.

While I didn't realize it at the time, I'd begun to follow the path foretold by Moore's law.

# CHAPTER 3

# LAKESIDE

Lakeside was the most prestigious private school in Seattle, and I wanted nothing to do with it. My Ravenna friends were moving on to seventh grade at Eckstein Junior High, the nearby public school, and I'd assumed I'd be with them. Worse yet, Lakeside was all boys, a grim prospect for a twelve-year-old.

But when my parents heard that I'd spent most of sixth grade reading on my own in the back of the room, they decided that I needed more of a challenge. They would have to sacrifice to pay the Lakeside tuition—$1,335, a lot for a middle-class family in those days. But they wanted me to have opportunities they'd missed out on in Oklahoma.

"*Why* do I have to go to private school?" I kept asking.

"Because you'll learn more," my mother replied. "And there will be a lot of other smart kids there. It'll be good for you."

Lakeside's entrance test was famously difficult. I decided to fail on purpose, and that would be that. It was a foolproof plan until I sat down with the exam: multiple choice, with lots of object rotations and pattern matching, a variation on a standard IQ test. *This is kind of interesting*, I thought. *Let's see how hard these questions are.* I decided to solve the first set, just to see if I could, and then compensate at the end with a bunch of wrong answers.

The next thing I knew, time was called: "Pencils down!" It was one of those tests that no one finished completely, and I hadn't gotten around to filling in those mistakes. But I was sure I wouldn't be admitted, anyway, since the odds were so slim.

I got in. And my parents were right. It was really good for me.

MODELED AFTER A New England prep school, Lakeside was a collection of old brick buildings on thirty acres near the Jackson Park Golf Course in north Seattle. I was thrown into a forty-eight-member class of the city's elite: the sons of bankers and businessmen, lawyers and UW professors. With scattered exceptions, they were preppy kids who knew each other from private grammar schools or the Seattle Tennis Club.

Just about everybody was smart at Lakeside, and they had skills and study habits that I lacked. The teachers were dynamic and demanding, prone to answering questions with questions. (The anomaly was Mr. Dunn, my volatile French teacher, who responded to careless conjugations with volleys of chalk and erasers.) For a while, I was tentative about raising my hand. I'd listen to the discussion and think my own thoughts, and then I'd chime in if nobody else did.

It took me most of seventh grade to get my bearings. Finally I clicked with Mr. Spock, my English teacher and the brother of Benjamin Spock, the world-famous pediatrician. "Paul has continued to be the most perceptive and thoughtful boy in my class," he wrote in my spring report card. Gradually I got used to being challenged. I'd grow more intellectually in my six years at Lakeside than in any other phase of my life.

IN EIGHTH GRADE, two events stood out. For a pregame football rally, I rigged up an oil heater transformer under a chair that held an effigy in the opposing team's colors. When the moment was right, the transformer set off a bunch of firecrackers stuffed in the dummy's arms. It looked like an electrocution, just as I'd planned.

My second big moment came when I was chosen to deliver the

graduation address for Lakeside's lower school. It was my first speech, and I slaved over it. As I rose before classmates, faculty, parents, and honored guests, I felt a strange sensation in my legs. My knees were knocking, just like a cartoon.

It was 1967, and artificial intelligence was the hot theme in science fiction. I'd read Isaac Asimov's *I, Robot,* with its First Law of Robotics ("A robot may not injure a human being or, through inaction, allow a human being to come to harm"), and *Colossus,* a 1966 British novel about a malevolent megacomputer that wound up ruling the world. Newspapers of the day were filled with headlines like "Computers Are Taking Over," or "Automated Government Is Here."

I began by hailing "the age of the computer" and a future that "holds for us the bright prospect of even more remarkable things to come." After acknowledging the specter of computers someday replacing human workers on assembly lines, I paid my respects to the machines' "amazing capabilities" in mathematics and their uses in banking, medicine, and the military. I pointed out that U.S. moon probes were in fact computer-run robots. But I was equally interested in what computers *couldn't* do: "They cannot have an original idea. They are unable to go beyond the limitations of their programming. . . ."

Were we on the threshold of a thinking robot? I closed with a prediction: "In fifty years, a robot with a fairly large brain cell capacity will be within reach." Today it appears that I was highly optimistic. With 2017 now around the corner, we're still not close to matching the abilities of the incalculably complex human brain.

When I recently reread that speech, it brought back the image of a boy who was fascinated by computers but had little practical knowledge beyond the flip-flop circuit. All I knew came secondhand from things I'd read. When I was growing up, few people outside major universities or big corporations had ever seen a real computer. It would have been hard to imagine that I'd ever lay my hands on one.

\*     \*     \*

WHILE LAKESIDE SEEMED conservative on the surface, it was educationally progressive. We had few rules and lots of opportunities, and all my schoolmates seemed passionate about something. But the school was also cliquish. There were golfers and tennis players, who carried their rackets wherever they went, and in the winter most everyone went skiing. I'd never done any of these things, and my friends were the boys who didn't fit into the established groups. Then, in the fall of my tenth-grade year, my passion found me.

My honors geometry teacher was Bill Dougall, the head of Lakeside's science and math departments. A navy pilot in World War II, Mr. Dougall had an advanced degree in aeronautical engineering and another in French literature from the Sorbonne. In our school's best tradition, he believed that book study wasn't enough without real-world experience. He also realized that we'd need to know something about computers when we got to college. A few high schools were beginning to train students on traditional mainframes, but Mr. Dougall wanted something more engaging for us. In 1968 he approached the Lakeside Mothers Club, which agreed to use the proceeds from its annual rummage sale to lease a teleprinter terminal for computer time-sharing, a brand-new business at the time.

On my way to math class in McAllister Hall, I stopped by for a look. As I approached the small room, the faint clacking got louder. I opened the door and found three boys squeezed inside. There was a bookcase and a worktable with piles of manuals, scraps from notebooks, and rolled-up fragments of yellow paper tape. The students were clustered around an overgrown electric typewriter, mounted on an aluminum-footed pedestal base: a Teletype Model ASR-33 (for Automatic Send and Receive). It was linked to a GE-635, a General Electric mainframe computer in a distant, unknown office.

One senior hunched over the machine and its khaki-colored keyboard, while another looked on and made an occasional cryptic comment. To the keyboard's right was an embedded rotary dial, for the modem; to its left sat the punch, which spewed a continuous stream of inch-wide, eight-column paper tape. Each character was defined by the configuration of holes punched out among the eight channels. (An inch length of tape held ten characters; a small program might run two or three feet.) In front of the punch, a paper-tape reader translated your programs and sent them to the GE computer.

The Teletype made a terrific racket, a mix of low humming, the Gatling gun of the paper-tape punch, and the *ka-chacko-whack* of the printer keys. The room's walls and ceiling had to be lined with white corkboard for soundproofing. But though it was noisy and slow, a dumb remote terminal with no display screen or lowercase letters, the ASR-33 was also state-of-the-art. I was transfixed. I sensed that you could do things with this machine.

That year would be a watershed in matters digital. In March 1968, Hewlett-Packard introduced the first programmable desktop calculator. In June, Robert Dennard won a patent for a one-transistor cell of dynamic random-access memory, or DRAM, a new and cheaper method of temporary data storage. In July, Robert Noyce and Gordon Moore cofounded Intel Corporation. In December, at the legendary "Mother of All Demos" in San Francisco, the Stanford Research Institute's Douglas Engelbart showed off his original versions of a mouse, a word processor, e-mail, and hypertext. Of all the epochal changes in store over the next two decades, a remarkable number were seeded over those ten months: cheap and reliable memory; a graphical user interface; a "killer" application, and more. Had anyone connected the dots, they might have foreseen the transformation of computers and how they would soon be used.

THE CLASSIC MAINFRAMES of my youth were the size of tractor-trailers and wildly expensive. Those early IBMs and UNIVACs had no more computing power than today's pocket calculators, but they took up entire rooms and threw off tremendous heat, even after transistors replaced vacuum tubes. They were overseen by trained operators who kept them running around the clock while the customers stayed outside, looking in. To gain access to computing, programmers used a keypunch machine to convert handwritten code into a deck of punch cards, one card per line. They'd snap a rubber band around the deck and bring it to an operator to have the cards read in.

Then the programmers returned to their offices to wait, because the work went on the operators' schedule. Depending on their job's priority, they'd pick up a printout hours or sometimes days later. If one card was bent or out of sequence, or a single comma in the wrong place, they'd get an error message and not much else. They'd have to deduce their mistake and start again.

"Batch processing," as this system was called, worked fine for large-scale information management tasks, like corporate payrolls. But it became so frustrating for programmers that they mounted a guerrilla movement for greater interactivity. In 1957, the visionary John McCarthy demonstrated a radical software prototype: a "Compatible Time-sharing System," as McCarthy called it, "that permits each user of a computer to behave as though he were in sole control." Instead of passively waiting for punch cards to be processed, users communicated with the computer through their terminal keyboards. You could "talk" to a mainframe, receive a prompt reply, then make your corrections. Programming became more like a conversation.

Time-sharing made computer time affordable by spreading costs among hundreds of users. Dozens of people could engage one computer simultaneously, with the central processing unit shifting from one person's work to the next in a fraction of a second. The new back-and-forth rhythm wasn't merely more efficient. It was a leap that made card decks superfluous and computer users far more productive. In 1965, General Electric packaged a refined version of McCarthy's system with the original Dartmouth BASIC and launched a commercial service. Three years after that, Bill Dougall and the Mothers Club brought it to Lakeside.

I was lucky to come of age in a time of fundamental change in the computer industry. Computing power, once the sole province of government and the wealthiest corporations and universities, could now be parceled out at an hourly rate. New technology delivered that power to scattered offices or schools. As usual, timing was crucial. If I'd been born five years earlier, I might have lacked the patience as a teenager to put up with batch-processing computers. Had I come around five years later, after time-sharing became institutionalized, I would have missed the opportunities that come from trying something new.

RATHER THAN MAKE programming a formal part of the math curriculum, Lakeside offered it as an independent study option. We were lightly supervised by Fred Wright, a young math teacher who'd taken a summer course in punch card programming at Stanford. Mr. Wright gave us a BASIC manual and a few starter problems to whet our appetites, and then he let us loose. Because we didn't know the "correct" way of doing things, we devised our own techniques. We became resourceful of necessity.

Only the most cursory documentation was furnished to help us. The BASIC manual was fifty-odd pages long, and I consumed it in a day or two. I memorized the twenty or so main keywords and how certain keys functioned on the Teletype. The language felt foreign for the first hour or two, and then it was—*Oh yeah, I get it.* BASIC was a lot easier than French: consistently logical, no irregular verbs, compact vocabulary. When I got stumped, I'd ask one of the seniors for help: How do you make that work? How do you print that? They were a month or so ahead of me and happy to show off what they knew.

In one of my first programs, borrowed from a manual, I graphed a sine wave. I watched the teleprinter's carriage swing back and forth to print a perfect pattern of asterisks, as though moved by an unseen, mesmerizing hand. Within days Fred Wright had little left to teach us. Now and then he'd pop his head in, smile, and say, "How are you guys doing?" Some of the stodgier teachers grumbled that we had too much freedom, but Mr. Wright loved riding that fine line between control and chaos, unleashing our enthusiasm.

It's hard to convey my excitement when I sat down at the Teletype. With my program written out on notebook paper, I'd type it in on the keyboard with the paper tape punch turned on. Then I'd dial into the GE computer, wait for a beep, log on with the school's password, and hit the START button to feed the paper tape through the reader, which took several minutes.

At last came the big moment. I'd type "RUN," and soon my results printed out at ten characters per second—a glacial pace next to today's laser printers, but exhilarating at the time. It would soon be apparent whether my program worked; if not, I'd get an error message. In either case, I'd quickly log off to save money. Then I'd fix any mistakes by advancing the paper tape to the error and correcting it on the keyboard while simultaneously punching a new tape—a delicate maneuver nowadays handled by a simple click of a mouse and a keystroke. When I achieved a working program, I'd secure it with a rubber band and stow it on a shelf until the next session.

For young people today, this process might seem hopelessly laborious, like cracking a walnut with a Rube Goldberg machine. But for high school students in the late 1960s, it was astounding to get "instant" feedback from a computer, even if you had to wait several seconds for the machine's next move in a game of Yahtzee. In a sense, that time-sharing terminal marked my start in personal computing years before personal computers. Programming resonated with my drive to figure out whether things worked or not and then to fix them. I'd long marveled at the innards of things, from transistors and integrated circuits back to that young-reader's book on road equipment. But crafting my own computer code felt more creative than anything I'd tried before. I sensed that there would always be more to learn, layer upon layer of knowledge and techniques.

Soon I was spending every lunchtime and free period around the Teletype with my fellow aficionados. Others might have found us eccentric, but I didn't care. I had discovered my calling. I was a *programmer*.

TWENTY OR SO students dropped into the computer room from time to time, but only half a dozen made it the hub of their universe. Although programming at its heart is a solitary venture, we became a nascent brotherhood. With no teachers to guide us, we traded commands and tricks of the trade. While a few of the acolytes were older students like Robert McCaw and Harvey Motulsky, I was one of four younger ones who formed the core. Ric Weiland, the son of a Boeing engineer, resembled Spock in *Star Trek* without the pointy ears: quiet, kind, meticulous. Ric built his own tic-tac-toe relay computer in the ninth grade, but never sought attention; he was happier in the background. Kent Evans, a minister's son two years younger than Ric and I, had frizzy hair, an intricate set of braces, and unflagging intensity. He was game for anything.

One day early that fall, I saw a gangly, freckle-faced eighth-grader edging his way into the crowd around the Teletype, all arms and legs and nervous energy. He had a scruffy-preppy look: pullover sweater, tan slacks, enormous saddle shoes. His blond hair went all over the place. You could tell three things about Bill Gates pretty quickly. He was really smart. He was really competitive; he wanted to *show* you how smart he was. And he was really, really persistent. After that first time, he kept coming back. Many times he and I would be the only ones there.

Bill came from a family that was prominent even by Lakeside standards; his father later served as president of the state bar association. I remember the first time I went to Bill's big house a block or so above Lake Washington, feeling a little awed. His parents subscribed to *Fortune* and Bill read it religiously. One day he showed me the magazine's special annual issue and asked me, "What do you think it's like to run a Fortune 500 company?" I said I had no idea. And Bill said, "Maybe we'll have our own company someday." He was thirteen years old and already a budding entrepreneur.

Where I was curious to study everything in sight, Bill would focus on one task at a time with total discipline. You could see it when he programmed—he'd sit with a marker clenched in his mouth, tapping his feet and rocking, impervious to distraction. He had a unique way of typing, sort of a six-finger, sideways scrabble. There's a famous photograph of Bill and me in the computer room not long after we first met. I'm seated in a hardback chair at the teleprinter in my dapper green corduroy jacket and turtleneck. Bill is standing to my side in a plaid shirt, his head cocked attentively, eyes trained on the printer as I typed. He looks even younger than he actually was. I look like an older brother, which was something Bill didn't have.

LIKE ALL TEENAGE boys, we loved games. Harvey Motulsky created a text-based version of Monopoly, with the computer's random number generator "rolling the dice." Bob McCaw put together a virtual casino program (including craps, blackjack, and roulette) that involved three hundred lines of code. We proudly mounted the printout up one wall, across the ceiling, and down the other.

Within a month, we'd run through the Mothers Club's budget for computer time for the year, so they allocated a little bit more. In early November, as computer blackjack began to pall, I got news from Harvey. A time-sharing company had opened in Seattle's University District. It needed people for acceptance testing of its new-model leased computer, a Digital Equipment Corporation PDP-10.

The next night I asked my father to take me to the Computer

Center Corporation, a ten-minute drive from our home. I peered through the plate glass, into a room that never went dark, at the mysterious puppy in the window: a black mainframe with cabinet after cabinet and panels of blinking lights. The CPU alone was about five feet wide. It was the first time that I'd seen an actual computer in the flesh, and it seemed not quite real that such a thing could exist just forty blocks from where I lived. All I wanted to do at that moment was log on, connect, and have at it.

Today's average laptop is thirty thousand times faster than the machine I was lusting after, with ten thousand times more memory. But in its day, the PDP-10 was the most advanced species of an evolutionary alternative to the batch-processing establishment. Founded by Ken Olsen and Harlan Anderson, DEC made its first splash in 1960 with the PDP-1, the first truly interactive, "conversational" computer. Less than a decade later, the PDP-10 became the mainstay for the Defense Department's ARPANET (the original Internet) and a time-sharing workhorse. It ran faster than GE's system at Lakeside and had a broader software repertoire, including FORTRAN and other languages, plus a rich array of online utilities.

Fortunately for me and my fellow Lakesiders, this wonderful hardware all relied on a new operating system, TOPS-10, that was apt to crash whenever it served too many users at a time. Computer Center Corporation (which we'd call C-Cubed) had taken delivery of its leased PDP-10 in October 1968, with a plan to start selling time in the New Year. In the meantime, their TOPS-10 needed to be debugged before the paying customers arrived. As an added incentive for C-Cubed, its lease payments would be deferred until the software functioned reliably. The company needed somebody to push the system to its limit, which was where we came in.

One C-Cubed partner was a Lakeside mother who'd heard about our little tech fraternity. A few days after my sneak preview, Fred Wright ushered us into the building to make introductions. A resident guru laid out the deal: We could have unlimited free time on their terminals, off-hours, as long as we abided by their ground rules. "You can try to crash the computer," he said, "but if it crashes from something you do, you've got to tell us what you did. And you can't do it again until we tell you to try."

The following Saturday, we met in the C-Cubed terminal room, a space three times the size of our cubbyhole at Lakeside. We were delighted to find a bank of a half-dozen ASR-33s: no more waiting to get on. Through another door lay the sanctum sanctorum, the computer room. Manned seven days a week by three shifts of operators, it was big and square and fluorescent-bright, with a shiny raised floor to keep the fat power and data cables out of harm's way. Whenever a bulky disk drive was installed, industrial-size suction cups were used to lift the floor and run new cables. Between the air conditioning and the hulking computer's fans, the place was so noisy that some operators wore hearing protectors, like workers on a factory floor.

For us, shifting from the GE-635 to the PDP-10 was like trading in a Corolla for a Ferrari. Saturdays were not nearly enough. We'd bus down to C-Cubed after school, cutting gym class to get there earlier, our junior briefcases in hand. (I doted on mine, which was brown leather and popped open at the lightest touch of my thumbs.) We were on the road to becoming *hackers,* in the original, nonfelonious sense of the term: fanatical programmers who stretched themselves to the limit. As author Steven Levy has noted, hacker culture was a meritocracy. Your status didn't hinge on your age or what your father did for a living. All that counted was ingenuity and your hunger to learn more about coding.

Every neophyte needs a master, and C-Cubed had three of them. They were world-class programmers all, with a nerdish élan and a tinge of the exotic. Unlike the business-side executives, they didn't treat us like nuisances; I suspect they may have seen in us their younger selves. At times it felt as though I'd jumped from high school into a postgraduate seminar in advanced systems programming.

Steve "Slug" Russell, the company's hardware chief, was short and round, with a wry sense of humor. Then thirty-one, he'd followed John McCarthy from Dartmouth to MIT. There Russell had created Spacewar, the first truly interactive computer game, on a PDP-1.

Bill Weiher, slim and bespectacled, never said much. Known for developing SOS (an acronym for Son of STOPGAP, one of the first great text editors), he looked like a scribe from the Middle Ages. I'd see him crunching away tirelessly at his terminal, building elaborate structures of intricate code.

Dick Gruen, an ex-DEC consultant who'd met Russell and Weiher at Stanford, was the most gregarious of the lot, a junk-food addict and Falstaffian jokester with a mop of curly hair. According to Gruen, the operating system had yet to be born that he could not crash, and he was clever enough that I believed him.

To them we were "the Lakeside kids" or "the testers." On occasion they'd have us simultaneously run a bunch of copies of a chess program to place an extra-heavy load on the system. Our assignment played to a teenager's impulse to wreck things just for fun, while channeling it into something positive. As I later told a Seattle journalist, "The most effective way to learn was going hands-on with what was the top machine of the time, learning about how it worked, what it took to 'make it or break it.'"

Another approach was to stress-test a piece of software until it failed, when we'd scribble down what happened on a piece of paper and move on. The ultimate coup was to crash the whole operating system, which would be apparent when the teleprinter froze and buzzed as you tried to type. Later Russell and Gruen would determine the source of the snag, happy as clams, knowing that their lease payment to DEC had been once again forestalled. We were happy, too. As long as we kept finding bugs, we'd extend our Camelot of free time.

When one of our mentors came by, I was almost too intimidated to speak. We adopted their jargon; a *kludge*, for example, was a baling-wire-and-gum sort of coding fix. They put up with our pestering, and every now and then threw us a bone from something they'd been working on. We were in awe of how efficiently they coded, a critical skill in an era of limited computer memory.

Mostly we were free to bang away on our own small projects. Bill worked on a war game; Ric grappled with FORTRAN. I wrote code for a matchmaking program. In the evening, we usually had the teleprinter room to ourselves. When we needed to pick up our listings, we'd knock on the computer-room door, say hello to the night operator, collect our printout, and return to our Teletypes. We might steal a glance at the PDP-10, but that was as close as we got.

THE KEY TO commercial time-sharing was permanent, high-speed data storage, a way to gain easy access to your work. C-Cubed limped along for months with old-generation disk drives that limited most customers to a couple dozen files of modest length. So there was great anticipation when Russell took delivery of a box about eight feet long by four feet high: a new moving-head disk drive from Bryant Computer Products in Walled Lake, Michigan. One of the company's field service representatives, a thick-accented Southerner, called it the Giant Bryant. The name stuck.

The drive was built to heroic dimensions. A massive electric motor at the center ran a thick shaft that supported a dozen oxide-coated steel disks, each more than three feet in diameter. They spun in unison while a set of hydraulic arms with magnetic heads, floating on thin cushions of air, moved across their surfaces to read the data. The drive could store around 100 million characters, an order of magnitude beyond anything else available. (Today's laptop drives typically store six hundred times as much data in 0.002 percent of the volume.)

Unfortunately, the Giant Bryant was flaky to a fault. Every so often, with as little provocation as a nearby footstep, a head would touch a disk and strip off the oxide: the ominous head crash, with data irretrievably lost and the disk damaged beyond repair.

For archival storage, C-Cubed used a less imposing device called DECtape. It came in four-inch canisters—small enough to slip into a pocket, large enough to hold a million characters. One 260-foot roll had the capacity of 2,500 feet of paper tape, or slightly more than the eight-inch floppy disks to be introduced by IBM five years later. Even within the limits of its motorized, reel-to-reel drive, DECtape was faster than paper tape and much sturdier, with dual redundancy and two layers of Mylar protecting the oxide. In demonstrations, DEC salesmen would punch a quarter-inch hole in the tape and then show that its data was intact.

Best of all, DECtape featured a directory structure, just like the Giant Bryant or the floppy drives to come. Traditional magnetic tapes were like sequential streams where stored information couldn't be safely updated; if you wrote something new in the middle of a tape, subsequent data would be lost. But DECtape was organized in discrete blocks of data, and one block could be rewritten without affecting any other. Now we could store half a dozen or more programs on a single tape, find all of them by name, and edit them independently or write over them. Up until I bought my own home terminal, my DECtapes were the first piece of computing technology that really belonged to me. We all wanted more of them—they were status symbols. Those little canisters made my work feel less ephemeral, more substantive, as though it had real and lasting value.

# CHAPTER 4

# ACOLYTES

As winter wore on, Bill and I exhibited the most stamina among the Lakesiders at C-Cubed. Typically my father would drive by to drag me home for dinner. I'd beg to stay—and won some and lost some. My parents worried that I was falling behind in school. Some of my grades were slipping, and my teachers seemed ambivalent about my new passion. In computer programming, Mr. Maestretti wrote, "Paul has been doing outstanding work on the computer. He has become tremendously interested in its workings, and has reached a sophistication far beyond . . . the average student." But in physics, where he gave me a midterm C+ (though I'd pull out an A in the spring), he bemoaned "the channeling of [my] efforts into work with the computer at the expense of other academic areas."

My English teacher, Mr. Tyler, dismayed by my chronic diffidence to homework, turned philosophical: "Paul is an 'enthusiast' (in the old religious sense) and when in the grip of an enthusiasm is almost totally irresponsible in other areas. How can one help such a student to see the error of his ways? I don't know. He could even be more right than we, who knows?" In fact, I was thriving in a professional environment, working hard at something I took joy in. What better experience could there be for a sixteen-year-old?

Left to ourselves, Bill and I would program until we were

starving and then walk across the street to a hippie enterprise called Morningtown Pizza. Next door was a convenience store with police cars out front and cops playing cards in the back room. We'd either wolf down our pizza at Morningtown or bring it back to C-Cubed and try to keep it from dripping oil onto our Teletypes. We'd keep at it until everyone but the night operator had left. Once I was on my own and lost track of time. The buses had stopped running and it was way too late to call my dad for a ride, leaving me an hour's walk home. A stray dog followed me all the way; my parents had to find it a home with friends of ours.

For me, the Holy Grail of software was the operating system, the computer's nervous system. It does the logistical work that allows the central processing unit to compute: shifting from program to program; allocating storage to files; moving data to and from modems and disk drives and printers. You don't think about it unless something goes wrong and it crashes.

At the time, operating systems weren't locked boxes as they are today. Manufacturers packaged their software with their hardware; any companies that bought DEC's computers were free to modify TOPS-10 as they saw fit. Bill and I knew that our mentors had access to TOPS-10 source code and were working to debug and enhance it. We also knew that it was off-limits to us, which made it ten times more fascinating than whatever we were working on. On weekends, after everyone had left, Bill and I would go Dumpster diving in the building's courtyard. We'd flip up the metal cover and I'd interlace my fingers to give Bill a boost—he couldn't have weighed more than 110 pounds. He'd lean down into the big container and scoop up anything that looked promising. After several trips, he found a treasure: a stack of stained and crumpled fanfold printouts. I can remember the smell wafting off the coffee stains and thinking, *This is a little gross, but I don't care.*

We took that precious hoard back to the terminal room and pored over it for hours. I had no Rosetta Stone to help me, and understood maybe one or two lines out of ten, but I was blown away by the source code's tightly written elegance. To grasp the architecture of an operating system like TOPS-10, I knew that I'd need to become fluent in its assembly code, the lower-level language that spoke directly to the machine. Seeing my interest, Steve Russell took me aside, handed me an assembler manual bound in glossy plastic, and told me, "You need to read this." In line with the do-it-yourself ethos of our world, nothing more had to be said.

Thrilled, I took the volume home and gobbled it up until I knew it backward and forward. One week and 150 pages later, I'd hit a wall; the manual described the mechanics for writing assembly code, but neglected to explain what those statements made the computer do. I went back to Russell and said, "I don't understand."

And he said, with a twinkle in his eye, "Oh, you better read *this*," and gave me another 150 pages in a white plastic cover: the system reference manual. It was a strain to get through it, and after two weeks I realized that something was still missing. Though I hated bothering Russell, I went to him again and said, "I still don't understand. How can I send characters to the Teletype?"

And he said, "Ah, there's one more manual you need," and he came back with what looked like a phone book: the operating system manual. To this day I'm not sure whether he was spoon-feeding or hazing me, but I'd needed all three manuals all along. It took several weeks more for me to take my first baby steps in assembler programming, and months before I felt confident. "This is fascinating stuff," I told Bill and the rest. But they were engrossed in their high-level languages, where they could write programs more quickly. So I continued alone.

In contrast to BASIC or FORTRAN, where each statement combined many instructions, assembly language was a direct, symbolic, one-to-one representation of binary machine code, converted into text and symbols that were easier to memorize than patterns of 0's and 1's. For example, a line of BASIC might read:

$A = B + C.$

When written in assembly code, the same statement might look like:

Load *B.*
Add *C.*
Store in *A.*

Assembly language programming was both less expressive and far more laborious than BASIC. And where programs written in high-level languages could be ported to different CPUs with minor variations, more or less like related dialects, assembly language was unique to each hardware platform, as distinct as German is from Portuguese. On the other hand, once inside the machine, assembly code could excecute up to hundreds of times faster. You were writing right to the hardware, down to the bare metal. You couldn't get faster than that.

A Lakeside schoolmate once said that I could read assembly code the way other people read novels, but I don't think it came more easily to me. It was simply the place I chose to focus, where the rubber met the road. I was finally beginning to understand how a computer worked at its most fundamental level. I'd made it into the guts of the machine.

NOTHING LASTS FOREVER, and there came the day when C-Cubed finished testing the PDP-10 and began to charge us for computer time. With the Mothers Club money depleted, Lakeside shifted its contract to C-Cubed. By that point, we had individual accounts. (I can still remember our account numbers: mine was 366,2634, while Bill drew 366,2635.) C-Cubed based its charges on a complex formula involving kilo–core ticks of CPU time and disk usage, and we constantly worried that we'd spent too much. Before mailing the monthly bills to our parents, Fred Wright would post a list above the Teletype in descending order of charges incurred, and you'd pray that your name didn't land in the top three. I cringed when I set the record at $78, the equivalent of nearly $500 today—how would I explain? To his credit, Dad took it in stride: "That's a lot, Paul. I know you're learning, but can't you cut back?" My parents saw my programming as a hobby, like my vacuum-tube radios or darkroom photography, only a lot more extravagant. Bill's parents felt the same way. We could sense their patience waning.

Late that spring, Bill and I got hold of a C-Cubed administrator password and logged on at Lakeside. Soon we found what we were looking for: the company's internal accounting file, named "ACCT. SYS." It was encrypted, but we knew that it contained every paying account and also the free ones. Our hope was to find a free account to tap into; we knew it was wrong, but we were desperate for untrammeled access. After a few futile attempts to find a specialized program that could read and modify ACCT.SYS, we copied the file to our directories, until we could try it again.

We never got the chance. A few days later, we were summoned to Fred Wright's office, where we were shocked to see Dick Gruen and another C-Cubed representative, an unsmiling man in a dark suit. We hoped we'd get off with a slap on the wrist, considering that we hadn't really done anything yet. But then the stern man said it could be "criminal" to manipulate a commercial account. Bill and I were almost quivering. Would we get suspended from school?

It was worse than that. "You stole the accounting file, and we're throwing you out," the man said. Our C-Cubed privileges were withdrawn through the summer. We were devastated.

Just when all seemed lost, I ran into a friend who knew a UW professor with a free C-Cubed account. Once Lakeside's spring term ended, I went almost daily to a terminal in the electrical engineering building. I picked up where I'd left off and read manuals over hamburgers at the student union. Life was good, but I kept mum about it all summer. I'd nearly reached my full height, a shade under six feet, but Bill and Kent still looked like junior-high-school students; I couldn't risk them jumping in and blowing my cover. Bill was furious when I finally told him, and I felt bad about it. But such was the lure of programming that I knew I'd do the same again.

IN THE FALL of my junior year at Lakeside, my sins forgiven and my sentence up, Steve Russell and I struck a bargain: In return for free computer time, I'd try to improve their BASIC compiler. As high-level languages had grown in popularity, compilers had become the indispensable middlemen. They were the translators that turned high-level source code into "object code," the binary bits and bytes that computers could actually execute. Like all DEC software, the PDP-10's BASIC compiler was open and extendable; you could freely layer on new features, which was the assignment I'd undertaken. It was a stiff challenge for someone who'd yet to enroll in his first computer science course. Printed out, the compiler's listings were as thick as an abridged dictionary, and it took me days to gain a sense of the whole and how it held together. Whatever assembly code I wrote needed to fit the program's logical flow, word by painstaking word.

For a while, I wondered if I'd bitten off too much. Too stubborn to ask for assistance, I used the previous programmers' comments as guideposts. For every ah-*ha* moment, there were days when I barely had a clue about the source code in front of me.

Fatigue is no factor when you're seventeen and caught up in something. I camped out at C-Cubed as long as my eyes stayed open, and as days became weeks, I began to eke out some progress. Since I'd found it painful to retype whole lines of BASIC programs whenever I made a small mistake, I adapted ideas from Bill Weiher's line editor to quickly search and insert single characters. And I religiously annotated every step, as per our mentors' protocol, for anyone who'd come along later to build on my work.

Again, I did all of this in the minutiae of assembly code, like an apprentice watchmaker squinting at the tiny wheels to understand their interplay. By the end, I probably knew more about that compiler than anyone at C-Cubed. Russell and Gruen seemed surprised that I'd gotten so far and were particularly pleased with my line editor, a beneficial tool for their customers. I'd become a true hacker. What I picked up over those two months formed the basis for my assembler work with microprocessors, when the stakes would be much higher.

Then as now, teenagers were often underestimated. Along with Bill and Ric and Kent, I'd shown how much young people could grow if given the chance. We were still years away from our mentors' level, but we weren't bad. And we were getting better.

DESPITE ITS ENGINEERING talent and first-rate time-share technology, C-Cubed was hobbled by a shaky business model. Only a handful of small-business people were willing and able to do their own programming, and few commercial programs were available to help them. The service became dangerously dependent on Boeing, Seattle's largest employer, where middle managers could lay off time-sharing fees on their expense sheets. In 1970, Boeing got slammed by a double whammy: a recession in the airline industry and a sharp cutback in NASA's Apollo program. There were layoffs and major cutbacks, including the company's external computing budget. Worse yet, Boeing established its own contract programming service. Over the span of a few months, it went from client to competitor.

C-Cubed cratered early that spring and filed for Chapter 11. As soon as Bill and I heard, we rushed to the terminal room to plead for time to finish some programs and back everything up on DECtape. Not long after we'd arrived, the moving men came to repossess the leased furniture. As we worked madly away at our Teletypes, we could see them going from room to room, piling desks into their trucks. Finally they got to us and said, "OK, boys, we've got to take the chairs." We knelt on the floor by our terminals to finish saving our programs.

Minutes later, I saw Bill staring out the window with his mouth open. One of the wheeled chairs had gotten loose and was rolling down Roosevelt Way with a moving man giving chase. We burst out laughing, but it was gallows humor, the end of a vital phase of our lives. My prospects for a summer job were gone, and my father was threatening to revoke my driving privileges if I didn't make up some missing chem labs. More seriously, the bankruptcy was a lasting reminder of how a business can plummet in a flash. Bill, in particular, never forgot that lesson.

IN RETROSPECT, the folding of C-Cubed was a blessing. By forcing the acolytes to scramble for computer access, it led us to broaden our experience. At the time, IBM controlled two thirds of the mainframe market. Its closest rivals were known as the Seven Dwarfs: Burroughs, Control Data, General Electric, Honeywell, NCR, RCA, and UNIVAC. Along with up-and-comers like DEC, they were fighting to expand their meager market share by beating the leader on price, power, innovation, or all three. The software sector was even more fractured. Today, after the inevitable shakeout that occurs in any maturing industry, there are basically three flavors of personal computer operating systems: Windows, Apple's Mac OS, and variants of Unix. Among 1970 mainframes, there were literally dozens. Every computer line was a software world unto itself.

One evening after school, early in my senior year at Lakeside, I brazenly walked through a door and into UW's graduate computer science lab. I picked up a manual and took my seat at a Teletype linked to a Xerox Data Systems Sigma-5, which I soon had figured out. Then a grad student approached to ask a question, and word got around that I seemed to know what I was doing. I was rolling along until an assistant professor called me into his office and said, "You don't look familiar. Are you in any of my classes?"

And I said, "No, sir, I'm not."

"As matter of fact, you're not even enrolled here, are you?"

I confessed that I wasn't. The professor smiled and said, "All right,

I'll tell you what. If you keep helping my students, you can stick around."

There was no turning back after that. I moved on to the Burroughs B5500 and a powerful language called ALGOL—my first brush with batch processing, a step backward in time that only deepened my appreciation of the PDP-10. I tried my hand at a Control Data CDC-6400 and an Imlac PDS-1, the pioneering graphical minicomputer, where I found a version of Steve Russell's Spacewar. I was a sponge, soaking up knowledge wherever I could. All of us were sponges then.

That November, a Portland time-sharing company called Information Services Inc. invited me and my three "colleagues" to meet to discuss a contract, a big step for us. Before driving to Oregon, we reconstituted ourselves as the Lakeside Programming Group, which sounded grown-up and official. ISI wanted a payroll program that had to be written in COBOL, a high-level language used in business applications. In return, they would credit us with free time on their PDP-10. We outlined our experience and submitted our résumés; Bill, just turned sixteen, had written his in pencil on lined notebook paper. We got the job.

As it turned out, our big break was unfulfilling. COBOL was a cumbersome, wordy language, and the accounting program a slog. We worked on it through the winter, using UW's computer science lab until we overstayed our welcome. In a letter dated March 17, 1971, a professor named Hellmut Golde complained that our work "tends to disrupt the intended use of the laboratory." He appended a list of violations, including our use of "the teletypes (at times all of them simultaneously) for prolonged periods of time, and occasionally unattended, to produce endless listings." The resulting noise level was "detrimental to the normal activities and also is not the intended mode of operation for a remote console."

"In view of these and other occurrences," Mr. Golde concluded, "I must ask you to turn in your keys and terminate your activities in the lab immediately." We figured that the grad students had complained to him, and moved to some Teletypes elsewhere to finish the job.

While we never saw any revenue from the payroll program, it felt like old times to be back on a PDP-10. And we began to see ourselves less as hobbyists and more as people who just might make a living by writing code.

HAVING HAUNTED THE stacks of UW's computer science library for some time, I naturally became the research arm of the Lakeside Programming Group. I spent countless hours buried in periodicals like *Datamation* or *Computer Design*, keeping up with the latest mainframe trends. I dived into esoteric technical reports from MIT and Carnegie Mellon, dense theoretical stuff that ranged from artificial intelligence to the latest algorithms. When I found something interesting, I'd check it out and show it to the group.

As my senior yearbook shows, I was reading other things as well. I'm pictured seated at a desk in my ubiquitous green corduroy jacket and what is most likely a blue oxford shirt. (You can't see my Beatles-style boots.) I have fashionably long hair, with thick sideburns and a Fu Manchu moustache. My chin rests atop a stack of eleven books, among them Joyce's *Dubliners, Modern University Physics, The Mexican War,* and the Holy Bible. I'm guessing that the photo was posed to satirize how much work our teachers threw at us. Still, it was a good illustration of my breadth of interests.

I was driven more by curiosity than by the compulsion to get good grades. When it came to Civil War trivia or the conjugations of *pouvoir,* I had trouble faking interest. "I am also very absent-minded (what a misnomer) and lazy (to put it mildly) towards things from which I derive no active or contemplative pleasure," as I wrote at the time. But give me a dynamic teacher and engrossing material, and I'd be insatiable. I can recall my Rimbaud phase, when I steeped myself in poems of profound longing and angst. I got enthralled by Assyrian history and my senior philosophy class.

It was there, in a discussion of Kant over a packed-lunch exchange with Holy Names School, that I met my first real girlfriend: Rita, a sharp and engaging redhead.

There were students hanging out in McAllister Hall who wore pocket protectors, who cared about BASIC and not much else. That wasn't me. I joined after-school blues jams on my acoustic guitar. I loved literature and movies and was fourth chair on the chess team. I never stopped rooting for UW's football and basketball squads, a loyalty inherited from my dad. And I moved in a range of social circles, with Lakeside's protohippies as well as the computer guys. I wasn't a nerd. I was just someone who happened to love computers, among many other things.

THREE DECADES AFTER teaching Bill and me at Lakeside, Fred Wright was asked what he'd thought about our success with Microsoft. His reply: "It was neat that they got along well enough that the company didn't explode in the first year or two."

There was always a push-and-pull with us. It manifested itself at Lakeside in the rivalry between Ric and me, on one side, and Bill and Kent on the other; they were two years behind us and had something to prove. At bottom, the Lakeside Programming Group was a boys club, with lots of one-upmanship and testosterone in the air. And while we were all bent on showing our stuff, Bill was the most driven and competitive, hands down. We were friends from the day we met, but there was an underlying tension, too.

Midway through twelfth grade, I was minding my own business in the school's computer room when Bill began taunting me: "Paul, there's something hidden here that you should know about, but I bet you can't guess what it is."

I said, "Oh, really, Bill? What would that be?"

And he said, "I can't tell you, but it's something you wish you had." Bill being Bill, this went on for a while. Unbeknownst to him, however, I knew his secret. Some weeks earlier, an auction had sold off C-Cubed's remaining assets, including dozens of DECtapes. Bill and Kent snapped them up for a few pennies on the dollar and never breathed a word of it. But Ric had spotted them hiding their booty in the Teletype's pedestal base, and passed the intelligence on to me. Later that day, after the others left, I scooped up the tapes, carried them home in a box, and hid them under my bed.

The next day, the worm turned. Bill was furious. "You knew those DECtapes were there the whole time," he said. "What did you do with them?"

"Really, Bill?" I said. "You had some DECtapes? Where did you get them?"

Bill was beside himself. Kent called me a thief and threatened to sue. It got loud enough that Fred Wright came in and took me aside, and I agreed to return the tapes.

That kind of conflict, though, was rare for Bill and me. In a series of senior-year essays about those near and dear to me, here is what I wrote about him:

> *A short, bright, smart, humorous and generally likeable person. Thinks school is a snap. Just as smart as me in most everything (but English) and very often superior even though he is only a sophomore. I know quite a bit more about the sciences and the world in general. Magically able to laugh at himself in almost any circumstance. Loves computers and gadgets as I do. Very suggestible and is ready to jump at any chance to have fun in strange ways. We fit together very well.*

AT MY LAKESIDE commencement exercise, a classmate named Stu Goldberg played the piano in virtuoso style. For a while I'd been weighing two possible career paths: rock guitar or computer programming? Hearing Stu, who would land with John McLaughlin and the Mahavishnu Orchestra the following year, reaffirmed my choice of computers.

After the ceremony, as I walked off with my parents, Fred Wright came chasing after us with a sheet of paper in his hand. It was my last time-sharing bill, somewhat north of two hundred dollars. My father grumbled a little as he made out the check. I was planning to major in computer science at Washington State University, but my parents were still dubious about the field's profession. They saw it as more of a sideline until I found my real future.

The Class of '71 was Lakeside's last as an all-boys' school; it merged with St. Nicholas to go coed that fall. As a parting gift, we left a tombstone that still rests on the campus. In misspelled Latin, it reads: *Vivat virgor virilis*, or, "Long live male virginity."

# CHAPTER 5

# WAZZU

I was glad to be on my own at Washington State (or Wazzu, as we called it), three hundred miles from home, but college life wasn't quite what I'd hoped. My intro courses were less than challenging. I missed my family and my girlfriend and got distracted by the social hubbub. Some people thrive when they first go out on their own, but I was not one of them.

I also missed the PDP-10. Early on, my nights were spent writing programs on batches of cards for an IBM mainframe. "It *is* different to be using IBM equipment but it really isn't bad at all," I wrote to Ric Weiland in November, putting a good face on it. New computers always intrigued me, even the baroque, slow, unwieldy ones. I read up and tried to think up tools to improve the IBM programming experience. My progress was slow.

The more rewarding part of college was the broader world I found there, especially at Phi Kappa Theta. A small underdog fraternity at the far end of the row, it perched on a slope so steep that it took two people to mow the lawn: one to push the mower and the other to hold the rope that kept it from rolling down the hill. Just behind the house was a switching yard where they put trains together at three in the morning. For the first two weeks I couldn't sleep, and after that I could sleep through anything.

But I loved that place. Thrown in with a lively mix of hippies, eccentrics, and ROTC cadets, I got a kick out of nearly all of them. There was Mike Flood, the frat president and wry ringleader who assigned me dishwashing duties; Gary Johnson, who saved on room fees by living with two dogs in his truck in the driveway; Simon Karroum, aka the Big Syrian, a massive, kindly soul whose English had been corrupted by a summer job on the Portland docks. We had to edit his papers and cross out the four-letter words, because he didn't know any better.

I was the computer guy, the one who would happily help you debug your homework; I could glance at a piece of FORTRAN code and quickly pinpoint what was wrong. But I also played hours of H-O-R-S-E in the driveway, where my notorious "matador" shot was hard to beat, and I snapped center on our intramural flag football team. Our quarterback, Jerry Morse, was a former New York Yankee farmhand with a gun of an arm. I wasn't blessed with great speed, so Jerry would tell me in the huddle, "Ten yards and turn around." If Simon and Mike were covered, he'd rifle it into my chest. I rarely dropped a pass.

Back from programming at one or two in the morning, I'd unwind with my electric guitar, a habit that annoyed some of my frat brothers. Mike Flood would ask me to stop, and I'd lay the guitar down after a final chord or two. But one night a muscular guy named George Shea burst into my room in a fury and hoisted me up against the wall. I looked at George and his clenched fist and considered the beating I was about to get. For someone who'd grown up in a family where no one ever got visibly angry, it was an out-of-body experience.

"Put him down." It was Mike Haspert, one of my guitar buddies, crouched in a karate stance. Word had it that he was a black belt. George weighed his options, dropped me to the floor in disgust, and stormed off.

A typical day at Phi Kappa Theta was less eventful: marathon hearts and chess games, *Star Trek* in the basement TV room, Pizza Shack and Taco Time. There were drives over the Idaho state line, where the legal drinking age was nineteen and beer was cheap. On Saturdays I'd join the throng to watch the Cougars get slaughtered by the likes of USC. I was mostly carefree until I drew 99 in the 1972 draft lottery, a number that could send me to Vietnam. By then the war looked grim, hardly worth dying for. But I would have served had they called me, as my father had in World War II.

As it turned out, they suspended the draft before my student deferment expired.

ON MAY 28, 1972, in a UW mountaineering class, my Lakeside friend Kent Evans was crossing a snowfield on Mount Shuksan when he slipped. Unroped and unable to check himself, he tumbled more than six hundred feet down the slope, hitting several large rocks. He was evacuated by a navy helicopter and died before he got to a hospital. Kent was seventeen years old.

Bill was torn up by Kent's death, just crushed. A few days after the funeral, Kent's parents asked us over to see if we'd want any of his computer things—a few manuals, nothing of importance. It was kind of them, but we felt strange sorting through Kent's belongings. We didn't stay long.

Bill had contracted with Lakeside to write a scheduling program in FORTRAN during summer vacation. "I was going to do it with Kent," he told me. "I need help. Do you want to work on it with me?" Though I wouldn't make much money, I was glad to step in and get reacquainted with a PDP-10. Bill stayed depressed for weeks, but his spirits gradually lifted as we immersed ourselves in the project, going at it full-bore in McAllister Hall like old times. Often we'd work past midnight and sleep on cots we'd brought to campus. The program was a challenge, with lots of moving parts: required courses, staggered sections, electives, double-period labs. I was impressed by how cleanly Bill broke the job into its component parts, and especially how he "preloaded" himself into an English class with a dozen or more girls and no other boys.

Bill and I became closer that summer. Our age gap no longer

seemed to matter; we had what I call high-bandwidth communication. Diving into a problem, we'd start "popping up the stack," computing jargon for the sequence for subtasks in the CPU: last in, first out. In conversation, the phrase meant that we'd shift from one topic to an earlier one without bothering to acknowledge the new context. Someone overhearing us would have made no sense of it:

"So then we can move this string . . ."

"You're right, the other thing will never happen if that's true. . . ."

"Exactly! That's the variable we used the last time."

Another strong commonality was our shared sense of the absurd. One night, after going far too long without sleep, we were grinding away for hours over some scheduling code—we just couldn't find the bug. Bill kept glaring at the problem page, and suddenly he said, "X!" and collapsed into helpless giggles. I took another look and saw what he meant: We'd left a meaningless hanging variable stuck in the middle of a line. "X!" I shouted. Then both of us were rolling on the ground, calling out "X!" in the empty building, exhausted and hysterical.

For breaks we'd go to the movies; we must have seen more than five hundred together over the years. My favorite theater was the Kokusai in Seattle's International District. It had double features with English subtitles, and the second film was always samurai. Bill didn't go in much for foreign fare, but one night he agreed to see "anything but one of those stupid movies with a little dog in it." No sooner had we settled into our seats for a contemporary Japanese drama than a noisy terrier was running across the screen.

"*Not* the little dog," Bill groaned out loud.

We had fun that summer, but we never stopped thinking about our next business opportunity. Bill had taken on a data processing job for a company that measured traffic flow patterns by counting the car wheels running over pressure-sensitive rubber tubes. At fifteen-minute intervals, a machine would punch a pattern of holes on special sixteen-channel paper tape, representing the number of cars. The tape had to be read manually, with the results recorded in longhand and then transferred to batch-loaded cards. The process was monotonous, inefficient, and murder on the eyes; Bill had farmed it out to younger students at Lakeside whom he paid fifty cents a tape to act as human paper-tape readers. One day he said, "Those kids are going blind trying to read those things. We've got to find a way to automate it."

I wondered aloud about using one of the modern minicomputers. The latest Texas Instruments models were especially compact and cost in the low four figures, but that was still too much money for us. Then I had another idea: What about Intel's new 8-bit microprocessor, the 8008? Based on what I'd read, the chip could run calculators, elevators, even smart terminals. Since its release that spring, little had been done to use it for data analysis. But if it worked as its specs suggested, the 8008 would be up to our task. "We could make our own chip-based system, that's the cheapest way to do it," I said. As Bill warmed to the proposal, I added a salient point: "We have to find someone to build the machine." Hardware was not our strength, so we'd need a third partner.

A mutual acquaintance told us about Paul Gilbert, an electrical engineering student at UW, and we tracked him down later that summer. After a few meetings, Paul had a workable sketch for Traf-O-Data, the name we'd use for both the traffic machine and our partnership. (Much later on, I asked Bill how he'd come up with it, and he said, "I got it from jack-o'-lantern." I thought that was really strange.) In that first flush of entrepreneurship, we had grandiose dreams about the money coming our way. Armed with our easy-to-read data charts on hourly traffic flow, municipalities would know just where to place their stoplights or to focus their road repairs. Wouldn't every public works department in the world want a Traf-O-Data machine?

Paul Gilbert wangled a UW discount and we special-ordered an 8008 chip at a local electronics store. Bill and I scraped together

$360 and drove by to pick it up. The sales clerk handed us a small cardboard box, which we opened then and there for our first look at a microprocessor. Inside an aluminum foil wrapper, stuck into a small slab of nonconductive black rubber, was a thin rectangle about an inch long. For two guys who'd spent their formative years with massive mainframes, it was a moment of wonder. "That's a lot of money for such a little thing," Bill said. But I knew what he was thinking: That little box contained the brains of a whole computer. We brought it to Paul Gilbert in the physics building, and he set to work.

In developing the Traf-O-Data software, Bill and I faced a dilemma. We knew that it would be painful, if not futile, to try to create software on the 8008 itself. We needed to build a set of development tools from the ground up, including a customized assembler, a program that could translate assembly language instructions into actual bytes. While the 8008 could address 16K bytes of memory, Bill and I could afford only a quarter of that in memory chips, not nearly enough for the tools.

So how would we program such a limited microprocessor on a machine that didn't yet exist? For me, the answer seemed clear: I'd *simulate* the 8008 environment on a mainframe. Simulators had first cropped up in the literature in the midsixties, when an engineer named Larry Moss devised a way for an IBM 360 to "emulate" earlier-model computers and run their software. Moss's work reflected a truism in technology circles that harkened back to the theories of Alan Turing in the 1930s: Any computer could be programmed to behave like any other computer. Software trumped hardware. Although I hadn't read about anyone simulating a microprocessor, I figured it should be easy enough—I'd simply trick a big computer into acting like a small one. In the meantime, we could exploit the big computer's abundant memory and advanced development tools.

We had no idea how much adversity lay in store for us. Using UW's lab equipment and facilities, Paul Gilbert went about constructing a fiendishly intricate prototype, with more than a thousand copper wires wrapped around dozens of gold-plated posts on two circuit boards. The box design and layout went smoothly, but Paul spent a year trying to get the noise-sensitive memory chips to work. Meanwhile, back at Wazzu, I struggled to build the simulation package on the IBM 360. Debugging on a batch-processing computer was downright Sisyphean, two steps forward and a step and a half back.

When Bill came out to Pullman during a hellacious cold snap that winter and we walked the two miles to the campus computer center, we noticed that a bank's reader-board thermometer was stuck at 13 below zero. The air was so frigid that it almost hurt to talk. By the time we reached our destination, my beard was stiff with ice. And Bill said, shivering, "Does it always get this cold in Pullman?"

I don't remember him coming out in the winter after that.

OVER CHRISTMAS, Bill got a call from Bud Pembroke, the guy who'd hired us to do the ISI payroll program. A massive software project for the Bonneville Power Administration's electrical grid was behind schedule, and Bud was scouring the region for programmers who knew their way around a PDP-10. I was not quite twenty and Bill was only seventeen, but age was not a criterion. "And you're going to be on salary," Bud said.

Bill said, "How much?"

And Bud said, "One hundred sixty-five dollars a week."

Four dollars an hour was a pittance for an experienced programmer, even then, but Bill and I couldn't believe our good fortune. Here was a chance to work together again on a PDP-10, and for pay! I was glad to take a leave of absence from Washington State. Bill had completed his required courses at Lakeside and got approval to pursue an off-campus senior project for his final semester. We told Bud to count us in.

Bill and I piled into his orange 1967 Mustang convertible and drove south to Vancouver, Washington, a land of strip malls, car washes, and a vintage A&W Root Beer drive-in stand where we'd become regulars. We found a cheap two-bedroom apartment and showed up for work on a Monday in January 1973. Our employer was TRW, a big aerospace company that had contracted with the Department of the Interior to set up a real-time operating and dispatch system, or RODS—the first system of its kind in the country, we were told. The government already had software that controlled Bonneville's generators along the Columbia River, distributing power to eight Western states. The point of RODS was to refresh that information each second and respond more efficiently to shifting power needs.

TRW management had projected that a handful of software engineers would need two years to finish the job, a drastic underestimate. Converting DEC's TOPS-10 into a real-time system was like turning an apple into an orange—and a new variety of orange, at that. More than a year into the project, with overrun penalties soaring, TRW's new software was still full of bugs. Wheeling into crisis mode, management went out to recruit every able-minded programmer they could find to get RODS up and running. By the time we got there, more than forty people were working on it around the clock.

Bonneville's hardened control facility was across the river from Portland, built mostly underground. They even had a shower room for washing off nuclear waste in the event someone pushed the button. Bill and I took the elevator down for what seemed like forever under the reinforced concrete. After passing several doors secured with combination locks, we were shown into a computer room with a raised floor and chilly air conditioning, the place where we'd test and run our code. I was excited to see that we'd be sharing the space with dual PDP-10's; I'd never worked so close to a computer.

Down the corridor was a control room as large as four basketball courts. An immense backlit grid covered two walls like something out of *Dr. Strangelove,* showing the status of every dam in the Northwest. If anything went haywire, a corresponding light would change from green to red. The Bonneville operators worked at color-display consoles with gargantuan keyboards that could call up any substation and paint it on their screens. There were meters showing dam outputs in *megawatts,* which I thought was pretty wild.

The programmers were a tight-knit if motley crew, from classic corporate types in white short-sleeve shirts and bow ties to free-wheeling characters like Bob Barnett, a Vietnam vet who showed us the ropes in a crazy-uncle kind of way. Bill was assigned a series of small jobs, while I was given a fair-size one, a recovery module to make the new automated system fail-safe. (When you're dealing with power for millions of people, going down is not an option.) If the primary PDP-10 failed, my system would tell the backup computer to take over.

Leaving nothing to chance, TRW performed all sorts of extreme tests, like gauging how a massive ground short might affect the computers below. After a quarter-inch steel cable was strung from a 250-kilovolt line to a stanchion planted in the earth, we came outside to watch someone throw a switch. A violent crack made us jump. The cable became a line of vaporized steel, and then it vanished. The computers, fortunately, were unfazed.

"Wow," I exclaimed, "that was really something."

And a TRW manager said, "No, what was *really* something was when Joe forgot to put his bucket down and drove his repair truck into that power line."

"What happened to him?"

"There were incredible sparks and the tires melted into the ground," the manager said, "and Joe freaked out. But he was OK because the truck became a Faraday cage." (In the 1830s, British physicist Michael Faraday demonstrated that an electrical current running along the exterior of a conductive structure had no effect on the interior.) The TRW guys burst out laughing as I thought,

*Oh my gosh, that's serious electricity.* With its bizarre personnel and sunless facility, RODS could seem very strange at times.

Bill and I were the youngest workers there, and surely the lowest paid, but Bob and the other managers cut us no special slack. At RODS we learned that we could hold our own with some of the top programmers around. I had to write a thousand lines of assembler code—not too heavy a load, but a tricky one. Two other programmers had taken a crack at it, but their code couldn't handle the "corner cases," like a simultaneous failure of two or more devices. I opted for a ground-up rewrite in the cleanly structured and annotated style that I'd learned at C-Cubed. I spent countless hours checking my work, which needed to be fail-safe. For the first time, I was writing directly on a running operating system. I found it fascinating.

Freed of school obligations and family constraints, Bill and I happily hunkered down for coding sessions and test cycles that ran twelve hours and more. We were both natural night people who would peak at ten or eleven P.M. and remain at optimal efficiency for quite a while after that. No matter how long it took, we'd stay to find that last bug. When Bill felt himself flagging, he'd grab a jar of Tang, pour some powder on one hand, and lick it off for a pure sugar high. (His palms had a chronic orange tinge that summer.) Often we would work for two days straight and then crash for eighteen or twenty hours, which Bill called "getting slept up."

But sleep was an afterthought. We had our Lakeside job to finish for the next term, and the graveyard shift at RODS seemed ideal for the purpose. The class scheduling program was CPU-intensive, and sometimes Bob Barnett came in late to find the PDP-10 slowed to a crawl. He'd stalk down the corridor booming in mock anger, "Gates and Allen, where are you? Shut your goddamn scheduling program down!"

When I wasn't writing code, I was playing acoustic guitar or catching up on the latest Watergate news at the apartment. Late-night diversions in Vancouver were pretty much limited to Denny's "classic breakfast," our go-to meal at three A.M.: eggs, bacon, a pancake, hash browns. For more excitement, Bill joined Bob at the dog track in Gresham, where they bet the animals' numbers based on license plates in the parking lot. I went along on a few trips to Portland Meadows, where Bob had inside information on a quarter horse named Red Robbie who'd been hopeless at a quarter mile. One night they entered him at a longer distance, and Bob persuaded us to risk our hard-earned money. Red Robbie jogged out of the gate, last as usual, before finding his stride midway through to win, going away at long odds.

Bill and I were regulars at the blaxploitation movies that played at a theater in northeast Portland. We had a great time watching *Super Fly* and the like until someone came up to us one night during the closing credits: "What are you white boys doing here?" That threw us, but we were back a week later. We just found those films enthralling.

Living with Bill, I saw a new side of him. My mother had a term for adrenaline junkies, people who would court risk for the thrill of it. "That person," she'd say, "is an edge walker." Bill Gates was an edge walker. He'd pride himself on making the 165 miles from Seattle to Vancouver in under two hours, putting the hammer down in his Mustang late at night. Where I was wary of physical danger, Bill seemed to enjoy it. When he entered our apartment one day in a full-leg cast, I asked him what had happened.

"Waterskiing with Barnett," he said. They'd run out that afternoon to Lacamas Lake. As Barnett tells the story, he'd taken his last run and wanted to get back to RODS, but Bill insisted on going one more time on a single ski. In his rush, he didn't bother to adjust the equipment, which can be a problem if you like to jump the wake of the boat. After Bill fell and snapped his leg, he was told to take six weeks to heal back in Seattle. He resurfaced in Vancouver, with a bluish leg and no cast, after three. "I'm going to water-ski with Bob," he told me. I couldn't dissuade him, and his leg somehow held up.

For the most part, the two of us got along well that spring and summer. But at times Bill could get edgy, especially during our chess games. I was a more methodical player, my openings more structured; Bill was an aggressive improviser. When I beat him one day, he got so angry that he swept the pieces to the floor.

"That was the stupidest move I ever made!" Bill shouted. After a few games like that, we stopped playing.

ONCE I'D DECIDED my approach, I was able to crank out the systems control panel code pretty quickly. The weak link was a buggy communications module that prevented my work from being tested in real time until after I went back to Washington State that fall. (RODS wouldn't be officially "energized" until more than a year later, in December 1974, after untold penalties against TRW.) Before leaving, I got some validation from John Norton, a legendary systems programmer who'd been parachuted in for a review. Norton could take an inch-thick listing, page through it in a day, then snap it shut. If you went to him later with a question, he'd close his eyes and say, "Go to page 57, you'll find the subroutine you're looking for." It was a proud day when my work survived his scrutiny.

In my off-hours I made progress on my Traf-O-Data simulator. The PDP-10's central processing unit weighed nearly a ton, but my program needed to get it to behave like a chip half the size of a pack of gum. My first task was to define a set of thirty or so "macros," the symbolic instructions that would generate bytes for the Intel 8008. Within a few days, I'd effectively performed a brain transplant. The PDP-10's assembler didn't know it, but it was now an 8008 assembler.

My next step was to build the simulator itself, a program to put this metamorphosis into action. Written in PDP-10 assembly language, the simulator would mimic the microchip's instructions. The coding went smoothly; it was as though everything I'd learned at C-Cubed and ISI had led me to this point. Fortunately, I was able to finish my week's work for Bob Barnett in about twenty hours, then focus on Traf-O-Data. After going hard for a week, I was done.

My third and final step was to modify the PDP-10's debugger to give Bill the ability to stop the program in midexecution and track the cause of any problem. The debugger was an ugly, hairy piece of code, full of trapdoors and cul-de-sacs, but three weeks after I'd begun, we had an unrivaled development suite for the 8008 chip. (My techniques proved so effective that Microsoft used them well into the 1980s, until microprocessors became fast and capable enough to host their own development tools.) Shortly before we returned to school, Bill finished the traffic analysis program. We tested it on the PDP-10 with hypothetical data, and the simulator generated an impressive bar graph printout. All that remained to be seen was whether Bill's program would work on Paul Gilbert's Traf-O-Data hardware.

Our dreams expanded; Bill talked about starting a real company. While I shared similar fantasies, mine centered more on the technology. It was clear to me that inexpensive computers would transform the future. But what could *we* do that was new and different? Where was it all headed? On one of Rita's visits to Vancouver, I took her up to TRW's microwave tower and expounded on its data transmission capability and what that might imply. Soon, I said, there would be high-speed links among people all over the world.

Another time, as Bill and I dined at a local pizza place, I had a thought: "What if you could get the news by reading from a computer terminal instead of buying a newspaper? You could even program it to find articles on whatever you wanted. Wouldn't that be great?"

And Bill said, "Come on, Paul! It costs seventy-five dollars a month to rent a Teletype and you can get a paper delivered for fifteen cents. How do you compete with that?" He had me there. But I couldn't stop thinking about a time when everyone would be digitally connected, with instant access to information and services. It would be a while before Bill and I defined our goal, in so many words, as "a computer on every desk and in every home." But the seeds of that motto—and my notion of a global network to join all those computers together—would be planted that summer among the strip malls and fast-food joints in Vancouver, Washington.

WE WERE MIDWAY through our work at RODS when Bill called home and got the news that he'd been accepted at Harvard University. He wasn't surprised; he'd been riding high since scoring near the top in the Putnam Competition, where he'd tested his math skills against college undergraduates around the country. I offered a word to the wise: "You know, Bill, when you get to Harvard, there are going to be some people a lot better in math than you are."

"No way," he said. "There's no *way*!"

And I said, "Wait and see."

I was decent in math and Bill was brilliant, but I spoke from experience at Wazzu. One day I watched a professor cover the blackboard with a maze of partial differential equations, and they might as well have been hieroglyphics from the Second Dynasty. It was one of those moments when you realize, *I just can't see it.* I felt a little sad, but I accepted my limitations. I was OK with being a generalist.

For Bill it was different. When I saw him again over Christmas break, he seemed subdued. I asked him about his first semester and he said glumly, "I have a math professor who got his PhD at sixteen." The course was purely theoretical, and the homework load ranged up to thirty hours a week. Bill put everything into it and got a B. When it came to higher mathematics, he might have been one in a hundred thousand students or better. But there were people who were one in a million or one in ten million, and some of them wound up at Harvard. Bill would never be the smartest guy in that room, and I think that hurt his motivation. He eventually switched his major to applied math.

By then we had ambitions beyond school. That December Bill and I redid our résumés. Not quite twenty years old, I listed a "working familiarity" with ten computers, ten high-level languages, nine machine-level languages, and three operating systems. I listed my objective as "systems programmer" and my desired salary as "open," though in parentheses I added "$15,000." Location: "Anywhere." I noted that I'd be available as of June 1, 1974, a sign that I was ready to leave school again for the right opportunity. I thought I knew what I wanted to do; I just lacked a firm plan for getting there.

In describing our work on Traf-O-Data, my résumé stated: "Designed and put together a system for traffic engineers to study traffic flow. The system is built around Intel's MCS-8008 microcomputer. The software and hardware setup has been fully tested using a prototype. Demonstrations to customers are planned for May 1974."

That summary was optimistic. True, Paul Gilbert had finally stabilized the noisy memory chips. And the Traf-O-Data machine certainly *looked* authentic, quite a feat on a $1,500 budget; Paul had modeled it after the popular PDP-8 minicomputer, with a similar layout for switches and LEDs. (The interior, with its rat's nest of posts and wires, was another story.) After hauling a Teletype over Snoqualmie Pass in the back of a Phi Kappa brother's pickup truck, I hooked up the machine by our kitchen sink in Pullman. Then I loaded in a small test program through the keys on the front panel, and it ran successfully. But we still couldn't be sure if it would run Bill's traffic analysis program, because we couldn't find an affordable reader for the oversize sixteen-channel tapes.

At wit's end, we turned to a local inventor who designed a contraption that read the tapes' holes with a conductive rubber pinch roller. It needed constant tightening and seldom fed the tapes through in a straight line, but it was the best we could do. At a demonstration that May for Seattle's King County Engineering Department, the tape reader malfunctioned—the whole thing was a fiasco. Bill finally broke down and spent serious money on a more reliable reader from Enviro-Labs. "Traffic Machine finally works (!)," I wrote to Ric Weiland in August 1974.

Charging two dollars per day of data collection, we found three clients: two smaller counties near Seattle and a district in British Columbia. They mailed their traffic tapes to Paul Gilbert's house, where he produced the graphs of hourly car flow. But just as we were getting under way, Washington joined a number of other states in offering the same service to cities for free. We didn't give up easily, even attempting (with no luck) to sell our wares in South America. According to six years of tax returns between 1974 and 1980, Traf-O-Data totaled gross receipts of $6,631 and net losses of $3,494. In 1982, when we closed our checking account, I received a distribution of $794.31. By that time Bill and I were preoccupied with running another company in Seattle.

In hindsight, Traf-O-Data was a good idea with a flawed business model. We had done no market research. We hadn't foreseen how hard it would be to get municipalities to make capital expenditures, or that officials would be reluctant to buy machines from students. For Bill, Traf-O-Data's failure would serve as another cautionary tale. Above all, we learned that it was hard to compete with "free." (Bill took that lesson to heart. Years later he'd become obsessed with Linux, the open-source operating system.)

But there were positives, too. Traf-O-Data bolstered my conviction that microprocessors would soon run the same programs as larger computers at a far lower cost. Looking ahead, my development tools for the 8008 would give us an invaluable foundation when that next-generation chip came along. In 2002, I purchased the one and only Traf-O-Data machine from Paul Gilbert and installed it in our STARTUP gallery at the Museum of Natural History and Science in Albuquerque. I wanted to pay homage to an obscure piece of hardware that played a critical role in the micro-processor software revolution.

In my experience, each failure contains the seeds of your next success—if you are willing to learn from it. Bill and I had to concede that our future wasn't in hardware or traffic tapes. We'd have to find something else.

# CHAPTER 6

# 2+2=4!

Through the spring semester of 1974, Bill kept urging me to move to Boston. We could find work together as programmers, he said; some local firms sounded interested. We'd come up with some exciting project—maybe an extension of Traf-O-Data, maybe something new. In any case, we'd have fun. Why not give it a try?

Still drifting at Washington State, I was ready to take a flier. I mailed my résumé to a dozen computer companies in the Boston area and got a $12,500 job offer from Honeywell. Bill received an offer there as well, and it seemed like an ideal arrangement; we could make a decent living while doing our own things on the side. Then, after I accepted the job and prepared to take another leave from Wazzu, Bill changed his mind and decided to go back to Harvard. I suspected heavy pressure from his parents, who had more traditional ideas. In a letter to Ric, Bill wrote, "They are more in favor of my taking up business or law—even though they don't say so."

I was still committed to the move. If Boston didn't work out, I could always return to school. In the meantime, I'd sample a new part of the country, and Rita had agreed to join me. We had grown more serious and wanted to live together as a trial run for marriage. Plus, Bill would be there. At a minimum, we could put our heads together on the weekends.

My dad was less than enthusiastic. "This software work seems to be a distraction," he said. "I don't agree with your choice, but you're old enough to make your own decisions." When the day came that August for Rita and me to leave, he got the family Chrysler washed and filled it with gas. Regardless of what they thought, my parents always did what they could to support me.

Driving cross-country with a girlfriend was an adventure. I remember how long it took to cross Montana, and how we reached New England in the thickest fog we'd ever seen, finally getting lost on Boston's roundabouts. We found an inexpensive apartment in Tyngsborough, up near the New Hampshire state line. Rita got work in a semiconductor plant nearby as I started at Honeywell, the company that made the thermostats in my childhood home.

If DEC was the cutting-edge leader among IBM's competition, Honeywell was a big cocoon where people punched the clock as though they were working for the phone company. The firm was known for its low-stress, informal work culture: no neckties, lots of bridge games at lunch. The managers had offices with windows, along the perimeter, while the programmers worked out of a large bullpen, two to a cubicle. My colleagues were nice guys in their thirties. They were solid software engineers, but nothing like the elite at C-Cubed or the crack hired guns at TRW. They had no hacker ethic.

I was assigned to a communications protocol that would link multiple Honeywell minicomputers, a small piece of a big project within a turn-the-crank environment. I sat in my light brown cubicle and wrote anonymous assembly code for a niche-market machine, and soon I got bored. I was happier in my spare time, when I could use Bill's password to hack around at Harvard and got my first exposure to Unix, the multitasking operating system from Bell Labs that had taken universities by storm. With short commands and a root-and-branch file system, Unix provided an easier way to organize files, and it could run on hardware costing as little as ten thousand dollars. Here was a parallel computing universe that seemed full of fresh ideas, and it made my work at Honeywell feel even staler.

Rita and I had come to New England knowing two people. One was Bart Johnson, a brilliant, troubled Lakesider who would insinuate that he was working for the Mafia. Bart had an unusual way of dealing with parking tickets; he'd buy a junker and park wherever he pleased in Back Bay, until the tickets overflowed his glove compartment. When the car got towed, as it inevitably did, he'd go out and buy another one.

Then there was Bill. We had him out to Tyngsborough in October for a birthday dinner for him and Rita, who always found Bill entertaining. Back in Pullman, she'd roasted a chicken one night for dinner and couldn't take her eyes off him. "Did you see that?" she said, after he'd left. "He ate his chicken with a *spoon*. I have never in my life seen anyone eat chicken with a spoon." When Bill was thinking hard about something, he paid no heed to social convention. Once he offered Rita fashion advice—basically, to buy all your clothes in the same style and colors and save time by not having to match them. For Bill, that meant any sweater that went with tan slacks.

That November Rita and I moved into Rindge Houses, a subsidized development in Cambridge with linoleum floors, steel doors, and legions of cockroaches. After my Chrysler began burning oil, I bought a used yellow Mustang convertible for $290. One morning I climbed in and turned the key. Nothing happened; someone had stolen the battery. A few days later, I went to Sears and returned with a new one. Again I opened the hood, and this time the engine was gone. I gave up on my convertible, which was ill-suited for that whistling Northeast wind anyway. Within weeks the car was up on blocks and stripped clean.

By Thanksgiving Rita had left her job and returned to Seattle to finish her degree at UW. Rita was my first love, my first slow dance, and without her I was lonely. I spent more time with Bill at Currier House before his nightly poker games with the local cardsharps. He was getting some costly lessons in bluffing; he'd win three hundred dollars one night and lose six hundred the next. As Bill dropped thousands that fall, he kept telling me, "I'm getting better." I knew what he was thinking: *I'm smarter than those guys.*

In my off hours, my thoughts turned to microprocessors. A few low-cost computers had been built around the Intel 8008, but none had made much headway. The French Micral N, marketed as a "microcomputer" in 1973, could be programmed only in binary and was used in highway tollbooths or for overseas agriculture projects. The Scelbi-8H, with just a thousand bytes of memory, was mostly ignored; the Mark 8 came in a kit for only the most manic do-it-yourselfer. With the advent of Intel's more capable 8080 chip in April 1974, technology seemed ready for a leap. But the springboard general-purpose machine had yet to be built.

I wondered if we might draw on the Traf-O-Data design to create an 8080-driven computer that would rival the PDP-8, but Bill found that unconvincing. Then I countered: What if we could string a hundred chips together to make something cheaper *and* more powerful than the minicomputers of the day? Or if we pooled a bunch of 4-bit processor "slice" chips to emulate the IBM 360 at a fraction of IBM's inflated prices?

Each time I brought an idea to Bill, he would pop my balloon. "That would take a bunch of people and a lot of money," he'd say. Or "That sounds really complicated." Our Traf-O-Data ordeal was still fresh in his mind. "We're not hardware gurus, Paul," he'd remind me. "What we know is software." And he was right. My ideas were ahead of their time or beyond our scope or both. It was ridiculous to think that two young guys in Boston could beat IBM on its own turf. Bill's reality checks stopped us from wasting time in areas where we had scant chance of success.

So when the right opportunity surfaced, as it did that December, it got my full attention.

\*     \*     \*

SOME HAVE SUGGESTED that our Altair BASIC was remarkable because we created it without ever seeing an Altair or even a sample Intel 8080, the microprocessor it would run on. What we did was indeed unprecedented, but what is less well understood is that we had no choice. The Altair was little more than a bare-bones box with a CPU-on-a-chip inside. It had no hard drive, no floppy disk, no place to edit or store programs. And even had the machine been up to it, debugging on the memory-challenged 8080 would have been slow and difficult at best.

Any other programmers vying to bring an 8080 BASIC to Albuquerque would be facing an uphill climb. For starters, they'd have to realize that they needed a simulator and then to create one from scratch on a mainframe or minicomputer. Bill and I had a big edge in speed and productivity with our Traf-O-Data development tools. But could we actually write a BASIC interpreter?

Our game plan echoed our work on Traf-O-Data. I would generate the tools, the macro assembler and simulator, while Bill took the lead in creating the interpreter's design. In contrast to a compiler, a memory hog that converts whole files of source code into assembly or machine language, an interpreter executes one snippet of code at a time, on the fly, which would minimize an Altair customer's outlay. At the time, 4K of memory was just under three hundred dollars retail—a fair sum in 1975, but not a deal-breaker for a crazed hobbyist. It would be tight, but we believed we could squeeze a pared-down interpreter into that 4K, with enough room left over for some small user-written programs.

One large piece of our BASIC was unaccounted for: the floating-point math code that was essential for manipulating large numbers and decimal points in scientific notation.* One night Bill and I were at dinner at the Currier House cafeteria, where advanced

---

*Scientific notation is a simplified way to handle very small or very large numbers using coefficients and exponents. For example: $83,700,000 = 8.37 \times 10^7$; $0.0072 = 7.2 \times 10^{-3}$.

math students would chat about hypercubes and five-dimensional geometry. I was worrying aloud that I'd have to write our math routines myself when a curly-haired freshman across from us piped up: "I've done those for the PDP-8." We promptly brought him to Bill's room to discuss what we needed, and that was how we found Monte Davidoff. (Monte negotiated a flat fee of $400 for his services, and several thousands more for follow-up work in Albuquerque.)

Quandary solved, we moved into Harvard's Aiken Computation Lab on Oxford Street, a one-story concrete building with an underutilized time-sharing system. The clock was ticking on us from the start. Bill had told Ed Roberts that our BASIC was nearly complete, and Ed said he'd like to see it in a month or so, when in point of fact we didn't even have an 8080 instruction manual. After we bought one, I set to work. The 8080 had more than twice as many instructions as the 8008, which meant that I'd need to create quite a few more macros. But the two chips shared a basic architecture, and my general approach was the same. Once again, I would be morphing PDP-10 software into an assembler for the microprocessor chip. I finished the macros in a day or two.

My 8080 simulator was larger but conceptually similar to the one for Traf-O-Data, and as before, I tweaked the PDP-10's debugger to allow us to stop and peer inside our BASIC as it ran. There are times in a programmer's career when everything clicks, when your brain is running full out; for me, this was one of them. I got a boost from Aiken's new video display monitor (or "glass teletype," in the jargon of the day), the DEC VT05. Access to a high-speed printer helped, as did storage on the PDP-10's hard disk drive. Within a month, we had development tools for the new chip that likely existed nowhere else. That 8080 package was quick and powerful, done about as well as it could have been. I'm still proud of that code today.

If my tools gave us our first big edge, Bill's conceptual talent as a programmer kept us quickly moving ahead. By the time I delivered my development suite, he'd already thought through the interpreter's structure. I can still see him alternately pacing and rocking for long periods before jotting on a yellow legal pad, his fingers stained from a rainbow of felt-tip pens. Once my simulator was in place and he was able to use the PDP-10, Bill moved to a terminal and peered at his legal pad as he rocked. Then he'd type a flurry of code with those strange hand positions of his, and repeat. He could go like that for hours at a stretch.

In building our homegrown BASIC, we borrowed bits and pieces of our design from previous versions, a long-standing software tradition. Languages evolve, ideas blend together; in computer technology, we all stand on others' shoulders. As the weeks passed, we got immersed in the mission. As far as we knew, we were building the first native high-level programming language for a microprocessor. Occasionally we wondered if some group at MIT or Stanford might beat us, but we'd quickly regain focus. Could we pull it off? Could we finish this thing and close the deal in Albuquerque? *Yeah,* we could! We had the energy and the skill, and we were hell-bent on seizing the opportunity.

We worked all hours, with double shifts on weekends. Bill basically stopped going to class. Monte overslept his one o'clock French section. I neglected my job at Honeywell, dragging into the office at noon. I'd stay until 5:30, and then it was back to Aiken until three or so in the morning. I'd save my files, crash for five or six hours, and start over. We'd break for dinner at Harvard House of Pizza or get the pupu platter at Aku Aku, a local version of Trader Vic's. I had a weakness for their egg rolls and butterflied shrimp.

I'd occasionally catch Bill grabbing naps at his terminal during our late-nighters. He'd be in the middle of a line of code when he'd gradually tilt forward until his nose touched the keyboard. After dozing an hour or two, he'd open his eyes, squint at the screen, blink twice, and resume precisely where he'd left off—a prodigious feat of concentration.

Working so closely together, the three of us developed a strong camaraderie. Because our program ran on top of the multiuser TOPS-10 operating system, we could all work simultaneously. We staged nightly competitions to squeeze a subroutine into the fewest instructions, taking notepads to separate corners of the room and scrawling away. Then someone would say, "I can do it in nine." And someone else would call out, "Well, I can do it in five!" At one point, after Monte laid his floating-point math routine on the floor, Bill sprawled next to the long tail of fan-folded paper to find a few last trims. We knew that each byte saved would leave that much more room for users to add to their applications. (Today we live in a different world, where sixteen *gigabytes* of memory—four million times our BASIC budget for the Altair—are packed into the base iPhone. Handcrafted code is by and large a lost art. People still try to make programs efficient, but they no longer fight to save that last byte, or even megabyte.)

A few years ago, when I reminisced with Monte about those days, he compared programming to writing a novel—a good analogy, I thought, for our approach to Altair BASIC. At the beginning we outlined our plot, the conceptual phase of the coding. Then we took the big problem and carved it into its component chapters, from the hundreds of subroutines to their related data structures, before putting all the parts back together. If a line didn't work, we'd re-edit our draft. The heart of the matter was to sustain the big structural picture while hammering out the details of a small subroutine, going back and forth between the two. It was the most demanding and stimulating mental challenge I had ever faced.

As we pushed on, our confidence grew. One day we called MITS to ask about the handshake subroutines on the Teletype for coding the Altair's input and output. We knew we were on the right track when Bill Yates, Ed Roberts's partner and lead engineer, told us that no one else had even posed the question. At that point we figured the job was ours to lose.

Returning to Aiken late one night after a fast-food run, we were stopped by the campus police and asked for our IDs. We'd considered our use of the facility harmless, especially since the PDP-10 was underutilized. But we didn't know that Harvard split the computer's maintenance costs with the U.S. Defense Department, based on usage. I'd relied on Bill's password account for my work on the simulator, which ate a lot of processor time. When the January bills came due, Harvard's share was up conspicuously, with one student the prime culprit: William Henry Gates III. (When he appeared before the university's administrative board that summer, Bill got off with a slap on the wrist.)

By late February, eight weeks after our first contact with MITS, the interpreter was done. Shoehorned into about 3,200 bytes, roughly two thousand lines of code, it was one tight little BASIC—stripped down, for sure, but robust for its size. No one could have beaten the functionality and speed crammed into that tiny footprint of memory: "The best piece of work we ever did," as Bill told me recently. And it was a true collaboration. I'd estimate that 45 percent of the code was Bill's, 30 percent Monte's, and 25 percent mine, excluding my development tools.*

All things considered, it was quite an achievement for three people our age. If you checked that software today, I believe it would stack up against anything written by our old mentors at C-Cubed. Bill and I had grown into crack programmers.

And we were just getting started.

AS I GOT ready to go to Albuquerque, Bill began to worry. What if I'd screwed up one of the numbers used to represent the 8080 instructions in the macro assembler? Our BASIC had tested out fine on my simulator on the PDP-10, but we had no sure evidence that the simulator itself was flawless. A single character out of place

---

*The opening credits embedded in our BASIC were as follows: "Paul Allen wrote the non-runtime stuff. Bill Gates wrote the runtime stuff. Monte Davidoff wrote the math package."

might halt the program cold when it ran on the real chip. The night before my departure, after I knocked off for a few hours of sleep, Bill stayed up with the 8080 manual and triple-checked my macros. He was bleary-eyed the next morning when I stopped by en route to Logan Airport to pick up the fresh paper tape he'd punched out. The byte codes were correct, Bill said. As far as he could tell, my work was error free.

The flight was uneventful up until the plane's final descent, when it hit me that we'd forgotten something: a bootstrap loader, the small sequence of instructions to tell the Altair how to read the BASIC interpreter and then stick it into memory. A loader was a necessity for microprocessors in the pre-ROM era. Without one, that yellow tape in my briefcase would be worthless. I felt like an idiot for not thinking of it at Aiken, where I could have coded it without rushing and simulated and debugged it on the PDP-10.

Now time was short. Minutes before landing, I grabbed a steno pad and began scribbling the loader code in machine language—no labels, no symbols, just a series of three-digit numbers in octal (base 8), the lingua franca for Intel's chips. Each number represented one byte, a single instruction for the 8080, and I knew most of them by heart. "Hand assembly" is a famously laborious process, even in small quantities. I finished the program in twenty-one bytes—not my most concise work, but I was too rushed to strive for elegance.

I came out of the terminal sweating and dressed in my professional best, a tan Ultrasuede jacket and tie. Ed Roberts was supposed to pick me up, so I stood there for ten minutes looking for someone in a business suit. Not far down the entryway to the airport, a pickup truck pulled up and a big, burly, jowly guy—six foot four, maybe 280 pounds—climbed out. He had on jeans and a short-sleeve shirt with a string tie, the first one I'd seen outside of a Western. He came up to me and in a booming Southern accent asked, "Are you Paul Allen?" His wavy black hair was receding at the front.

I said, "Yes, are you Ed?"

He said, "Come on, get in the truck."

As we bounced over the city's sun-baked streets, I wondered how all this was going to turn out. I'd expected a high-powered executive from some cutting-edge entrepreneurial firm, like the ones clustered along Route 128, the high-tech beltway around Boston. The reality had a whole different vibe. (On a later trip to Albuquerque, I came down from a plane and got hit in the head by tumbleweed on the tarmac. I wasn't in Massachusetts anymore.)

Ed said, "Let's go over to MITS so you can see the Altair." He drove into a low-rent commercial area by the state fairgrounds and stopped at a one-story strip mall. With its brick facade and big plate-glass windows, the Cal-Linn Building might have looked modern in 1955. A beauty salon occupied one storefront around the corner. I followed Ed through a glass door and into a light industrial space that housed MITS's engineering and manufacturing departments. As I passed an assembly line of a dozen or so weary-looking workers, stuffing kit boxes with capacitors and Mylar circuit boards, I understood why Ed was so focused on getting a BASIC. He had little interest in software, which he referred to as variable hardware, but he knew that the Altair's sales wouldn't keep expanding unless it could do something useful.

When I arrived, there were only two or three assembled computers in the whole plant; everything else had gone out the door. Ed led me to a messy workbench where I found a sky-blue metal box with ALTAIR 8800 stenciled on a charcoal gray front panel. Modeled after a popular minicomputer, with rows of toggle switches for input and flashing red LEDs for output, the Altair looked like a slightly smaller version of our Traf-O-Data machine, about seven inches high by eighteen inches wide. It seemed fantastic that such a small box could contain a general-purpose computer with a legitimate CPU. But I had no doubt that the Altair was the real McCoy. The only mystery was whether it would work with the paper tape stowed in my briefcase.

Hovering over the computer was Bill Yates, a sallow, taciturn string bean of a man with wire-rimmed glasses—Stan Laurel to Ed's Oliver Hardy. He was running a memory test to make sure the machine would be ready for me, with the cover flipped up so I could see inside. Plugged into slots on the Altair bus, an Ed Roberts innovation that was to become the industry standard, were seven 1K static memory cards. It might have been the only microprocessor in the world with that much random-access memory, more than enough for my demo. The machine was hooked up to a Teletype with a paper-tape reader. All seemed in order.

It was getting late, and Ed suggested that we put off the BASIC trial to the next morning. "How about dinner?" he said. He took me to a three-dollar buffet at a Mexican place called Pancho's, where you got what you paid for. Afterward, back in the truck, a yellowjacket flew in and stung me on the neck. And I thought, *This is all kind of surreal.* Ed said he'd drop me at the hotel that he'd booked for me, which I'd thought would be along the lines of a Motel 6. I'd only brought forty dollars; I was chronically low on cash, and it would be years before I'd have a credit card. I blanched when Ed pulled up to the Sheraton, the nicest hotel in town, and escorted me to the reception desk.

"Checking in?" the clerk said. "That will be fifty dollars."

It was one of the more embarrassing moments of my life. "Ed, I'm sorry about this," I stammered, "but I don't have that kind of cash."

He just looked at me for a minute; I guess I wasn't what he'd been expecting, either. Then he said, "That's OK, we'll put it on my card."

Alone in my room, I called Bill and said, "They've got the computer working." We were excited but also nervous, because the next day would tell the tale.

The following morning, with Ed and Bill Yates hanging over my shoulder, I sat at the Altair console and toggled in my bootstrap loader on the front panel's switches, byte by byte. Unlike the flat plastic keys on the PDP-8, the Altair's were thin metal switches, tough on the fingers. It took about five minutes, and I hoped no one noticed how nervous I was. *This isn't going to work,* I kept thinking.

I entered my twenty-first instruction, set the starting address, and pressed the RUN switch. The machine's lights took on a diffused red glow as the 8080 executed the loader's multiple steps—at least that much seemed to be working. I turned on the paper-tape reader, and the Teletype chugged as it pulled our BASIC interpreter through. At ten characters per second, reading the tape took seven minutes. (People grabbed coffee breaks while computers loaded paper tape in those days.) The MITS guys stood there silently. At the end I pressed STOP and reset the address to 0. My index finger poised over the RUN switch once again. . . .

To that point, I couldn't be sure of anything. Any one of a thousand things might have gone wrong in the simulator or the interpreter, despite Bill's double-checking. I pressed RUN. *There's just no way this is going to work.*

The Teletype's printer clattered to life. I gawked at the uppercase characters; I couldn't believe it.

But there it was: **MEMORY SIZE?**

"Hey," said Bill Yates, "it printed something!" It was the first time he or Ed had seen the Altair do anything beyond a small memory test. They were flabbergasted. I was dumbfounded. We all gaped at the machine for a few seconds, and then I typed in the total number of bytes in the seven memory cards: 7168.

**OK**, the Altair spit back. Getting this far told me that 5 percent of our BASIC was definitely working, but we weren't yet home free. The acid test would be a standard command that we'd used as a midterm exam for our software back in Cambridge. It relied on Bill's core coding and Monte's floating-point math and even my "crunch" code, which condensed certain words (like "PRINT") into a single character. If it worked, the lion's share of our BASIC was good to go. If it didn't, we'd failed.

I typed in the command:

**PRINT 2+2**

The machine's response was instantaneous:

4

That was a magical moment. Ed exclaimed, "Oh my god, it printed '4'!" He'd gone into debt and bet everything on a full-functioning microcomputer, and now it looked as though his vision would come true. He couldn't get over the fact that Bill and I had solved the puzzle without any of the hardware—that was astonishing to him. But Ed wasn't as surprised as I was that our 8080 BASIC had run perfectly its first time out of the chute. The Altair's one-digit response, the classic kindergarten computation, proved that my simulator was on target. I was quietly ecstatic and deeply, deeply relieved.

"Let's try a real program," I said, trying to sound nonchalant. Yates pulled out a book called *101 BASIC Computer Games,* a slim volume that DEC brought out in 1973. The text-based Lunar Lander program, created long before computers had graphics capability, was just thirty-five lines long. Still, I thought it might build Ed's confidence. I typed in the program. Yates launched his lunar module and, after a few tries, settled it safely on the moon's surface. Everything in our BASIC had worked.

Ed said, "I want you to come back to my office." Through a flimsy-looking doorway, I took a seat in front of his desk and the biggest orange glass ashtray I had ever seen. Ed was a chain smoker who'd take two or three puffs, stub the cigarette out, and light the next one. He'd go through half a pack in a single conversation.

"You're the first guys who came in and showed us something," he said. "We want you to draw up a license so we can sell this with the Altair. We can work out the terms later." I couldn't stop grinning. Once back at the hotel, I called Bill, who was thrilled with the news. We were in business now, for real; in Harvard parlance, we were *golden*. I hardly needed a plane to fly back to Boston.

From Honeywell I'd call Ed periodically with updates. One day he interrupted me: "Stop, stop. How would you like to move down here to New Mexico and run our software group?" Albuquerque felt foreign to me, and I'd only just learned that it wasn't in Arizona. But the salary was $16,000, a bump from what I was making at Honeywell, and it was hard to refuse an offer to work on the code we'd created. Besides, Bill and I agreed that one of us probably needed to be there to service our customer and ride herd over software distribution. I was the freer agent, and the one who'd received the invitation, so it fell to me.

I called Ed back and said, "When do you want me to start?"

To a man, my coworkers declared that I was making a big mistake. It was crazy, they said, to ditch an established firm for some fly-by-night start-up selling hobbyist kits in the desert. "Your job's safe at Honeywell," they kept telling me. "You can work here for years."

I knew that my move was a risk, but I was disappointed in my colleagues. I wanted to hear something like: *Good luck, young fellow, and more power to you.* I'm afraid that I was less than gracious in my going-away party speech: "I guess I don't have anyone to congratulate me for leaving except myself."

CHAPTER 7

# MITS

$E$d Roberts was my senior by twelve years, a fact that shaped his first encounter with computers. When he was stationed at Kirtland Air Force Base in Albuquerque in the 1960s, its weapons lab had one of the world's most powerful computer installations: two Control Data Corporation 6600s, the fastest mainframes in captivity. But Ed never got to touch them. He had to hand his batch cards over for processing, "and I always thought it was a bad way to go," as he later explained. "I thought everybody ought to own their own computer, and I thought that for years and years."

In 1969, when I was at C-Cubed, Ed founded a new company in his garage: MITS, for Micro Instrumentation and Telemetry Systems. He began in the model rocket electronics business, then shifted to handheld electronic calculator kits. When Texas Instruments killed the market with cheap mass-produced models, and MITS was about to go under, Ed turned to the idea that had nagged at him since Kirtland: "a real, fully operational [personal] computer that . . . could do anything that a general purpose minicomputer of the time could do." His "ultimate gadget," as he called it, would be a sensation if he could pull it off. There was nothing close to it on the market.

Like me, Ed was following the chips. When he got wind of the 8080 microprocessor, he wangled some handwritten data sheets from an Intel rep before the release date. Looking at the specs, Ed could see that the microprocessor was fast and powerful enough to support the type of computer he'd been talking about, a machine he could sell in kit form for under $400. He made a deal with Intel for a thousand chips at $75 apiece, a steep discount. To get a loan, he told his bank that he could sell eight hundred machines in the first year, or four times as many as his private estimate.

Within weeks of the *Popular Electronics* bombshell, prepaid orders flooded into MITS from two thousand customers. Many sent cash for what was basically a proof-of-concept prototype, a bare-bones machine with no keyboard, no display, and just 256 bytes of memory. Because Bill Yates had yet to design the interface cards for a Teletype or audiocassette hookup, the only way to get data into the Altair was through the front-panel switches. A tiny 50-byte program required hundreds of settings in just the right order. But some people didn't care; they figured they'd buy the Altair now and decide what to use it for later.

The mail in Ed's office piled nearly to the ceiling. The balance in his checking account swung a half-million dollars from red to black in six weeks. His skeleton staff, cut from ninety to fewer than twenty after the calculator meltdown, was swamped. Ed found himself at the head of a movement to give people the technology they'd wanted for a long, long time. In the words of David Bunnell, MITS's vice president of marketing, the Altair "liberated that technology to make it available to anybody who had a brain."

I RETURNED TO Albuquerque as MITS's "director of software development" just after Easter, in April 1975. After asking for two weeks' salary in advance, I moved into the Sand and Sage Motel on Central Avenue, the old Route 66, just across the street from the Cal-Linn building—a strong selling point, because I had no car. (I'd left the Chrysler with Bill, who lent it to an acquaintance. It disappeared for good after that.)

The MITS software department was at the far end of the

building, next to a vacuum cleaner repair shop. Our space was maybe a thousand square feet: a walk-in reception area with our terminals along one wall, and then a row of doorless cubbyholes that barely held a desk and two chairs apiece. I took the one at the front—I had my pick, as I had no staff. A month later, I'd be joined by Gary Runyan, whom Ed had hired to create an internal accounting system, and a month after that, I got a secretary. To keep the office from getting too noisy, Gary would wheel the Teletype into the bathroom whenever he printed out a listing.

I'd come at a frenetic time, with all hands on deck to answer customer phone calls and sort through the growing order backlog. A few days after I arrived, the company published the first issue of *Computer Notes,* edited by David Bunnell, one of the first periodicals devoted to microcomputers. On his inaugural front page, David hailed our software's arrival: "Altair BASIC—Up and Running." Though we were still months from shipping, Ed Roberts knew that our software gave the Altair a strategic edge over the competition that was sure to follow. Our relationship was perfectly symbiotic. Bill and I benefited from Ed's distribution and marketing networks, while MITS, a classic early innovator, got out front with our programmer-friendly language and dedicated support and upgrades.

While Bill cranked away at Harvard to build our BASIC's more powerful 8K and 12K versions, I spent my days consulting with Bill Yates and helping with technical questions from our growing client base. I put the machine through its paces for visiting reps and took an unending stream of calls from frustrated buyers. It wasn't easy to assemble an Altair, which required more than a thousand solder connections before you could power it on. Some of our customers were engineers, but others were lawyers and dentists and car mechanics with no background in computer technology. After taking months to finish the assembly, they'd labor to toggle in a small demo routine. Then they'd call me.

CUSTOMER: I don't think my Altair works.

ME: Are all the lights on in front?

CUSTOMER: Yes, they're all on, but it still doesn't work.

ME: OK, you're going to have to buy some memory.

CUSTOMER: Oh yeah, memory. What's that?

Here was the problem: To boost its profit margin, MITS had stopped shipping the minuscule 256-byte memory card that was bundled with the first batch of $398 kit machines. When you booted up a machine without a card, all the lights went on simultaneously, a bad sign. I'd tell the poor customers that they'd need at least 1K static memory ($176 in kit form) or a 4K dynamic memory board ($264). Few seemed irritated or angry at the news. They were just happy to have their own computer, and I knew how they felt. I'd been thrilled when Ed gave me an Altair to use at home.

Some callers were a little odd. One began, "I'm having a problem, listen to this." The next thing I heard was the sound of a dial-up modem, a horrendous screech that nearly ruptured my eardrum. The caller said, "Does that sound like RS-232 to you?" I told him that I couldn't diagnose his problem by ear, then walked him through the solution.

Eddie Currie, Ed Roberts's general manager and milder alter ego, got one customer who insisted that his Altair wouldn't work right because he and the computer had a personality conflict. Eddie said, "Well, how do you think we can resolve this?"

And the customer said, "Maybe you could send me another Altair with a personality more like mine."

AFTER HARVARD LET out for the summer, Bill and Monte joined me in Albuquerque. We rented a furnished two-bedroom apartment on the ground floor of the Portals, a five-minute drive from MITS. It was a standard medium-rise apartment building, with shag carpeting and a courtyard swimming pool that we never used.

Later we added Chris Larson, a younger Lakeside student who'd originally been conscripted for Traf-O-Data. Bill and I each took a bedroom, while Monte and Chris made do with the couch or floor.

In need of transportation, I bought my first new car, a metallic blue hatchback Chevy Monza. Bill came with me to pick it up, and we had a hilarious time getting it home. I'd never used a stick shift before, and I'd pop the clutch and stall every twenty feet. Bill tried, with similar results. The Monza was a high-powered little number with a V-8 engine and an undersize clutch that I'd burn out once a year.

I did MITS business all day, then stayed on as Bill, Monte, and Chris trickled in to work on our BASIC. I'd arranged a cheap time-sharing deal with the local school district, which made its PDP-10 available late in the afternoon. After editing our programs on the trusty ASR-33 Teletype, we'd have someone shoot down each day to the schools' office and pick up our listings from their fast line printer. Later on we'd lease a DECwriter terminal and install it in our living room.

Our day's highlights were our meals: Furr's Cafeteria for chicken-fried steak; Mr. Powdrell's Barbecue for beef sandwiches, with old Mr. Powdrell still tending the smoker; Long John Silver's when we missed Seattle seafood. After hours, we'd often wind up at Denny's, where we'd be so revved up from our work that we'd freak out the waitresses. I remember a night when one of them looked from one pale face to the next and asked, "Are you guys speeding?"

"No," Monte replied, "we're programmers."

After dinner we often took in the latest action movie before heading back to the office to code for hours. When I finally got home, I'd unwind by plugging in my Stratocaster and trying to play along with Aerosmith or Jimi Hendrix. (Monte preferred Emerson, Lake & Palmer; Bill played R & B or sang at the top of his lungs to Frank Sinatra's "My Way.") One night, as I lay in my bed in the dark, someone pushed through my window and into my room. I shouted and he fled. A few nights later, I found my prized Stratocaster gone.

As the summer wore on, Bill and Monte fell into the habit of working until sunup or whenever the school system said we had to stop. I can picture Bill debugging BASIC on a Teletype in the corner, flipping through the printout listing in his lap and typing with fierce intensity. He lived in binary states: either bursting with nervous energy on his dozen Cokes a day, or dead to the world. He'd work until drained and then curl up on the floor in his office and be asleep within fifteen seconds. Sometimes I'd return to MITS in the morning and see Bill's feet sticking out of his office doorway in a pair of scuffed loafers.

Working the equivalent of two jobs and programming on the weekends, I logged crazy hours myself. One day blurred into the next, as my journal attests:

> *7:30 AM—left work for home. Ate omelet. Sleep.*
> *4:00 Work. Meet w/Eddie & Chamberlin. Want to know*
>    *royalty situation.*
> *6:00 Dinner.*
> *7:00 Work—organic stuff. Can't find notebook, where is*
>    *it?!*
> *9:45 Go home for a while. Sleep.*
> *2:00 Wake up. Go to work. Put tables in BASIC.*

That was life in Albuquerque: so much code, so little time.

BY JULY 1975, our 4K and 8K BASICs were ready to ship. Prepping the orders with a hand-powered winder, I'd thread in the paper tape, hook my finger in one of the winder's holes, and spin, a big advance over rolling by hand. We were thrilled to see those tapes boxed for shipping—our baby, going out into the world.

In Boston and the Bay Area, in labs and corporations like Honeywell, microcomputers were viewed as a passing fad. But the doubters didn't faze us. We were certain that the tech establishment was wrong and we were right, and the proof came each day in the mail sacks bulging with orders for the Altair and our BASIC. In that little ramshackle building in Albuquerque, it felt as though anything was possible.

OUR ONE PRODUCT was 8080 BASIC, and MITS was our only customer; our interests were aligned. We'd been working on a handshake with Ed for months, but now we were ready to formalize the relationship. After some back-and-forth on the numbers, Bill went to a local attorney to have the papers drawn. In return for "the exclusive right and license" to sell our BASIC worldwide for ten years, MITS would give us $3,000 up front, plus per-copy royalties of $30 to $60, depending on the version. We'd receive 50 percent of gross receipts from BASIC licenses bought without hardware sales. Sublicenses to third-party OEMs, the original equipment manufacturers who made their own computers, would also be divided fifty-fifty. Since Bill and I retained ownership of our software, we were free to initiate these deals.

Our lawyer inserted one other clause to protect us. Paragraph 5, titled "Company Effort," stated: "The company agrees to use its best efforts to license, promote, and commercialize the PROGRAM. The company's failure to use its best efforts as aforesaid shall constitute sufficient grounds and reason for termination of this agreement by Licensors. . . ."

One day that July, Ed came in waving the contract and saying, "I trust you guys. I'm going to sign this right now. I don't even have to read it."

Bill and I just looked at each other. Though we didn't think we were ripping Ed off, the contract was clearly crafted in our favor. Bill said, "You don't want another lawyer to review it?"

Ed said, "No, I'm sure it's fine."

In the life of any company, a few moments stand out. Signing that original BASIC contract was a big one for Bill and me. Now our partnership needed a name. We considered Allen & Gates, but it sounded too much like a law firm. My next idea: Micro-Soft, for *micro*processors and *soft*ware. While the typography would be in flux over the next year or so (including a brief transition as Micro Soft), we both knew instantly that the name was right. Micro-Soft was simple and straightforward. It conveyed just what we were about.

From the time we'd started together in Massachusetts, I'd assumed that our partnership would be a fifty-fifty proposition. But Bill had another idea. "It's not right for you to get half," he said. "You had your salary at MITS while I did almost everything on BASIC without one back in Boston. I should get more. I think it should be sixty-forty."

At first I was taken aback. But as I pondered it, Bill's position didn't seem unreasonable. I'd been coding what I could in my spare time, and feeling guilty that I couldn't do more, but Bill had been instrumental in packing our software with "more features per byte of memory than any other BASIC we know," as I'd written for *Computer Notes*. All in all, I thought, a sixty-forty split might be fair.

PASSING BY THE MITS loading dock one day, I saw boxes stacked high with eight-inch floppy disk drives, the new storage devices recently introduced by IBM. Each one had a capacity of 243K (nearly a quarter of a megabyte), which would "enable the Altair 8800 to function as a really sophisticated computer system," as *Computer Notes* promised that July. Floppy disk drives were a giant step toward a personal machine that rivaled minicomputers for functionality. An 8K program that took thirteen minutes to load using paper tape, or five minutes with an audiocassette, needed only a few seconds on a floppy.

But Altair owners wouldn't be able to use the new drives until Bill wrote our stand-alone Disk BASIC, so called because of its primitive internal file system, and I was getting nervous. As summer drew to a close, I kept prodding him to get started: "Bill, it's almost time for you to go back to school and you haven't written a single line of code."

"It's OK, I'm thinking about it," he'd say. "I've got the design in my head."

Then it was: "Bill, you're leaving in ten days. Can you really get this done?"

"Yeah, I can do it. Don't worry about it."

Shortly before Labor Day, Bill checked into a hotel with three legal pads and ten pencils. Five days later he came out with thousands of bytes of assembly language code. He typed it into a terminal, handed me the legal pads, and said, "OK, you're gonna have to finish debugging it. I've got to go." Then he was off to Harvard.

Later on, as the company grew and his executive duties multiplied, Bill would get fewer opportunities for such high-wire creativity. In a way, that was too bad—he had a rare gift for programming.

IN SEPTEMBER 1975, I flew east to observe Ed Roberts's latest marketing ploy in action. A college student named Mike Hunter was on a six-month, sixty-city tour in a Dodge camper van known as the MITS-Mobile, showing off the marvels of the Altair. I joined him at a Holiday Inn in Huntsville, Alabama, where Mike set up three computers on a folding table. By six o'clock, most of the sixty chairs were filled at ten dollars a head, then five times the cost of a movie. The crowd was heavy with dyed-in-the-wool hobbyists and engineers from central casting: pocket protectors, slide rules, horn-rimmed glasses, crew cuts. It felt as though we'd traveled back in time to 1962.

Mike began with a three-hour seminar, using Ed's homemade slides: an hour on the history of computer hardware; an hour on our software; an hour on the Altair. After a Q & A, the engineers got to play with the computers. "Is that a dummy model?" someone asked. In retort, Mike swiftly toggled in the bootstrap loader and ran Lunar Lander with our 4K BASIC. Doubters would check under the table, looking for cables to some minicomputer they imagined had to be hidden behind the partition. They found it hard to believe that such a little box could run a real program, or that you could buy a bona fide computer for the cost of a high-end scientific calculator. But once they saw it was real, the engineers became almost giddy with enthusiasm. Mike won over a lot of customers that night.

Back in Albuquerque, with Altair sales smashing the $1 million mark in its first year on the market, MITS expanded back to nearly a hundred employees. I continued to tune our BASIC, and took pains in writing its user manuals. I loved getting responses like this one, from a happy customer in Washington State:

> *I've seen and used other BASICs, but byte-for-byte, Altair is the most powerful BASIC I've seen. . . . The level of your documentation is, for me though, the high point. Sections for those who know nothing and sections for those who know a lot, plus sections that "normal" people can read and understand.*

In a number of phone calls to Harvard, I pressed Bill to help me take Micro-Soft to the next level. I projected that our royalties would soon support him in Albuquerque, and in November Bill convinced his parents to allow him to take a leave of absence. But when our 1975 royalty statement arrived, we were sorely disappointed. Our revenues totaled a mere $16,005. By Bill's calculation, fewer than one in ten Altair buyers were purchasing BASIC. It was hard to fathom, because the machine was next to worthless without it.

Finally we figured out why our sales were so low. People had a good reason not to buy our software.

Many of them were getting it for free.

THE PROBLEM BEGAN with Ed Roberts's pricing policy. With the base Altair kit costing around four hundred dollars, Ed barely broke even on the machines themselves. The real money for MITS was in peripherals, like the memory cards that plugged into the Altair's bus. When Intel and Texas Instruments ran short of memory chips, Ed turned to an off-brand called Signetics, whose chips were hopelessly flaky. I started getting calls, less friendly this time, from people who'd invested in 4K of memory and still couldn't load BASIC. I'd see Bill Yates tearing his hair out in the engineering department over defective Signetics cards. As David Bunnell and Eddie Currie later acknowledged in *PC Magazine,* ". . . the probability of getting a 4K memory board to work when assembled from [an Altair] kit was remote. And the likelihood that it would continue to work would easily have been rated zero."

Meanwhile, a new wave of computer clubs had been energized by the MITS-Mobile and *Computer Notes.* At the Homebrew Computer Club in Silicon Valley, a carpenter named Steve Dompier programmed the Altair to "play" a song by generating interference on an adjacent radio that was tuned between stations. (Dompier's opening number was the Beatles' "Fool on the Hill.") But Altair buyers soon wanted more than tinny renditions of pop tunes, and they needed our BASIC. But why purchase it for $75 when a facsimile could be churned out for no charge?

Hobbyists had a hard time accepting software as intellectual property, a concept with little precedent. It wasn't until the year of the Altair's release that a national commission declared that computer programs, "to the extent that they embody an author's original creation, are proper subject matter of copyright." The Homebrew Computer Club wasn't far removed from the hippie ethos of Haight-Ashbury. Members freely shared software like "Tiny" BASIC, a minimalist program out of Stanford, and why should our program be any different? During a MITS-Mobile stop in Palo Alto, one Homebrew associate reportedly helped himself to our BASIC interpreter and punched out fifty duplicates to distribute at the club's next meeting. And that was only the beginning.

David Bunnell was a former antiwar activist who came from

a newspaper family in Nebraska and didn't mind stirring up controversy. (He'd later become the preeminent publisher of personal computer magazines, including *PC Magazine, PC World,* and *Macworld.*) In September 1975, David used *Computer Notes* to admonish "a few of our customers for arrogantly, and I think foolishly . . . ripping off MITS software." The following month, Ed Roberts wrote that anyone "who is using a stolen copy of MITS BASIC should identify himself for what he is, a thief." But nobody seemed to be listening, and our royalties languished into the New Year.*

"This just isn't right," Bill said. "We've worked so hard on this thing, and people are just ripping us off." I felt the same way—would all those eighteen-hour days be for naught? Fed up, Bill penned "An Open Letter to Hobbyists" for the February 1976 issue of *Computer Notes.* Identifying himself as "General Partner, Micro-Soft" (likely the first published use of the name), he explained how we'd developed our BASIC and how our royalties thus far amounted to less than two dollars per hour of our time.

> *Why is this? As the majority of hobbyists must be aware, most of you steal your software. Hardware must be paid for, but software is something to share. Who cares if the people who worked on it get paid?*
>
> *Is this fair? . . . One thing you do [by stealing software] is prevent good software from being written. Who can afford to do professional work for nothing? . . . The fact is, no one besides us has invested a lot of money in hobby software. . . . Most directly, the thing you do is theft.*

Although Bill had gone no further than David or Ed, he provoked a much angrier reaction. Maybe it was his stinging sarcasm,

---

*The theft of Altair BASIC foreshadowed the wholesale piracy of copyrighted material that plagues the entertainment industry today. Once a song or movie or piece of software was reduced to binary bits, it became easy to copy, even more so with the ascendance of the Internet.

or the fact that David got Bill's letter published in half a dozen hobbyist periodicals. The Southern California Computer Society threatened a class action suit for defamation. Jim Warren, editor of *Dr. Dobb's Journal of Computer Calisthenics*, wrote:

> *There is a viable alternative to the problems raised by Bill Gates in his irate letter to computer hobbyists concerning "ripping off" software. When software is free, or so inexpensive that it's easier to pay for it than to duplicate it, then it won't be "stolen."*

Though we received no checks from repentant pirates, the debate became part of a gradual climate change. While theft remained common, both end users and commercial firms began to accept that software, like hardware, had intrinsic value.

Ed Roberts was furious that Bill's letter had gone out on MITS letterhead without his authorization. He insisted on a follow-up in *Computer Notes* two months later, in which Bill stuck to his position "about the stealing that was going on," but made clear that he was not a MITS employee. (Earlier, after Bill had lobbied for compensation for his work on Altair software, Ed briefly put him on the MITS payroll. According to a pay stub dated September 19, 1975, Bill received $90 for a forty-hour week, or $2.25 per hour.)

Ed's friction with Bill had been simmering for some time. Though still in his early thirties, Ed seemed like someone from our parents' generation. His five sons called him "sir," and he could intimidate you in a fatherly way. But nobody intimidated Bill, who wouldn't feign politeness if he thought someone was wrong. When Bill pushed on licensing terms or bad-mouthed the flaky Signetics cards, Ed thought he was insubordinate. You could hear them yelling throughout the plant, and it was quite a spectacle—the burly ex-military officer standing toe to toe with the owlish prodigy about half his weight, neither giving an inch.

Ed was troubled, too, by the countercultural ambience in his growing software department, where we'd crank up Hendrix or Blue Oyster Cult for energy. Apart from my beard, which I grew long in Albuquerque, my own style was conventional: dark slacks, blue shirts, and loafers. But a fair number of my staff considered shoes optional, along with shaves, haircuts, and hygiene. "You can bring the customers in to see Paul," Ed would tell his people, "but keep them away from the rest of that department."

Beneath the surface, Ed and Bill had a lot in common. They were equally driven and persistent, and both thought they were smarter than just about everyone else. (Usually they were right.) Ed respected people who were creative and productive, and he understood our value to MITS. One day he brought an old friend to our office and said, "I can't control these guys. But they're so smart I've got to keep them. They're just so good at what they do."

AROUND THE TIME of Bill's letter, the Altair boom enabled MITS to move into larger quarters near the airport. I received a promotion to "vice president of software," though I don't recall getting a raise. A month later, MITS staged the World Altair Computer Convention at the Airport Marina Hotel. For three days, Albuquerque was the undisputed capital of the personal computer subculture. People came from nearly every state—and from Japan, Taiwan, and Australia—to exchange ideas and share their excitement. The star panelist was Ted Nelson, the wild-eyed author of the underground sensation *Computer Lib*. (Nelson also co-invented hypertext, by which words in one article can link to a related page, a pervasive aspect of today's Web.) He summed up his wild philosophy in four maxims: "Most people are fools, most authority is malignant, God does not exist, and everything is wrong."

The convention was Ed Roberts's finest hour, save for one ominous development out of Silicon Valley. Processor Technology rented a suite at the hotel to promote their more reliable static memory cards, which plugged neatly into the Altair's open-architecture bus. When David Bunnell ripped up their sign in the hotel lobby, I realized that MITS had stronger competition than it had banked on. Early innovators rarely stay way out in front for long. Everybody sees what's been done and starts to copy the heck out of it, and sometimes the followers do a better job. One year after the Altair's breakout in *Popular Electronics,* IMS Associates started shipping the IMSAI 8080, an aluminum-cased Altair clone with commercial-grade plastic paddle switches, a snap-in front panel, and a superior 20-amp power supply. The following summer brought contenders like Processor Technology's Sol, with an integrated keyboard and handsome walnut frame. A dozen others waited in the wings.

Ed Roberts no longer had the microcomputer market virtually all to himself. In February 1976, a MITS ad claimed that there were "more Altair computers up and running than all the other general-purpose microcomputers combined." But by the time MITS came out with the improved Altair 8800b that spring, it had lost precious ground. By the end of the year, its market share would fall to 25 percent, against 17 percent for IMSAI and 8 percent apiece for Processor Technology and Southwest Technical Products. The trend was not encouraging for Ed. But for two young men in the software business, it was the sound of opportunity knocking.

IN APRIL 1976. Micro-Soft hired its first salaried employee: Marc McDonald, an old friend from Lakeside. He moved in with us at the Portals, soon to be followed by Ric Weiland. By summer, Bill was back from school. After borrowing my car one night, he woke me from a sound sleep. "They put me in a holding cell and you're my phone call," he said. "Can you get me out? It's terrible in here!" Picked up for speeding on Central Avenue, he'd given the arresting officer a hard time and was thrown in with the drunks. He wasn't thrilled with his fellow inmates, in particular the inebriated one who was throwing up next to him. I was short on cash for the bondsman, so I went to Bill's room and grabbed a mound of change on his dresser. It was just enough to spring him.

Sometimes I wondered why Bill drove so fast; I decided it was his way of letting off steam. He'd get so wound up in our work that he needed a way to stop thinking about the business and the code for a while. His breakneck driving wasn't so different from table stakes poker or edge-of-the-envelope waterskiing. They were all needed escapes.

"The weather here is exceptional," I wrote home that spring. "The sun is shining but there are always cool breezes—and all the plants are just starting to bloom. I'm sure Dad would enjoy it!" But had my parents seen my complexion, they'd have known I wasn't getting much sun. My work was so all-consuming that the rest of my life went on hold, and Rita and I canceled our plans for marriage. At age twenty-three, I just wasn't ready.

The personal computer market was exploding, with new machines emerging by the month. Later that year, we made our first sales to third-party manufacturers: Data Technology Corporation, National Cash Register, Citibank, General Electric. All were for flat fees, which locked us in as the exclusive provider of BASIC for their machines. Our strategy was to price our products so low that it wouldn't pay for hardware companies to develop their own BASIC, especially since it would delay their entry into the market to do so. But after a $50,000 sale to GE, Bill had seller's remorse. As he wrote to me:

> *I think we got bargained down to a very very low level in the GE deal and unless we get the [royalty] protection we need in that, I don't think it is a good deal for MITS or us. . . . The main idea is to get a good deal that doesn't require much work for as much money as possible without being too inconsistent with other sales of BASIC. . . .*

A short time later, we licensed BASIC to NCR for $175,000. Even with half the proceeds going to Ed Roberts, that single fee would pay five or six programmers for a year. Though we still relied on MITS's marketing team to help with OEM sales, our business was growing fast. Over time, as Microsoft became *the* language development company for the personal computer industry, its partners divided the labor to play to their strengths. Bill focused on legal and contract issues, drummed up new business, and navigated our license sales. Whenever I pointed him to a new microcomputer, he'd be all over it to try to sell our software.

It was my task to guide our programmers as we crafted BASIC for a mushrooming OEM clientele, adding features and fixing bugs. I did a good deal of the grunt work myself and made sure that our products got delivered and properly implemented and upgraded. But my most vital charge was to chart our future. Where Bill eyed tomorrow's markets, I looked to a more distant horizon. What would our customers want six months or a year from now, and what did we need to do to get it to them before anyone else?

Our primary task was to adapt BASIC, our bread-and-butter product, for a new group of microprocessors now competing with the Intel 8080. This work had kicked off the previous fall, when MITS announced an Altair for Motorola's new 8-bit chip. It gathered steam with the release of the 6502 chip from MOS Technology at an unheard-of $25. For each new microprocessor, I created a new set of development tools on the PDP-10, while Ric helped with the BASIC interpreter rewrites. Though the work was a grind, I was glad to extend our company's reach. Bill and I aimed to provide all language software for every microcomputer on the market. Those BASIC adaptations would be the bedrock of our revenue for years to come.

I also kept pushing to extend our work into other programming languages. In August we hired Steve Wood to develop an 8080 FORTRAN compiler to broaden our clientele among scientists and engineers. When our FORTRAN-80 was released the following April, we were no longer just "the BASIC company." We had a second product line.

*     *     *

BY OCTOBER 1976, Micro-Soft had outgrown our living room. We ordered swivel chairs and desks from a discount house and moved to our first real headquarters, a leased suite of four offices just off Central Avenue. The decor was modest and the offices small, but they had spectacular views of the thunderstorms scudding across the desert valley.

As business pressures weighed on Ed Roberts, our interests grew less complementary. To maximize Micro-Soft's revenue, we needed to distribute our software as widely as possible; in Ed's perfect world, we'd sell it to Altair owners exclusively. Our relationship became strained when he jammed me to release a version of BASIC that had fallen behind schedule.

"But it's got bugs in it," I told him. "You can't ship something with so many problems. The customers are going to kill us." We might deliver late, but I always wanted our products to be top quality before they were released. I'd seen what had happened to MITS with its off-brand memory cards, and how a lemon could permanently tarnish a company's reputation. After a shouting match, Ed gave in. In November I resigned from MITS and moved full-time to Microsoft, the trade name we had registered with the State of New Mexico around that time. With Bill about to quit college for good and Chris Larson back on board, we leased another four offices early in 1977. We were at full strength now, our forces joined, ready to rock 'n' roll.

# CHAPTER 8

# PARTNERS

Bill's intensity was nonstop, and I couldn't keep working with him and living with him, too. It was time to leave the Portals. I rented a rambling three-bedroom house in the suburbs with Ric and Marc, while Bill and Chris Larson took an apartment near the air force base. When Bill asked me for a walk and talk one day, I knew something was up. We'd gone a block when he cut to the chase: "I've done most of the work on BASIC, and I gave up a lot to leave Harvard," he said. "I deserve more than 60 percent."

"How much more?"

"I was thinking 64–36."

Again, I had that moment of surprise. But I'm a stubbornly logical person, and I tried to consider Bill's argument objectively. His intellectual horsepower had been critical to BASIC, and he would be central to our success moving forward. That much was obvious. But how to calculate the value of my Big Idea—the mating of a high-level language with a microprocessor—or my persistence in bringing Bill to see it? What were my development tools worth to the "property" of the partnership? Or my stewardship of our product line, or my day-to-day brainstorming with our programmers? I might have haggled and offered Bill two points instead of four, but my heart wasn't in it. So I agreed. *At least now we can put this to bed,* I thought.

Our formal partnership agreement, signed on February 3, 1977, had two other provisions of note. Paragraph 8 allowed an exemption from business duties for "a partner who is a full-time student," a clause geared to the possibility that Bill might go back for his degree. And in the event of "irreconcilable differences," paragraph 12 stated that Bill could demand that I withdraw from the partnership.

Later, after our relationship changed, I wondered how Bill had arrived at the numbers he'd proposed that day. I tried to put myself in his shoes and reconstruct his thinking, and I concluded that it was just this simple: *What's the most I can get?* I think Bill knew that I would balk at a two-to-one split, and that 64 percent was as far as he could go. He might have argued that the numbers reflected our contributions, but they also exposed the differences between the son of a librarian and the son of a lawyer. I'd been taught that a deal was a deal and your word was your bond. Bill was more flexible. In my experience, he believed that agreements were open to renegotiation until they were signed and sealed. There's a degree of elasticity in any business dealing, a range for what might seem fair, and Bill pushed within that range as hard and as far as he could.

THE MOMENTUM IN personal computers shifted for good in 1977, away from self-made trailblazers like MITS and IMSAI and toward big brand-name companies. Three second-generation machines, the "1977 Trinity," were released over a span of six months: the Apple II, the Commodore PET, and Tandy's TRS-80. All were fully assembled, out-of-the-box computers with built-in keyboards. The Commodore and Tandy threw in integrated monochrome monitors and cassette recorders, and were bargain-priced at around $600. The higher-end Apple II, at $1,298 and up, was easily expandable and offered color graphics capability. (By contrast, an assembled Altair 8800b—with no monitor, keyboard, memory, or data-storage device—sold for $1,070.)

The newcomers were plastic builds with ersatz space-age stylings, and none of them bowled me over. The PET had a horrible "Chiclet" keyboard; the TRS-80 was awkward to expand. The Apple II had a better design, but it was pricey and came without a monitor. None of the three were packaged at the start with floppy disk drives. But despite their flaws, they offered more computer for less money than anything before them, and they all sold well. It wouldn't be long, I thought, before turnkey machines—better turnkey machines—were everywhere. And as computer hardware kept getting smaller and faster and cheaper, better software would be needed to create a compelling package.

Even as I tracked the computer flavor of the month, I never stopped thinking about the advances to come and how people would use them. Here's an excerpt from my column in *Personal Computing*, circa January 1977, four years before the Osborne I became the first portable computer: "I expect the personal computer to become the kind of thing that people carry with them, a companion that takes notes, does accounting, gives reminders, handles a thousand personal tasks."

A few months later, in an interview with Microcomputer Interface, I took my train of thought further. Fifteen years before the World Wide Web, I imagined a computerized society that was far-flung yet intimately linked:

> For machines like the [Commodore] Pet that aren't con-
> nected to any central network, I don't see much of a future. I
> don't see the housewife really learning to program in BASIC.
> What I do see is a home terminal that's connected to a cen-
> tralized network by phone lines, fiber optics or some other
> communication system. With that system you can perhaps
> put your car up for sale or look for a house in a different city
> or check out the price of asparagus at the nearest grocery
> market or check the price of a stock. . . .

The technology wasn't nearly there yet, and I didn't use the phrase in so many words, but that was my first public intimation of what I'd later call the Wired World.

THE 1977 TRINITY effectively doomed the Altair. Ed Roberts was a man of huge vision but weak execution; he'd set off the revolution but couldn't keep his company in front. Most of all, Ed lacked the relentless price-cutting mindset you needed in a company selling to a mass market. But even had he done everything right, MITS's days were numbered from the start. As microcomputers became more functional, hobbyists were finding ways to use them at their jobs as stockbrokers, research scientists, and engineers. And as the market became more lucrative, big companies swooped in, just as Texas Instruments had with handheld calculators. There was no way for MITS to match Apple's innovation or Tandy's economy of scale and its RadioShack distribution network. Ed got overwhelmed and burned out.

For Bill and me and our compatriots at the young Microsoft, on the other hand, this should have been the best of times. The makers of the Trinity knew that they couldn't develop their own BASIC quickly enough, certainly not one as good as ours. Apple tried to get by with a homegrown version, but customers complained that it lacked floating-point math. The company wound up licensing our 12K BASIC interpreter, burned it into read-only memory (ROM), and branded it Applesoft. (Whereas RAM is reusable and can accommodate any number of programs, ROM is a fixed-memory chip on a computer's motherboard.) Just two years out of the gate, Microsoft was establishing the industry standard for microprocessor languages. In a news report that spring on Albuquerque's KOB-TV, a local expert marveled that it was "getting to the point where software will cost as much as the machine." Our company seemed poised to prosper. Until, that is, we were threatened with the loss of our keystone product.

As MITS's market share eroded, and Ed Roberts became desperate to retain a competitive edge, he began killing deals to license our software to Altair rivals. He maintained that he was under no blanket obligation to sublicense our source code to competitors. That was a big problem for Microsoft, because he perceived just about every microcomputer company as a competitor. The issue became acute after Ed decided to sell MITS to Pertec, a Southern California manufacturer that believed it was buying all rights to BASIC. In April 1977, as the deal with Pertec was closing, Ed canceled two of our third-party sales. After we threatened to terminate the MITS contract, MITS/Pertec filed for arbitration. They got a judge to bar any new BASIC sales while the decision was pending. We were frozen out of our main source of revenue.

In June, with our cash flow drying up, Bill and I prepped for our testimony with our attorney, Paull Mines. After each session, we'd race down to the garage to see who could get back to our office first without a traffic ticket. My Monza was quick but no match for Bill's Porsche. I had to be crafty to beat him, taking shortcuts through alleyways and parking lots, and even then I'd be hard-pressed to win one time out of four. One day I left a session to get a document from Bill's car. At the end of the afternoon, Bill and I looked at each other and nodded, our signal that the race was on. I tore out of the garage and won easily, though I thought it was strange that I hadn't seen the Porsche the whole time. Then I felt in my pockets and found Bill's car keys. After I returned to the law office, Bill shook his head in disgust. "That's the only way you beat me," he said.

The hearing was grueling. It was disquieting to see Pertec line up their three lawyers against our one, and tough to watch Ed testify against us. The arbitrator's leanings seemed to shift from day to day. It gradually dawned on us that he had little understanding of software, a mostly untested arena for litigation. After ten days of testimony, he took the case under advisement with no telling when we'd get a final ruling.

A lot rode on the outcome. If Pertec won the rights to our source code, it would mean the end of Microsoft BASIC as we knew it, along with the lion's share of our business. We'd have to write a new BASIC from scratch or move on to a different kind of software. Our future would be imperiled.

Meanwhile, the restraining order was starving us. As summer turned to fall, we struggled to make payroll and to cover our rent and time-share expenses. It reached the point where we had to borrow $7,000 from Bob Greenberg, a Harvard classmate of Bill's whom we'd hired to write a BASIC for a new Texas Instruments chip. We owed our lawyer and could be liable for the costs of the hearing if we lost. The other side figured they could use their deeper pockets to outwait us, and I began to wonder if they might be right. "Look, we're just about out of money," I told Bill over dinner one night. "I think we should consider settling."

And Bill said, "You've got to trust me on this one. I talked to my dad, and he thinks we've got a good chance to win." When pressed, Paull Mines took the same position. So I swallowed hard and hung in there, and it was the best advice Bill never took from me. In November, seven long months after the process began, the arbitrator handed down a twelve-page decision. The special clause in our contract, those papers that Ed never checked, had made all the difference. "The testimony was undisputed that MITS never really embarked on what could be considered best efforts in marketing the source code," the decision read. By vetoing our sublicense sales, MITS/Pertec "materially breached its best efforts obligation. . . . I find this an act of corporate piracy not permitted by either the language or any rational interpretation of the Contract."

The ruling was a total victory for Microsoft. Our contract with MITS was terminated, with Pertec held accountable for all unpaid royalties. Most crucially, Bill and I recovered all rights to our BASIC interpreter and could now sell it to whomever we pleased—and better yet, keep all the revenue. Our one big roadblock was gone.

Not long after that, Ed Roberts quit Pertec after the company rejected his design for a laptop computer. "We're not convinced that people need personal computers on their desks," an executive told him, "but we're sure as hell convinced that they don't need them in their laps." (Like me, Ed could be too early with a promising idea.) In 1978, the TRS-80 shipped 100,000 units; the Commodore PET, 25,000; the Apple II, 20,000; the IMSAI, 5,000; the Altair, 3,000. Soon after, Pertec discontinued the Altair brand in favor of its own label. It closed the Albuquerque plant in 1980 and moved production to California.

As always, Ed found something else to do. He bought a vegetable farm in Georgia, entered medical school in his midforties, and became a country doctor. Though he lived a rich life after MITS, he felt bitter to be left out of the history books. "We created an industry," he said in *Triumph of the Nerds,* a 1996 documentary, "and I think that goes completely unnoticed." He was half right. Ed did indeed create the first truly commercial personal computer, the first widely affordable general-purpose machine. He spearheaded every aspect of microcomputer marketing, from publications and conventions to a retail dealer network. His imagination was boundless. The Altair even debuted a digital camera interface back in 1976.

And he gave two college dropouts the opportunity of their young lives.

But Ed was wrong about being forgotten. When he passed away in April 2010, his obituary made the front page of the *New York Times.* (The photo showed him leaning over the Altair 8800 in his doctor's whites.) I'd made up with Ed a long time before, and he and Bill had gotten past their differences. When Bill flew out to see him a few days before he died, Ed was talking about the latest nanotechnology and how he might work with it. He was looking ahead all the way to the end.

AFTER WINNING IN arbitration, we repaid Bob Greenberg with interest and closed our BASIC deals for the Commodore PET and

the TRS-80. The flat-fee price tags on those licenses were whatever the market would bear, because no one knew for sure what
the personal computer would become. I flew to Fort Worth to meet
Bill for a demo at Tandy, which had taken a lot of heat for using
Tiny BASIC in an initial manufacturing run of the TRS-80. We
were ushered into the sprawling office of John Roach, a tall, plain-
spoken Texan who was en route to becoming Tandy's chairman
and CEO. He was not a man to be trifled with.

"Now," Roach said in a thick drawl, "can you boys really deliver a BASIC interpreter that works for our computer?"

"We believe we can," Bill said, and then he rattled off some of
our software's outstanding features.

Roach nodded and said, "And how much is this going to cost
me?"

And Bill said as coolly as he could, "Fifty thousand dollars."

"That," Roach said flatly, "is the biggest pile of horseshit I ever
heard."

Bill and I looked at each other, wide-eyed. We'd heard a lot of
bargaining tacks, but this was something new. Afterward Bill said
to me, "Well, maybe I did ask for a lot, but *horseshit*?"

We didn't back down, though, and eventually got our price. I always marveled at Bill's bravado; he'd come on superconfident, and
people like John Roach never knew how much we feared losing
the deal. Our near-disaster in arbitration was one more lesson for
us. Going forward, we would aim for maximum market share in
any sector we entered. You could never have too many customers.

In any event, Tandy did well by our arrangement. With our
BASIC inside, the TRS-80 became the hottest-selling computer in
the world until Roach got outflanked by Apple. But we were used
to the shifting landscape ·of the hardware market by then. Machines came and went; good software lived on.

FREED OF MY obligations to MITS, I fell into the programmer's
natural cycle and coded long into the night, when distractions are

fewest and you can submerge into a problem. Then I'd crash for six or seven hours and drag in close to noon. Our office culture was much the same as at MITS, with loud rock and casual attire. We weren't much for corporate trappings. When Texas Instruments came to confer one day, we had to send someone out to buy two guest chairs for the reception area.

"Hope you are not working too hard," my father wrote me. "You need to take it a little easy and get away for a time, otherwise you will burn yourself out. Also hope you decided to buy the nice leather coat." The truth was that time and money were both in short supply. I continued to make $16,000 in salary, plus a low-five-figure distribution as a partner—as in most start-ups, we plowed our profits back into the business. Three years after Ed Roberts sprang for my hotel room, I still didn't have a credit card. In February 1978, the Albuquerque National Bank rejected my application for a MasterCharge, citing "insufficient credit file." Offended, I appealed: "I am particularly interested to know how much of a factor my religion is in your continued rejection of my application." (When asked to designate my denomination, I usually checked "None.")

In general, money wasn't an issue because there wasn't much to spend it on. Albuquerque, as I used to say half-jokingly, was a repeating pattern of a 7-Eleven, a gas station, a movie theater, and a fast-food joint. Bill and I never missed a blockbuster opening; I remember *Superman* and especially the first *Star Wars* and its epic opening battle scene. There were occasional concerts, like Ted Nugent or the Marshall Tucker Band, where I'd watch the guitarists to see how I might copy their licks. That was about it.

After renting a house within walking distance of the office, I splurged and bought an Advent front-projection television, one of the first of its kind, with a twenty-four-square-foot screen. Bill would come by to watch any Muhammad Ali fight, shadowboxing along with the champ. Others joined me for *Saturday Night Live,* or I'd visit Marc, who'd invested in another avant-garde technology coinciding with the Altair: the Betamax videocassette recorder. He built a library of fastidiously labeled movies and *SNL* episodes; we never tired of the "Czech Brothers" skits with Steve Martin and Dan Aykroyd, who later became a close friend.

Marc was an outstanding programmer who talked a thousand miles a minute and got cantankerous at times. He liked to be different. He kept a pet iguana and swore by Saabs and their floor-mounted ignition switches. He stuck by Betamax until the bitter end and was almost apoplectic when it got supplanted by VHS, an inferior technology.

We had close to a dozen people on staff, and most of us were single and in our early twenties. Programmers tend to be loners, but Steve and Marla Wood would gather everyone to hang out from time to time. Marla volunteered as a docent at the local zoo and became the foster parent of a bull snake and a baby reticulated python. The python was only about five feet long, but it could startle people the first time they noticed it wrapped around her neck. Once she sat down next to Ric, who was oblivious for a minute. Then the snake moved and Ric levitated off the couch.

We had our share of characters. Bob Wallace was a wry jokester who later helped originate shareware and funded research on psychedelic drugs. Jim Lane owned a broadsword and rarely missed a medieval fair. But no one was more idiosyncratic than Gordon Letwin, a brilliant nerd's nerd who would lock himself in his office and generate reams of flawless code. Gordon trusted nobody. He would use a different name on every magazine subscription—A. Gordon Letwin, B. Gordon Letwin, and so on—just to track down the source of any junk mail. He married a woman named Rose, and they adopted a baby pig that they treated like a member of the family. The pig grew to be seventy pounds or more, and would blast through its pig door into their home like a fullback going off tackle. Years later I heard that Gordon was taking it around with him on his Learjet.

\* \* \*

TO RECRUIT TALENT, we published a help-wanted ad with my contact number in hobbyist magazines: "Microsoft is hiring systems programmers to work on APL, BASIC, COBOL, and FOR-TRAN. . . . Microsoft is the leader in microcomputer systems programming." In June 1978, Intel introduced the 8086, one of the first 16-bit microprocessors and the next evolutionary step in personal computer technology. I was in regular contact with Intel and had the 8086 data sheet and instruction set well ahead of the official release. By then it was old hat for me to create development tools for chips from their specs, sight unseen.

The 8080 handled up to 65,536 bytes in memory; the new chip could address up to a megabyte. One million bytes—at the time, it seemed unlimited. I saw the potential for powerful word processing, with plenty of headroom for improved video and graphics and a full-featured operating system running underneath. To me, it was inevitable that future microcomputers would become so useful and usable that they'd be de rigueur in the corporate world.

Though there was no 16-bit hardware on the horizon, I was determined not to wait as we had for the Altair. I set to work to simulate the 8086 on the PDP-10 and rewrote my macros for the larger instruction set. When the next-generation boxes materialized, we'd be ready.

Our 8-bit business was booming, and we ran late on our deadlines as new work kept pouring in. With Bill always worried about meeting expenses, we'd make commitments with little regard for our capacity to fulfill them. People had no choice but to work longer and harder—even Miriam Lubow, Bill's secretary, who sneaked in on weekends to do her filing without telling her husband. We maxed out what we could do on the school district's PDP-10 and switched to a faster one in Denver. My own job became a little easier when CP/M, the operating system developed by Gary Kildall at Digital Research, began to gain traction as a de facto standard. Once I adapted BASIC to it, we no longer had to customize our software for each new computer.

Bill consciously aspired to be "hardcore," a favorite adjective dating back to this Harvard days. He'd gulp his Cokes and work in his office deep into the night, and come in the next day cranky and bloodshot. When he really wore down, he'd take a catnap. Just after Miriam started, she was alarmed one Monday morning to find her boss sprawled on the carpet. She ran to see Steve Wood, who'd taken over from Ric as office manager, and cried, "Help me! Bill's on the floor, and it looks like he's unconscious!"

Steve puffed calmly on his pipe and said, "Ah, he was probably here all weekend, don't worry about him. Just go back to work."

"But what do I do if somebody calls for Mr. Gates? What do I tell them?"

"Tell them he's out," Steve said, "and you won't be lying."

Microsoft was a high-stress environment because Bill drove others as hard as he drove himself. He was growing into the taskmaster who would prowl the parking lot on weekends to see who'd made it in. People were already busting their tails, and it got under their skin when Bill hectored them into doing more. Bob Greenberg once put in eighty-one hours in four days, Monday through Thursday, to finish part of the Texas Instruments BASIC. When Bill touched base toward the end of Bob's marathon, he asked him, "What are you working on tomorrow?"

Bob said, "I was planning to take the day off."

And Bill said, "Why would you want to do that?" He genuinely couldn't understand it; he never seemed to need to recharge.

Our company was still small in 1978, and Bill and I worked hand in glove as the decision-making team. My style was to absorb all the data I could to make the best-informed decision possible, sometimes to the point of overanalysis. Bill liked to hash things out in intense, one-on-one discussions; he thrived on conflict and wasn't shy about instigating it. A few of us cringed at the way he'd demean people and force them to defend their positions. If what he heard displeased him, he'd shake his head and say sarcastically, "Oh, I suppose that means we'll lose the contract, and then what?"

When someone ran late on a job, he had a stock response: "I could code that in a weekend!"

And if you hadn't thought through your position or Bill was just in a lousy mood, he'd resort to his classic put-down: "That's the stupidest fucking thing I've ever heard!"

Good programmers take positions and stick to them, and it was common to see them square off in some heated disagreement over coding architecture. But it was tough not to back off against Bill, with his intellect and foot-tapping and body-rocking; he came on like a force of nature. The irony was that Bill liked it when someone pushed back and drilled down with him to get to the best solution. He wouldn't pull rank to end an argument. He *wanted* you to overcome his skepticism, and he respected those who did. Even relatively passive people like Bob Wallace learned to stand their ground and match their boss decibel for decibel. They'd get right into his face: "What are you saying, Bill? I've got to write a compiler for a language we've never done before, and it needs a whole new set of runtime routines, and you think I can do it over the weekend? Are you kidding me?"

I saw this happen again and again. If you made a strong case and were fierce about it, and you had the data behind you, Bill would react like a bluffer with a pair of threes. He'd look down and mutter, "OK, I see what you mean," then try to make up. Bill never wanted to lose talented people. "If this guy leaves," he'd say to me, "we'll lose all our momentum."

Some disagreements came down to Bill and me, one-on-one, late at night. According to one theory, we'd installed real doors in all the offices to keep our arguments private. If that was the case, it didn't work; you could hear our voices up and down the eighth floor. As longtime partners, our dynamic was unique. Bill couldn't intimidate me intellectually. He knew I was on top of technical issues—often better informed than he, because research was my bailiwick. And unlike the programmers, I could challenge Bill on broader strategic points. I'd hear him out for ten minutes, look him straight in the eye, and say, "Bill, that doesn't make sense. You haven't considered $x$ and $y$ and $z$."

Bill craved closure, and he would hammer away until he got there. On principle, I refused to yield if I didn't agree. And so we'd go at it for hours at a stretch, until I became nearly as loud and wound up as Bill. I hated that feeling. While I wouldn't give in unless convinced on the merits, I sometimes had to stop from sheer fatigue. I remember one heated debate lasting forever, until I said, "Bill, this isn't going anywhere. I'm going home."

And Bill said, "You can't stop now, we haven't agreed on anything yet!"

"No, Bill, you don't understand. I'm so upset that I can't speak anymore. I need to calm down. I'm leaving."

Bill trailed me out of his office, into the corridor, out to the elevator bank. He was still getting in the last word—"But we haven't resolved anything!"—as the elevator door closed between us.

I was Mr. Slow Burn, like Walter Matthau to Bill's Jack Lemmon. When I got mad, I stayed mad for weeks. I don't know if Bill noticed the strain on me, but others did. Some said Bill's management style was a key ingredient in Microsoft's early success, but that made no sense to me. Why wouldn't it be more effective to have civil and rational discourse? Why did we need knock-down, drag-out fights?

Why not just solve the problem logically and move on?

WITH THE COMPANY en route to its first million-dollar year and having outgrown the bank building, Bill and I faced a decision: stay or go? After three years in New Mexico, I was ready to move. It was hard to recruit top-flight programmers to Albuquerque, not exactly a hotbed of research or technology. After the sale of MITS to Pertec, there was no real business reason to stay.

On a personal level, there were many things to love about Albuquerque: the sunsets, the climate, the clean desert air. But if you grew up around water and trees, a high desert city can never feel completely like home. I missed the green of the Pacific Northwest, and I missed my family, too.

Bill came to my house to discuss our options. He was dead set against moving to the Bay Area. He'd seen how people in Silicon Valley changed jobs every year or two, which couldn't be good for our long-term projects. That left Seattle, because Bill missed his family, too. We could fly out to our Bay Area customers in ninety minutes, and the rainy days were a plus; they'd keep programmers from getting distracted. We agreed to finish out our lease and move home at the end of the year.

Which is the story of how Seattle inherited what is now its second-largest employer.

On Pearl Harbor Day, 1978, the Microsoft staff convened on the second floor of a shopping center for a group portrait. Despite a rare and raging snowstorm in Albuquerque that day, eleven of thirteen made it to Royal Frontier Studios. Ric Weiland was house-hunting in Seattle, and Miriam Lubow's husband told her she'd be crazy to drive the three miles into town. (Miriam was the only employee who wouldn't make the move with us, though she'd follow later on.)

When I look at that iconic photograph today, I see a group of young people excited about their future. Back in Boston, Bill and I had been searching for the next big thing, little knowing that we'd find it in this remote city in the Southwest. Now we had a real team behind us, and a firm sense of direction. In four years, we had come a long way.

If you look closely at that photo, you'll see just about everyone smiling. That captures our spirit back then. When I talk about the early days at Microsoft, it's hard to explain to people how much *fun* it was. Even with the absurd hours and arguments, we were having the time of our lives.

I had to leave two weeks before the others to set up the main-frame we'd bought for our software development. I scanned the map and saw that the shortest route went through Utah and Idaho, and then into Washington. I didn't bother to check the forecast, and it was snowing like the dickens by the time I reached the Four Corners area in Utah. I was sliding all over the place in my rear-wheel-drive Monza. At one point I was listening to Earth, Wind & Fire when I spun clear off the road, which scared the heck out of me.

I tend to be obstinate in adversity. I put chains on my tires. By the time I reached a mountainous stretch between Utah and Idaho called Dead Man's Pass, the highway was one solid sheet of ice. I passed lines of semis that had either skidded off the pavement or swerved onto an escape ramp. Most sensible people would have turned back. But I white-knuckled it down that mountain, half-sure that I was going to shoot through the guardrail.

When I finally reached Seattle (and it took close to a week), I sent word back that people should take the California route instead. They all had smooth sailing, except for Bill. He reportedly collected three speeding tickets, two of them from the same cop.

# CHAPTER 9

# SOFTCARD

I bought my first house in the Seattle suburb of Bellevue, a four-bedroom, split-level contemporary that backed onto the woods and came complete with field mice. It had big picture windows and a spacious deck overlooking Lake Sammamish. I bolted my couch together and set up the big-screen, then unpacked my Laser-Discs and audiocassettes. My sister moved in with me for a while, and it felt as though I was home again. I'd traded in my Chevy Monza for a little black Mazda RX-7, which was fast and nimble and got me to home-cooked meals at my parents' house in half an hour. Life was good.

With our new downtown Bellevue office to myself for a few days, I fired up our spanking new 2020, DEC's smallest main-frame. For Microsoft, that purchase was both a rite of passage and a key to boosting our productivity: no more sharing time with junior high schools, no disruptions when some other operation monopolized or crashed the machine. Our new location resembled our old one in Albuquerque, on the eighth floor of a ten-story building owned by Old National Bank. We'd expanded from ten offices to maybe fifteen, with a good-size foyer for a receptionist. But we still had to walk single file in the corridors, sidling by boxes stacked with incoming hardware. My office was next to Bill's, and we shared a secretary.

In April 1979, our BASIC interpreter became the first micro-processor software product to surpass a million dollars in sales. With more than three hundred thousand users in the United States and abroad, it was installed on more machines than any other single program. But we didn't pause to celebrate. A jumble of 8-bit computers, many of them prototypes, crowded a group of tables near the programmers' offices. I'd need to get BASIC ported onto each of them to consolidate Microsoft's dominance in high-level languages.

If a hardware company used a BASIC that wasn't ours, we'd disassemble it to see if they'd reverse-engineered our copyrighted code. If our suspicions were confirmed, a stern letter or two usually sufficed. If the code came from another company, we'd press the point that our BASIC was light years better. And it was, because we'd never stopped striving to add features and improve it.

Convinced that our future lay in the 16-bit world, I began work on a stand-alone 8086 BASIC with Bob O'Rear, an air force veteran who became my de facto deputy for development. We were still working on faith, since the first 16-bit microcomputer had yet to appear. That May I took a call from Tim Patterson, a young designer at a local hardware shop called Seattle Computer Products (SCP). He'd built a prototype computer with the 8086 chip mounted on a processor board and was hunting for software to test it. I told him, "Bring it on up. We've got something that might work." Tim was an engineer after my own heart, someone who'd roll up his sleeves and dive into the knottiest problems. After a week of tinkering, both hardware and software passed a run-through. It was a useful collaboration that would lead to a more important alliance down the road.

That early 8086 initiative was just one example of our trying to stay ahead of an ever-accelerating game. We constantly feared that someone might be gaining on us. In those early years in Seattle, I had a disturbing, recurrent dream: Bill and I on the flight deck of a B-17, struggling to get hold of the plane while turbulence buffeted us all over the sky. We never crashed, but we never gained complete control, either. And there was no bailing out. We were strapped in for the duration.

THE JAPANESE MARKET was exploding, thanks in large part to Kazuhiko (Kay) Nishi, our flamboyant agent in East Asia. Kay published a chain of glossy computer magazines that worked hand in glove with his nonstop salesmanship for Microsoft. In August 1979, after he snagged a big contract with NEC, Bill and I went to Japan to help drum up more business. It was my first trip outside North America and everything was new to me, from our futon mats with wooden headrests to the multicolored plates of sushi and boiling pots of shabu-shabu.

We traveled first to Kobe, where Kay's parents owned a girls' school with an outdoor swimming pool. There were two diving platforms, one three meters high (plenty for me) and another at ten meters. A bunch of the girls watched between classes as Bill climbed to the top of the high dive. He jumped, feet first, and they screamed. He must have hit the water at a slight angle—when he pulled himself out, the whole front of his body was bright red. It must have stung, but it didn't stop him. Bill kept jumping, and the girls screamed each time.

We took a bullet train to Tokyo, where we noted a development that had yet to catch on in the United States: the computer "superstore." After checking in at the Hotel Okura, I ordered a hamburger with mustard from room service. I took a large bite, and instantly my sinuses began to burn. As I gasped, I saw Bill laughing at me. Even the mustard was different here.

As we headed out for our first meeting, the elevator stopped and a couple squeezed in: a long-haired guy with Coke-bottle eyeglasses and a Japanese woman with curly black hair. Could it be John Lennon and Yoko Ono? I leaned against the side of the elevator, trying to look casual, and inadvertently pressed an intermediate floor button. We stopped, the door opened, and the guy with the glasses said, "Nobody 'ome." Now I *knew* it was John Lennon. I desperately wanted to say something but my brain froze. After we reached the lobby and the couple walked off, I said to Bill, "Did you see that? That was John Lennon and Yoko Ono."

"Really?"

"Yes, look, there they go!"

And Bill said, "Oh, yeah, you might be right." He wasn't a *Rolling Stone* reader like me. He knew bits and pieces of popular culture, but he was thinking about the software business first, second, and third.

Kay Nishi was an unusually Westernized and entrepreneurial Japanese, a high-octane maverick who flew his own helicopter to business meetings. He was a big spender, piling up huge debt. (On a later trip, Bill was not amused after Kay excitedly took him by a Tokyo train station to show him "the dinosaur": a $1 million, life-size, concrete brontosaurus built to promote a new joint PC format, with Microsoft on the hook for part of the bill.) Kay worked against the grain of Japan's conservative business culture but opened many doors for us, including Matsushita Electric, now Panasonic. A junior technical person met us in reception to escort us to the top floor, where the chief technology officer awaited. As our elevator ascended, our guide looked more and more uncomfortable. I said, "Have you ever been to the top floor before?"

"Oh, no, never," he said.

"Have you ever met with Mr. —— before?"

"Oh, no, never." The poor man was sweating bullets.

The meeting room contained two large tables facing each other about six feet apart. There were a dozen people on Matsushita's side; the chief took the middle chair, while the others flanked him in descending order of status. They smoked like chimneys and drank rocket-fuel coffee. Bill and I sat at the other table with Kay, who would fill us in later about any byplay among the Japanese.

"So, Mr. Gates," the chief said, "how do we know that you'll deliver on time?" They grilled us for four hours, standard procedure in Japan; they wanted to be sure that we could make good on our promises. Bill was confident and assertive. He'd go into his rocking mode and say, "Well, we've done this with Apple and this with Tandy. . . ." No one seemed to care that he was twenty-three years old. The more technical or speculative questions came to me: "So tell us, Mr. Allen, how do you see the future of the personal computer industry?" (After we got to know each other better, I'd become Allen-san.)

We toured the plant until five o'clock, at which point the air conditioning shut down and the company song was piped in over a sound system. Kay motioned for us to stand along with our hosts, who sang together, full out. When it was over, I asked Kay if they were going home now. "Oh, no," he said. "They'll work until eight o'clock and then go out to eat with their buddies, and then they'll start again really early tomorrow." I was thinking: *These guys are working a lot harder than the average American. How in hell can we keep up?* And for the most part, we couldn't. The migration of consumer electronics manufacturing out of the United States was already well under way.

Each night we'd get taken out by Japanese executives on expense accounts. They chose European restaurants, a big treat for them, until we finally pleaded for some Japanese food. Toward the end of our stay, one executive said, "That was a great meeting. I'd like to invite you to something special, a geisha house or a really great dinner. You choose." Bill looked at me and I knew without asking that he'd vote for the geishas. "A nice dinner sounds great," I said. The man reserved a private room at one of the top spots for the four of us. There were endless courses of spectacular sashimi and cooked dishes, and the service was outstanding. As our host took the check, Kay got really quiet and began shaking his head. I sensed that something extraordinary had just taken place. As we left the restaurant, I said, "Kay, how much did that dinner cost?"

He thought for a second and said, "Six thousand dollars."

"Six thousand for four people? How is that possible?"

"Best fish," Kay said. "Big room." Someone had gone to the immense Tokyo fish market and selected the top specimens. Quality and privacy came at a premium in Tokyo.

Before returning home, we took in *Alien* at a downtown movie theater. I'd seen it in Seattle, where I gasped like everyone else when the alien popped out of John Hurt's chest. But in Tokyo, no one made a sound except Bill and me. Afterward I asked Kay if the audience had liked it. "Such a monster," he said, shaking his head. "Such a terrible monster." Kay looked nauseated—he'd been immersed in the film like everyone else, but they did not react. They held it all in.

In Japan we saw firsthand that our ambition to become *the* software language company had real potential. With China still closed and Korea not yet a player, to dominate Japan was to rule Asia. Back in Bellevue, the bullpen table grew cluttered with more 8-bit Japanese hardware. It was a preview of where personal computer design was headed—how a company like NEC, for example, was implementing color graphics that went miles beyond the Commodore PET's.

The Japanese market was fiercely competitive. Late one night, we surprised a bespectacled engineer who'd sneaked into our office to snap Polaroid pictures of the competition. Another time, some Ricoh reps came by to ask what we had available. We ran down our list of every language on our shelf and one or two that weren't ready yet. The reps kept nodding, and at the end they said, "We'll take them all." When their prototype machine malfunctioned and we failed to meet our delivery date, the head rep was distraught. "Mr. Allen, I *promised* to deliver," he said, almost sobbing. He camped out at our office for days to help me get the software running. His honor was on the line.

Many of the Japanese machines were unconventional, with strange key placements, and a thought began to gnaw at me. Coming off my experience at MITS, I believed that we could build an 8-bit system superior to anyone else's, including Apple's, and customize it to run our software. Kay was pushing us to join forces with a Japanese company that would manufacture under the Microsoft name. He wanted to approach Sony, which was known for televisions and audio speakers but had no track record in computers. As Kay saw it, a Microsoft/Sony computer would be completely new and different, a true multimedia machine with state-of-the-art audio and video, the sort of thing I'd been talking about for years. Vern Raburn, the president of our consumer products division, was in favor. But Bill was adamant about staying out of hardware. "We'd be in conflict with our customers," he told Kay. More than fifty companies were licensing our 8080 BASIC alone by that point, and the last thing Bill wanted was to turn those clients into competitors.

Our growing confidence made it easier to reject a mid-seven-figure purchase offer that summer from H. Ross Perot, the Dallas billionaire. It just felt way too soon for us to cash out. "Our conclusion is that at present we wish to remain independent," Bill wrote to Mort Meyerson, Perot's number two. "We see the potential to double the size of our organization and earn over $2 million per year before taxes." Bill was on the mark: Microsoft's year-end revenues would total $2.4 million in 1979, and our staff would more than double, to twenty-eight.

IN JUNE 1979, we made our first trip to New York City for the National Computer Conference. We took a two-bedroom suite at the top of the Plaza Hotel, the perfect spot for launching bottle rockets over Central Park. Kay Nishi came up with a request: He had friends in from Japan with no place to stay. Could they bunk in with us? Sure, we said—we didn't want to be rude. A few minutes later, Kay showed up with half a dozen businessmen, all very polite, from Fujitsu, Toshiba, and NEC. I called the front desk and said, "How many rollaway beds do you have available?"

"I think we have six, sir."

"OK, bring them all up."

Soon there came a knock on the door. Six chuckling bellhops lined the corridor with six rollaways, a less than typical request for a high-priced suite. The beds filled the living room until you could hardly inch past them. The next morning, I had to fight my way through a forest of socks hanging in the bathroom, which the Japanese had left out to dry. But our hospitality paid off. One of our guests snapped open his briefcase, filled to the brim with U.S. currency. He was so eager to buy our BASIC interpreter that he'd brought cash for a down payment on the license, over ten thousand dollars. Bill wrote out a receipt on his business card.

The annual event was where suits from firms like IBM and DEC pitched their latest mainframes and minicomputers. Microcomputer companies were the new kids on the block, shunted to a small annex in a hotel by the main arena. Eddie Currie, Ed Roberts's old number two at MITS, had moved to Lifeboat Associates, a software distribution company in New York, and he invited us to share his ten-foot-square exhibition space. We'd brought Tim Patterson along to help us debut our BASIC-86 on Tim's prototype machine. No one else had a 16-bit BASIC, and ours would shortly be in the market. I was feeling pretty good until I stopped by the booth of a Massachusetts outfit called Personal Software. They had an Apple II running something I'd never seen before, on any class of computer: an interactive accounting spreadsheet. They called it VisiCalc.

Though the booth wasn't drawing much of a crowd, it did grab the attention of an electronics analyst who later became the venture capitalist behind Compaq Computer. Ben Rosen understood that he was looking at the first "killer app," an application that would dominate and redefine its category. As Rosen wrote the following month in the *Morgan Stanley Electronics Letter:*

*Today, virtually the only user of personal computers who is satisfied with the state of the software art is the hobbyist. And he does all of his programming himself. But for the professional, the home computer user, the small business-man, and the educator, there is precious little software avail-able that is practical, useful, universal, and reliable.*

*Enter VisiCalc . . . a new concept in software. . . . Though hard to describe in words, VisiCalc comes alive visually. In minutes, people who have never used a computer are writing and using programs. Although you are operating in plain English, the program is being executed in machine lan-guage. But as far as you're concerned, the entire procedure is software transparent. You simply write on this so-called electronic blackboard what you would like it to do—and it does it.*

Rosen described a dividend discount valuation model that had taken him twenty hours to program in BASIC; he created a more flexible version of the same thing with VisiCalc in fifteen minutes. "Who knows?" he concluded. "VisiCalc could some day become the software tail that wags (and sells) the personal computer dog."

That was our philosophy, too; we believed that software was more valuable than hardware. But we hadn't counted on someone outflanking us with a whole new approach. To that point, business programs had been written almost exclusively for higher-end mi-crocomputers like Tandy's TRS-80 Model II, machines marketed to small businesses that did their own data processing. Apple com-puters were viewed as toys for educational programs and games. But once VisiCalc enabled nonprogrammers to do financial mod-eling on the Apple II, all that was about to change.

At Microsoft we'd had good excuses for putting off a move into applications software. The field was competitive and highly fragmented, and Bill and I had decided that we wouldn't enter a market unless we knew we could be number one. And with our programmers straining to fulfill our language contracts, it was hard to see how we could plunge into a whole new sector. Still, I'd had pangs as I watched WordMaster evolve into WordStar, the first widely accepted application of its kind. I knew in my gut that word processing would become a major revenue source. Were we missing the boat?

VisiCalc was another wake-up call. We'd licensed Applesoft BASIC on a fixed-fee basis, so we had nothing to gain from a spike in Apple II sales. Worse yet, our other languages ran exclusively on CP/M, which was incompatible with the microprocessor used by the Apple II: the MOS Technology 6502, Intel's cut-rate competitor. With VisiCalc boosting its sales geometrically, Apple would be positioned to carve out a big slice of a growing market, one Microsoft couldn't penetrate. And we didn't need to read Ben Rosen to realize that people could use the new spreadsheet program without our software.

From the start, we'd built Microsoft around the premise that our products would be universal. Wherever the general-purpose microcomputer market went, we'd be there. But as personal computing matured from an enthusiast subculture into a mass medium, I came to see that languages would soon be outweighed by applications. Our mission could be at risk unless we built our own spreadsheet, and our own word processor and database, as well. The Altair had taught us how quickly fortunes in the tech world could rise and fall.

As Microsoft's technical leader, I faced a more immediate bind: How could we get our existing products onto the Apple II platform? In theory, we could develop new compilers for the Apple in FORTRAN, COBOL, Pascal, and the rest. But the job would require years of coding by several programmers. It would leave us understaffed in our core business of porting BASIC to new 8080 machines, not to mention the 8086 computers just around the corner. Morever, the Apple work would saddle us with a new catalog of assembly code to debug and enhance, a costly, labor-intensive proposition. All told, the expense and distraction of full-scale development could cripple our still-small company. It was a dilemma that begged for an original solution.

A few months after seeing VisiCalc, heading to lunch in the back of Steve Wood's pickup truck, I got one of those ideas that fortuitously flash into my head, a mix of inference and extrapolation. Instead of rewriting our entire software catalog, why not turn the Apple II into a compatible system? If we designed an 8080 circuit board to plug into the Apple, the machine could run CP/M from a floppy disk and all our languages on top of it. By importing a CP/M-friendly CPU, we'd avoid a massive recoding project and get into the Apple II market at least six months sooner.

In effect, I'd turned a software problem into a hardware problem—an elegant shortcut, a sort of Hail Mary pass. At first Bill wondered if it might be a distraction. But he came to agree that this was one Microsoft hardware effort that might be worth the trouble.

There are two phases to any invention. The first is the moment of inspiration. The second is the execution, which is less exciting but more than challenging in its own right. I had no idea whether my idea was actually doable. I called Tim Patterson and said, "Can you design this thing?"

And Tim said, "I think it's possible." A few weeks later, he came back with a circuit board containing a Z-80 chip, a cheaper equivalent to Intel's 8080. It was simple enough to undo the plastic snaps and pop the lid off an Apple II, then slide the card into an expansion slot wired to the CPU. The native MOS Technology 6502 still ran the Apple's peripherals (display, keyboard, printer) but otherwise went into a state of suspended animation. The Z-80 SoftCard, as we called it, took over most of the actual processing. We'd turned the Apple II into something that Steve Jobs wouldn't have imagined: a CP/M computer.

Tim understood the Z-80 well, and the card's general design was more than adequate, but getting two processors to coexist was a nightmare. The thing would work fine for a while, but then the native CPU would crash and take our SoftCard with it. In March 1980, we rolled out the prototype at the West Coast Computer

Faire in San Francisco, fretting that it would go down at an inop-
portune moment. I can recall Steve Jobs passing by with a scowl.
He had to be irritated that we'd barged into his Apple II walled
garden and thrown the gate open to the whole CP/M software
community.

To eradicate the SoftCard's gremlins, I brought in an Apple-
savvy engineer named Don Burtis and paid him $8,000 for a
ground-up redesign. He quickly found the defect in the hardware's
architecture. On April 2, 1980, we issued a press release entitled
"Cornucopia for Apple Computer Owners":

> *A product that will allow the more than 75,000 Apple com-
> puter owners to use a vast array of new software, including
> business packages, was announced today by Microsoft Con-
> sumer Products. . . .*
>
> *"Most of the existing 8080/Z80 programs require a five
> thousand dollar or more computer," says Paul Allen, Mi-
> crosoft Vice President and Z-80 SoftCard creator. "After
> hearing about the Z-80 SoftCard, several business people
> have told us they plan to bring home their word process-
> ing, accounting or statistical programs to run on their home
> Apple computers at night. That makes Apple computers tax
> deductible."*

We bundled the SoftCard with diskettes for CP/M and our
BASIC interpreter, and priced it at $349. It started shipping that
fall to strong demand. As we thought it might, VisiCalc helped to
drive Apple's sales through the roof; Jobs had nearly a year's head
start before the spreadsheet was developed for other microprocessors, and he exploited his lead well. The Apple II went from 35,000
units in 1979 to 210,000 in 1981, lagging only the Atari 400/800
and the TRS-80. It became a hit on college campuses and made a
notable dent in the small business market.

My invention allowed Microsoft to share in that success. We

sold approximately 25,000 SoftCards in 1981 alone, worth about $8 million in sales, and continued our strong run into 1983 before imitators cut into our margins. For Apple II owners who'd been limited to a thin catalog of native applications, the SoftCard gave them two computers in one. Suddenly they had access to tens of thousands of CP/M-compatible programs written in BASIC, FORTRAN, or COBOL. On the flip side, the SoftCard represented a huge windfall for Peachtree Software, creator of the popular Peachtree Accounting, which with no development costs had a new market handed to it. And of course, our new product was a boon to Gary Kildall and Digital Research. More copies of CP/M would be sold for use in the Apple II, a hitherto incompatible machine, than for any other computer.

For Microsoft, the SoftCard provided a point of entry into the Apple environment. It gave us a new and substantial customer base for our Disk BASIC and other languages. Moreover, the SoftCard turned computer-pricing strategy on its head. In the old world, everyone from IBM to MITS had bundled software as a throw-in with the machine. Now we were bundling a cheaply made piece of hardware to help us sell BASIC and our expensive suite of software. The SoftCard was the razor; our languages were the blades.

The SoftCard lent Microsoft a needed revenue boost in an awful recession year. Perhaps most important, it gave us comfort in abandoning the 8-bit development world and turning our energies to software for the 8086 chip, a shift that would prove critical in landing our big contract with IBM less than a year later. As Bill noted in a 1993 interview for the *Smithsonian*:

> [The] question was, "Should we spread those products over to other 8-bit chips, like the 6502 that runs in [the Apple II]? Or, should we immediately move up and do 16-bit software?" And I said, "No, we are going to do 16-bit software." Everybody was a little bit disappointed because it meant that we wouldn't be able to sell onto these machines. That

*is when Paul invented the idea of the SoftCard, so that we could actually take our Intel software and run it on this machine, and, at the same time, go ahead and devote our resources to being way ahead of everybody else in developing software for the 8086.*

I had already been instituting the move to 16-bit software, but Bill wasn't wrong about the SoftCard's importance. Under the circumstances, I felt that our 64–36 partnership split was out of whack. Bill had set a precedent by claiming extra equity for his work on Altair BASIC, another exceptional contribution. Now it was time, I thought, to augment my share. A modest adjustment in the ratio seemed only right.

But when I made my case, Bill would have none of it. "I don't ever want to talk about this again," he said. "Do not bring it up."

In that moment, something died for me. I'd thought that our partnership was based on fairness, but now I saw that Bill's self-interest overrode all other considerations. My partner was out to grab as much of the pie as possible and hold on to it, and that was something I could not accept. I didn't have it out with Bill at the time. I sucked it up and thought, *OK . . . but one day I'm out of here.*

MICROSOFT NOW COMMANDED the CP/M 8-bit market in programming language software, and the SoftCard gave us a secure beachhead with Apple. But as we grew, our need for more help became glaring. Neither Bill nor I had a lot of experience as managers, and both of us had other areas of responsibility—Bill in sales, I in software development. Steve Wood had filled in admirably as general manager, but he, too, was a programmer by background. Bill came to see that we needed someone to help him run the business side of things, just as I ran technology. He chose Steve Ballmer, a Harvard classmate who'd worked in marketing at Procter & Gamble and was now studying at Stanford's business school. Bill sold him hard to me: "Steve's a supersmart guy, and he's got loads of energy. He'll help us build the business, and I really trust him."

I'd run into Steve a few times at Harvard, where he and Bill were close. The first time we met face-to-face, I thought, *This guy looks like an operative for the NKVD.* He had piercing blue eyes and a genuine toughness. (Though as I got to know him better, I found a gentler side as well.) Steve was someone who wouldn't back down easily, a necessity for working well with Bill. In April 1980, shortly before leaving town on a business trip, I agreed that we should offer him up to 5 percent of the company, because Bill felt certain that Steve wouldn't leave Stanford unless he got equity.

A few days later, after returning from my trip, I got a copy of Bill's letter to Steve. (Someone apparently found it in the office's Datapoint word processing system, and it had made the rounds.) Programmers like Gordon Letwin were furious that Bill was giving a piece of the company to a person without a technical background. I was angry for another reason: Bill had offered Steve 8.75 percent of the company, considerably more than what I'd agreed to.

It was bad enough that Bill had chosen to disregard me on a partnership issue we'd specifically discussed. It was worse that he waited till I was away to send the letter. I wrote him to set out what I had learned, and concluded: "As a result of discovering these facts I am no longer interested in employing Mr. Ballmer, and I consider the above points a major breach of faith on your part."

Bill knew that he'd been caught and couldn't bluster his way out of it. Unable to meet my eyes, he said, "Look, we've got to have Steve. I'll make up the extra points from my share." I said OK, and that's what he did.

# CHAPTER 10

# PROJECT CHESS

By 1980, having sold more than half a million copies, our BASIC drew the attention of the largest computer maker in the world. After ignoring personal computers for years, IBM had awoken to their emergence as a platform for business. Big Blue knew that its four-year development cycle for mainframes wouldn't fly in the fast-changing world of microcomputers. In a sharp departure from company tradition, it moved to outsource to companies that could help get a new product to market faster.

Microsoft was about to make the big time.

That August, a three-piece-suited contingent led by Jack Sams approached us about Project Chess, the code name for what would become IBM's PC. After we talked them out of an 8-bit machine and won them over to the Intel 8086 (or as it turned out, the cheaper but virtually identical 8088), they wanted everything in our 16-bit cupboard, including FORTRAN, COBOL, and Pascal. Aside from BASIC, none of these products were even close to being ready for the 8086 platform. It would take a wild scramble to get them all done on IBM's tight timetable.

Then, in late September, Sams asked us if we could provide a 16-bit operating system. We referred him to Digital Research, which we'd heard was far along in building one. Bill called Gary Kildall and said, "I'm sending some people over to you, and I want you to be good to them, because you and I are both going to make a lot of money on this deal." He didn't mention IBM by name because the company insisted on maximum discretion and secrecy. We'd had to sign a nondisclosure agreement before they'd even sit down with us.

As Kildall himself later acknowledged, he was off flying on business when the Project Chess group arrived. His wife, who was also his business partner, refused to sign the nondisclosure and offered a Digital Research document instead. That was something you did not do with IBM. Sams came back to us and said, "I don't think we can work with those guys—it would take our legal department six months to clear the paperwork. Do you have any other ideas? Could you handle this on your own?"

After the fact, there would be endless rumors about Microsoft's dealings with Digital Research. Kildall theorized that IBM chose to work with us because we were willing to license an operating system for a flat fee, while Kildall insisted on a per-copy royalty. But I had a front-row seat, and this is what happened: We tried to do Digital Research a favor, and they blew it. They dropped the ball. I vividly remember how furious Bill was at what had transpired. He couldn't believe that Kildall had blown this golden chance and placed the whole project in jeopardy.

Bill called an emergency meeting with me and Kay Nishi. What could we do to resuscitate the deal? There was silence for a moment, and then I said, "There's another operating system that might work. I don't know how good it is, but I think I can get it for a reasonable price." I told them the story of Tim Patterson and Seattle Computer Products, which began shipping its 8086 machine earlier that year but had found sparse commercial interest. The missing link was an operating system. Kildall had promised a CP/M-86 by the first of the year, but he hadn't delivered; his company lacked the typical start-up's urgency. No one knew when his 16-bit software would make it to market.

Tim Patterson had gotten frustrated waiting. Our BASIC-86

was fine for writing programs, but his customers couldn't run a word processor or other applications on top of it. So Tim had cobbled together a provisional 16-bit operating system to help his company sell a few computers until Kildall came through. (As Tim later said, "We would have been perfectly happy having somebody else do the operating system. If [Digital Research] had delivered in December of '79, there wouldn't be anything but CP/M in this world today.") He called the program QDOS, for Quick and Dirty Operating System, which he'd managed to cram into 6K of code. Once it was mostly done, he changed the name to 86-DOS.

Tim had made strong strides with his software, and I felt confident in telling Bill and Kay that it would probably work. Though we'd still need to finish and adapt it for the IBM PC, 86-DOS would give us a running start. At least we'd have a shot.

After I finished, Kay cut in. "We've got to do it!" he kept shouting. Selling our BASIC in Japan, he'd seen firsthand the enormous interest in CP/M-80 from computer hardware firms. If Microsoft was to govern its future, we had to have our own operating system.

I agreed. Ever since Altair BASIC, our objective had been to establish standards and then to license our programs throughout the industry. Now, thanks to a fluke, we'd been handed the opportunity to create the pivotal product of the era. With IBM's unmatched power and reach, we might even be able to unify the microcomputer software market. As a bonus, as Kay pointed out, a 16-bit Microsoft operating system would dovetail neatly with our language development business.

Bill was less enthusiastic. He didn't know Tim Patterson, and we'd be betting our deal with IBM—the most critical one we'd ever have—on an unknown quantity once called Quick and Dirty. But Bill realized that we might lose the whole contract unless we came up with something, and he went along.

I called Rod Brock, who owned Seattle Computer Products, to work out a licensing agreement. We settled on $10,000, plus a royalty of $15,000 for every company that licensed the software—a total of $25,000 for now, as we had only one customer. The next day, a Microsoft delegation (Bill, Steve, and Bob O'Rear) met with IBM in Boca Raton and proposed that Microsoft coordinate the overall software development process for the PC. Five weeks later, the contract was signed. IBM would pay us a total of $430,000: $75,000 for "adaptations, testing, and consultation"; $45,000 for the disk operating system (DOS); and $310,000 for an array of 16-bit language interpreters and compilers.

Bill and I were willing to forgo per-copy royalties if we could freely license the DOS software to other manufacturers, our old strategy for Altair BASIC. Already enmeshed in antitrust litigation, IBM readily bought this nonexclusive arrangement. They'd later be slammed for giving away the store, but few people at the time discerned how quickly the industry was changing. And no one, including us, foresaw that the IBM deal would ultimately make Microsoft the largest tech company of its day, or that Bill and I would become wealthy beyond our imagining.

AS I LOOK back at my life, I'd propose that my successes were the product of preparation and hard work. Yes, I was lucky to get early programming opportunities in high school and at C-Cubed; to have a father with the keys to a major library system; to find a partner in Bill who could take my ideas and magnify them; to cross paths with Ed Roberts, who needed to buy what we were able to build, just at the right time.

But it was no accident that I was positioned to take advantage of those breaks. IBM came to Microsoft in the first place because we had pushed the frontier for microcomputer languages with more prescience and boldness than anyone else. I had ties to Tim Patterson because I'd hustled to develop an 8086 BASIC and later hired Tim to take a first pass at the SoftCard. I was drawn by nature to people who, like me, were eager to see what might come next and wanted to try to make it happen. From my youth, I'd never stopped thinking in the future tense.

One part of my job description had not changed: I was still the research arm of our organization. I kept up with *Electronic News* and *Computer Design* and their ilk, and regularly dropped by UW's computer science library to check on anything I might have missed. I'd long been fascinated by the work of Douglas Engelbart, who had invented the pointing device he called a mouse in 1963. His work influenced technologists at the Xerox Palo Alto Research Center, or Xerox PARC, the lab that would anticipate nearly every major trend in personal computing by a decade or more. (PARC's breakthroughs were mostly ignored by its mother company, which had no idea what to do with them and squandered an opportunity to define the personal computer market.)

Xerox PARC was an ivory tower with a moat around it; you knew amazing things were going on there, but it was hard to get a handle on them. By the late 1970s, however, a few journal articles divulged some of PARC's innovations. Even before we moved back to Seattle, I was putting a bug in Bill's ear about the graphical user interface (known as GUI, pronounced "gooey"), a computer experience that went beyond conventional typing and character-based displays to new modes of interactivity. Linked to a mouse, a GUI would allow ordinary people to use computers intuitively; its potential impact on our market couldn't be overestimated. Microsoft was preoccupied with Project Chess, but I knew that we'd need a GUI—and GUI applications—in our arsenal before long.

Whenever I showed Bill material like "Alto: A Personal Computer," a technical report published by Xerox in 1979, he responded as he had to my pre-Altair excitement over the 8080 chip. "It looks intriguing," he said, "but who's going to build the hardware and sell it at a price that works?" The Alto was a research prototype that addressed a bold question: What could you create if you trusted Moore's law and reimagined the state of the art with no cost constraints? But the machine was far too pricey for the home market. For a pragmatist like Bill, the whole idea must have seemed premature.

His view began to change in September 1980, when Charles Simonyi, one of PARC's lead programmers, came in for a job interview. Bill was tied up when he arrived, and Steve Ballmer sent him to me. A soft-spoken man with a mild Hungarian accent, Charles had grown restless with pure research and wanted to move into product development. He knew us as "the language company" and brought some ideas in that area. But I was more interested in the work he'd been doing at PARC. I paged through his portfolio, and it blew me away.

Two months earlier, in a strategy memo for Microsoft R & D, I'd pushed for development of "a word processor which stands above the rest in terms of features, ease of use, and adaptability." Now I was holding that very thing, or at least a fair description of it, in my hands. Charles had led the development team for Bravo, the first WYSIWYG (what you see is what you get) word processing software to feature proportional fonts. Unlike predecessors like WordStar, Bravo presented text on the screen exactly as it would appear on the printed page. While I didn't grasp all of the technical details at first, it was plain that I was looking at the future of word processing software, and at the person who could guide us there.

Charles came back a second time after meeting with top Xerox executives who wanted very much to keep him. We must have said something right, because he decided to throw in with us instead. "The contrast couldn't have been sharper," he'd say later. Xerox was "an old company in an old industry going downhill, walking in the dark. It's not that they didn't know the answers. That's normal. But they didn't know the questions." Charles's decision shocked his PARC colleagues, who couldn't believe he was moving to such an obscure software operation. (Six years later, the two companies' market values would cross. As of late 2010, Xerox was worth $15 billion, or about 7 percent as much as Microsoft.)

Later that fall, before his deal with us was finalized, Charles invited me to his lab in Palo Alto for a demonstration. As he sat before an Alto and put it through its paces, I was amazed. It was one thing to read about a true breakthrough, something else to see it in action. Now I knew how people must have felt at Engelbart's Mother of All Demos in 1968: as though beamed by transporter into the future.

The Alto wasn't technically a microcomputer because it didn't use a microprocessor. But it was compact for its time, with the cabinet holding the CPU and hard drive was the size of a dorm room refrigerator. The desktop unit consisted of a keyboard and an integrated monitor proportioned like a sheet of standard copy paper, taller than it was wide. Where commercial computers of the day offered low-resolution displays of white or green or amber characters on a black screen, the Alto had been rethought from the ground up. As Charles typed on the black-on-white, bitmapped display, I saw for the first time everything we take for granted in today's word processors: bold and italic and underlined fonts of different sizes, curved lines and justified text. I watched transfixed as Charles "cut" and "pasted" sections of his document. Xerox PARC had not oversold the Alto. It did indeed replicate the flexibility of pen and ink, but with digital ease and speed.

To the side of the keyboard, Charles rolled a rectangular box with three buttons in a horizontal row: a mechanical mouse. When he moved aside, I sat down for a turn. It took a few moments to coordinate the movement of my hand with the position of a cursor on a screen. But soon the mouse felt like an extension of my arm, and it was then that I realized how a GUI interface could make people so much more productive.

Charles took over again and dragged an icon representing a document file to a printer icon. A laser printer known as the Dover hummed into action. At the time, dot matrix and daisywheel printers were the bane of personal computer users: slow, loud, and prone to jamming, with just one standard font. But in the magical world of Xerox PARC, I had within seconds a perfect copy of the memo that summarized our meeting with Charles in Seattle: "*What is our business?* Produce and sell software for micro-mini systems on the mass market. . . ." The printer was the one PARC brainchild that Xerox, a copier company at heart, would successfully bring to market. A single Dover cost about $200,000, Charles said, but we both knew the price would soon plunge.

Charles drew my attention to a yellow cable running out the back of the machine, an umbilical cord to a local area network that connected several Altos using Ethernet, yet another patented PARC technology. This nexus of personal computers had all the benefits of old-style time-sharing (a common printer and a file server for additional storage), but none of the drawbacks (slow connections, crippling networkwide crashes).

*Wow!* I thought. *This is going to change everything.* PARC's achievement seemed both startling and commonsensical. Surely people would want what I'd seen and touched at Charles's lab. *Of course* you should be able to interact with a computer with a pointing device, or drag a file to a different folder, or push a button to print what looked like a page from a book. That afternoon in Palo Alto was a thunderclap. Once GUIs went commercial, computers would become so natural and organic that anyone's mother would learn how to use them. At that point, it seemed to me, nothing could stop their universal adoption. They'd be like television sets; they'd be irresistible.

PROJECT CHESS WAS so hush-hush that even industry insiders had no clue what we were doing. When I mentioned it to Charles after he started work for us around the New Year, he thought it was one of Vern Raburn's consumer game products and wasn't impressed. "We've got to *focus*," he said. Then I told him about IBM's move into the personal computer market.

That was a different story, Charles agreed.

We were so tight-lipped that we wouldn't even mention the famous corporate acronym by name. We referred to our customer as HAL, after the computer in *2001: A Space Odyssey.* (As movie buffs know, HAL is IBM moved one letter down the alphabet.)

New levels of security were needed. When the PC prototype arrived at our office around Thanksgiving, it was closeted in a small, windowless backroom, under strict lock and key. Access was limited to a handful of people.

A third of our staff worked on some aspect of Project Chess, but the central developments unfolded in this airless ten-by-fifteen-foot space. My direct responsibility was BASIC-86. To conserve the PC's limited memory, IBM had directed us to embed BASIC in the machine's ROM. Though we'd done this earlier with Applesoft BASIC, I was nervous as hell about it. The only way to fix a faulty ROM chip was by recalling the machine, and what if our new BASIC had bugs? I knew that you didn't release complex, first-generation software and have it banged on by hundreds of thousands of users without something bad turning up.

I hit upon a novel solution: to insert a hundred or more coding "hooks," so that any part of the BASIC code could be patched or updated from a floppy disk. (For an analogy, think of open envelopes taped to key sections of a book, allowing new material or corrections to be inserted without reprinting the entire volume.) Those hooks turned out to be lifesavers.

To make sure that DOS would pass IBM's tests, I chose the steady Bob O'Rear. He would make sure that Tim Patterson's DOS was compatible with IBM's BIOS (basic input/output system), the built-in software that controlled the computer's keyboard and display. In addition to IBM's prototype, our high-security room contained a blue box called the ICE-88 (for Intel circuit emulator), a diagnostic device to expedite the debugging. The machines generated tremendous heat, and Bob and I sweated like pigs in our Bermuda shorts and T-shirts. In an unused space across the hall sat Bill's friend Andy Evans, a volatile securities trader in need of a desk and business telephone. Whenever the markets took a turn against him, Andy screamed and hurled his phone against the wall, which could be disconcerting.·

We were working on a crash schedule with a client who was

famously intolerant of slipped deadlines. We'd overnight floppy disks with each day's progress to IBM in Boca Raton, where the software was tested. If some setback made a day unproductive, one of our programmers (unbeknownst to me) would "accidentally" reformat the disk before shipping. When IBM called to complain that they'd gotten a blank disk, he'd apologize for the error and correct it in the next shipment, buying time.

One big problem was the flaky IBM prototype. Bob kept re-soldering loose connections, but it could be hard to trace the source of the defect: hardware or software? Precious days were lost. More delays came from IBM's fastidious testing protocol, and Bob spent a discouraging amount of time filling out corporate forms. (We joked that IBM's slogan should have been "Better products through better paperwork.")

The original mid-January deadline to have DOS and BASIC working came and went, and we began to worry that IBM might pull the plug if they couldn't make their scheduled August rollout. Rumor had it that a parallel workgroup in Japan stood ready to replace us if we faltered. On January 19, 1981, Bob expressed our concerns in writing to an IBM manager named Pat Harrington:

> *Microsoft is continuing its efforts to bring up 86-DOS and BASIC on the prototype hardware but, due to problems with both hardware and software provided by IBM we have yet to be successful. . . . These problems have left us several weeks behind schedule.*

Six nights later, Bob got the software up and running. He broke the news to me the following morning, and I'd never felt so relieved. We still had bugs to address, and the IBM printer they sent us didn't work, but we knew that we were on our way. On May 1, Tim Patterson left SCP to come to work for us. He was a critical reinforcement because he knew 86-DOS inside and out.

Late that spring, Bill and Kay Nishi made another trip to Japan. For a solid week they were besieged by Japanese computer makers clamoring for a 16-bit operating system. Despite a leak in one of the trade magazines, Project Chess remained top secret, and Bill couldn't say a word about the DOS we were developing in Seattle. Even so, that trip was telling. Microsoft's biggest plum, it became apparent, wasn't the version we'd made specifically for IBM PCs. The real bonanza was the compatible system that we'd call MS-DOS—the product that could be sold over and over again worldwide, under our own name, to companies that would follow IBM's flying wedge into the 16-bit market. Between the interest in Japan and IBM's domestic ripple effect, we began to realize that MS-DOS would be the international centerpiece of personal computer technology.

So it was crucial for us to gain as much control over DOS as we could. In June, I returned to Seattle Computer Products to try to modify our deal for 86-DOS, offering a flat fee of $30,000 for any future licensing. Rod Brock countered by asking for $150,000 for an exclusive license. I upped our offer to $50,000 for exclusive rights and then proposed an outright purchase, throwing in favorable terms on subsequent upgrades of our 16-bit languages. That was the sales agreement that Brock and I signed on July 27, 1981, a contract that laid the foundation for what Microsoft would become. I knew it was a coup, and that a free-and-clear DOS would be a valuable asset. But I cannot say that we knew just how valuable it would be.

As I stated in a deposition sometime later:

*Bill was very adamant that we should make the contract an agreement of sale. . . . Bill thought we should have complete ownership and control of the product. . . . [He] felt it was always better, if you wanted to control and benefit from the evolution of a product, to own it as compared to license it. . . . [He] said it would just make everything cleaner. . . .*

If Brock had known about IBM, he undoubtedly would have held out for more, and we certainly would have upped our offer. But he was happy to sell. He'd been hit hard by the recession and needed cash, and no one twisted his arm. Brock's priority was to increase his hardware sales by bundling a reliable operating system with his new computers. SCP wasn't equipped to partner with IBM as the industry moved into the next era of personal computers— that was never in the cards.* (Five years after the PC's rollout, Brock fell on hard times and sued Microsoft in an attempt to regain control over the operating system that he'd sold us. Given the uncertainties of a jury trial, Microsoft settled.)

IBM's personal computer was announced on August 12, 1981, and shipped ahead of schedule in November. Everyone expected the PC to do well, but no one had anticipated that it would rule the PC market so quickly. Within four years, with Apple's machines the sole exceptions, any microcomputer that was incompatible with the PC and MS-DOS standards would be irrelevant.

I was proud of our team, of course. MS-DOS quickly became the cornerstone of the company's success, and it was deeply satisfying to have played a central role in its delivery to market. But I was equally proud of 86-BASIC, our old warhorse now running on a new processor chip. While I'd tweaked and improved the vintage code that we'd originally handcrafted for the Altair, it survived mostly intact in the PC. It still had some gas left in the tank, after all.

AS MICROSOFT GREW to nearly a hundred employees, we knew we had to follow the Silicon Valley model and share some equity to keep our top people. We weren't yet ready to take on the

---

*Earlier that summer, when we were still licensing 86-DOS under a nonexclusive contract, Brock was approached by Eddie Currie on behalf of Lifeboat Associates. As Currie tells the story, he offered Brock $250,000 for any rights to 86-DOS that Microsoft didn't control. Brock chose instead to stay with us. He didn't want to antagonize Bill or lose his long-term, cut-rate access to our software.

complications of a public offering, as Apple had in 1980, but it was time to incorporate. We strengthened our board of directors by bringing in David Marquardt, a young venture capitalist who would ease our entrée into the financial markets. In June 1981, we filed our papers with the State of Washington.

With the pie cut into more pieces, our stakes were slightly diluted. Under the new ownership split, Bill kept 51 percent of the equity and I retained 30 percent. The other stakeholders were Steve Ballmer, 7.8 percent; Marquardt's Technology Venture Investors, 5.1 percent (for an investment of $1 million); Vern Raburn, 3.5 percent; Gordon Letwin, 1.3 percent; and Charles Simonyi, 1.3 percent. I kept my title as vice president, later amended to executive vice president According to my formal employment agreement, I would receive a base salary of $100,000 as a corporate officer on top of my $60,000 manager's pay. Bill got $25,000 more as president.

The incorporation didn't immediately change anything, but it made our business feel more serious. That fall we moved into a larger space near Lake Washington and Burgermaster, a fast-food favorite. Bill and I took adjacent offices with a shared secretary and a short passageway between us. I could hear his every shouting match, including the battles royal with Steve Ballmer. Steve complemented Bill as a sounding board on business strategy, as I did on technical strategy. Bill remained the big-picture tactician, but Steve made us more disciplined and systematic. The two of them could get adversarial at times, with Steve's arm-waving histrionics feeding into Bill's pitiless dissections of what he thought everyone else was doing wrong. They were both ultracompetitive, super-high-IQ, maniacally relentless people with a tendency toward melodrama.

Over time, their disagreements seemed to get more frequent and intense, like face-offs between bull elephants—especially when Steve tried to push Bill to ramp up hiring, the only way to keep our customers and sustain Microsoft's growth. Not long after coming on board, he told Bill that Microsoft needed another thirty people right away, doubling our staff. I was all for it, but Bill considered it heretical. He liked to take on overhead slowly and incrementally, which could miss the boat in the tech industry. He started yelling at Steve: "Do you know what you're doing when you ask for thirty people? Are you trying to bankrupt this company?"

Steve bellowed back, "We don't have a choice! We've got commitments and delivery dates! If we don't make these hires, we'll blow the contracts!"

And Bill said, "What if the business slows down while we're paying all these people? We'll be wiped out! Are you crazy? We could destroy this company! Do you want to destroy us?"

I gave Steve credit for not backing down; he kept working Bill over until he got what we needed. After an hour of back-and-forth, he said, "That's OK, Bill, it's on me, damn it, but we've got to get those people in here or we're screwed."

Steve was sincere and straightforward—theatrical, maybe, but not manipulative. We didn't always agree about the business, but we generally stayed out of each other's way. Sometimes we'd go on recruitment trips and share a twin room in the frugal Microsoft tradition. One morning I awoke to a series of grunts. I cracked my eyes open to find Steve doing push-ups by the dozen at seven in the morning. I thought, *This guy is really hardcore.*

Typically we'd tour the top computer science schools at the best universities: MIT, Cal Tech, Harvard, Yale, Stanford. (I can recall a packed lounge at MIT where students were chanting the actors' lines in unison during a *Star Trek* rerun.) Bill thought it was better to get programmers when they were young and enthusiastic, before they were ruined by working somewhere else. After my stint at Honeywell, I couldn't disagree. We wanted freshly minted bachelor's degrees, occasionally a master's, rarely a PhD. Above all, we were after the brightest lights. A great programmer can outproduce an average one by ten to one; with a genius, the ratio might be fifty to one.

Fortunately, with its water and nearby mountains and urbanized core, Seattle was an easier sell than Albuquerque. And once IBM announced the PC, anyone could see that we were offering unparalleled opportunities. We might pay slightly under the norm, but our pitch was persuasive: Would you rather work on some process-control project for Dow Chemical or a state-of-the-art word processor for the IBM PC? An ambitious young software engineer wouldn't think twice about joining us.

Steve's efforts finally got Microsoft growing in line with its revenues, from 40 employees in 1980 to 128 in 1981 and 220 in 1982. When a company doubles or triples in size each year, it can't possibly stay tight-knit. But I still hung out with people from work, going for dinner at Casa Lupita or downtime at a pub called the Nowhere, where I built on my Wazzu skill set at foosball. When our six-day workweeks allowed it, there were volleyball games and barbecues at Bob O'Rear's, with Marc McDonald serving batches of his homemade daiquiris.

My life was more rounded than before. I bought a small sailboat. I invited musicians to my house on Lake Sammamish, where we'd make a single blues jam last an hour. And I hosted a memorable Halloween party, where I dressed as a wizard and Bill did chest slides on the balustrade from my upper floor down toward the kitchen. He'd run as fast as he could, throw himself on the banister, and glide to the parquet below. He was still edge-walking. One day he borrowed Andy Evans's Porsche 928 and spun and bottomed the car out, nearly totaling it; the repairs took more than a year. Bill got so many speeding tickets that he had to hire the best traffic attorney in the state to defend him. He finally switched to a sluggish Mercedes turbo diesel just to stay out of trouble.

In our farewell company photograph back in Albuquerque, nine of the eleven people were programmers, a bunch of young hackers having fun together. That changed in Seattle as we brought in MBAs to support an increasingly lucrative set of product lines. Many were hired for sales and advertising; others handled end-user testing on new features. This was basic business practice, but it inevitably funneled resources away from development. As a technology company grows, it must balance the need for innovation with the imperative to bolster existing products and keep the profits flowing. As Microsoft expanded far, far beyond the thirty-five programmers that once seemed like a pipe dream, it would get more and more difficult to keep that balance.

# CHAPTER 11

# BORROWED TIME

A week after we completed work on the PC, a form letter came from IBM: "Dear Vendor, you've done a fine job. . . ." Gary Kildall gave us a less favorable review. Some time before the August 1981 rollout, Bill and I met with him at Boeing Field, south of downtown Seattle. He'd heard rumors about our involvement with PC-DOS and wanted to feel us out—and to make an appeal for the old spheres of influence. "In a perfect world," Gary said, "you guys should do languages and we should do operating systems."

Digital Research had recently acquired CBASIC, which ran under CP/M-80. As Gary talked, CBASIC sounded like a shot across the bow; if Microsoft came up with a DOS, Kildall would open fire on us in the language business. But we were past the point where a competitor could knock us back on our heels, and certainly not in languages, where we had supreme confidence. At the time, CP/M-80 was running on hundreds of computer models. Its sales amounted to more than $5 million a year. But with 8-bit technology soon to be eclipsed and IBM secured as our 16-bit platform, Digital Research was destined to be an also-ran.

Kildall did not go gently into the night. Shortly after the PC's announcement, he claimed that we'd ripped off his software. The charge wouldn't hold up, however. The commands that Tim Patterson had copied from CP/M-80 were both nonproprietary and common knowledge—the keyword to open a file on a disk, for example, or to send it to the printer. Tim had never seen CP/M's source code, and he'd built QDOS (and then 86-DOS) in 8086 assembly language, from scratch. His program was a different animal, as anyone who'd used both the 8-bit CP/M-80 and the 16-bit 86-DOS could attest. For starters, Tim's system could read or write files up to six times faster. MS-DOS had borrowed no more from CP/M-80 than Kildall had taken from DEC's DOS-11 operating system when he created CP/M years before.

After Kildall made noise about suing for copyright infringement, a move his lawyers apparently discouraged, IBM offered his long-delayed CP/M-86 as an alternative for the PC. But it was obvious that IBM had no wish to support two sets of application software or to revisit the chaos of the 8-bit market. It priced our DOS at $40 and CP/M-86 at $240, a premium that reflected Kildall's insistence on per-copy royalties. Once it became clear to users that IBM's own software would run only on DOS, the independent software vendors ignored CP/M-86 and kept flocking to our operating system en masse. Our relationship with IBM made MS-DOS's supremacy a fait accompli.

THE IBM PC was imperfect. It was expensive and looked corporate and soulless. But it was also the best personal computer of its time, with the most powerful processor, a superior keyboard, and reliable floppy disk drives. Executives didn't wait for their IT officers to take the plunge into microcomputing; they went out, bought their PCs, and plugged them in. IBM had projected the sale of 250,000 units within five years, and they were off by a factor of ten.

The PC marked the official close of the hobbyist era in computing, as the consumer market that we'd seeded with the Altair now came of age. Pretty much anyone who'd used an electric typewriter felt that they could handle this new class of computer. Within a few years of its release, in a development IBM had failed to anticipate, there would be dozens of PC "clones," fully compatible (and generally cheaper) computers that captured most of the home market after licensing MS-DOS. Soon our operating system was bringing in more revenue than all our languages combined.

By 1984, the industry had converged around a single standard: MS-DOS twinned to the IBM specification. Legions of applications were developed to run on top of it. Hobbled by inferior hardware and limited software, other platforms could not compete. The TRS-80 was extinct by 1986; the Commodore 64 and Atari ST died a few years later. Only Apple survived, carving out a premium niche in the U.S. market that would hover around 10 percent.

Down the road, Microsoft would suffer from the distraction of OS/2 until the company jettisoned the jointly created operating system in 1990 and signaled the end of its development partnership with IBM. Nevertheless, our original deal with Big Blue was critical both for Microsoft and for the industry as a whole. The PC phenomenon gave personal computers credibility in the business world. It became the launchpad for Windows and GUI applications like Word. Charles Simonyi, who has flown twice to the International Space Station, likes to use a rocket analogy. IBM gave Microsoft an essential boost before becoming a drag that we needed to shed.

Or put another way: Before DOS, Microsoft was an important software company. After DOS, it was the essential one.

For me, the poignant postscript to this story was the fall of Digital Equipment Corporation, the company we idolized in our youth. Early on, its top management had resisted the shift to personal computers. As late as 1977, its president told the World Future Association, "There is no reason anyone would want a computer in their home." Five years later, DEC swallowed its pride and released a well-designed microcomputer called the Rainbow 100, but shot itself in the foot by using the old 8-bit CP/M system. When DEC finally got around to implementing MS-DOS, the company required a customized version that was incompatible with thousands of PC applications, and it flopped.

In the mainframe and minicomputer worlds, DEC had achieved small miracles by marching to its own drummer. If, ten years earlier, you had told us that IBM would forge a new path for microcomputers and that the maker of the PDP-10 would straggle in late and be unable to adapt, we would never have believed you.*

As IBM PC sales exploded, the national media took notice of Microsoft, and particularly of Bill as its president. He became the face of our company and the logical source for any journalist, which was fine with me. (I'll do my share of publicity but I don't seek it out, my recently opened Twitter account notwithstanding.)

One thing didn't change: Bill was as headstrong as ever. Once I flew with him to San Francisco to visit a few customers. For efficiency's sake, we conducted separate meetings before rendezvousing back at the airport. I reached the gate several minutes before takeoff, but Bill was late as usual. They issued the final boarding call—no Bill. I was resigned to finding the next flight when he rushed up to the gate, out of breath. It was too late; the plane was already inching away from the jetway. But Bill never stopped running, through the boarding gate and into the jetway itself, with me trailing. Upon reaching the motor control panel, he did a quick scan and began pushing buttons. Then I realized what was happening: *Bill was trying to move the jetway back up to the plane so we could board.*

Aghast, I called out, "Don't do that!" An airline agent rushed over; I was sure that we would both be arrested or, at the very least, escorted from the terminal. But the man said, "Sir, sir, hold on. We'll get the plane to come back." To my astonishment, that is exactly what happened. They returned the plane, allowed us to board, and we got home on time.

---

*As minicomputers were undercut by ever more powerful microprocessors, and by the PC in particular, DEC went into a fatal tailspin and was acquired by Compaq in 1998.

In general, I had less to do than ever with the business side of Microsoft. With Steve Ballmer on board, I was free to anchor our technical work. My management style was to wander the halls and peek in on the programmers:

"What problems are slowing you down?"

"Have you thought about trying it this way?"

"What happens if I pull the disk out when you're doing that?"

We'd talk for a few minutes as I probed, one of my strong suits. Then I'd let them solve the rest of the problem themselves—unless someone hit a roadblock and got stuck, when I'd drill down to help get things moving again. The programmers liked having one of their own in a decision-making position, and I'm sure it was a relief to report to someone with a technical background. Often I'd get valuable information about some unexpected problem; they'd be loath to tell Bill for fear of getting yelled at, but they felt more relaxed with me. I loved working with my guys, and I think they knew it.

But though my role may have narrowed, Bill kept running big decisions by me. Our dynamic was more intertwined than the partnership at Apple, where Steve Jobs was the grand thinker and Steve Wozniak the crack hardware designer. Bill and I were both generalists at heart. That was a big strength for Microsoft, but it also meant that no subject escaped debate.

BACK IN FEBRUARY 1980, after I'd grown convinced that we needed a more powerful operating system, we licensed AT&T's Unix software, and renamed it Xenix to abide by trademark restrictions. Our goal was to find a niche among midsize companies that wanted a heavier-duty system than MS-DOS without paying for a minicomputer or using a time-sharing service. But while Xenix made some money for Microsoft, it fell short of expectations. Even a scaled-down version of Unix was too demanding for the 8086 chip, and there were financial issues, too. AT&T was unwilling to lower its license fees for high-volume sales, so their royalties cut deeply into our profit margin. Microsoft wound up selling its interest in the software a few years later.

Xenix was still on my mind in the spring of 1982, when IBM asked us for a next-generation DOS that could manage the upcoming PC-XT and its 10-megabyte hard disk drive, a vast amount of storage at the time. (It's about enough for three uncompressed digital photos today.) By that point, DOS 1.1 was like a one-story, one-bedroom house—it kept the rain out, but it sorely needed remodeling. I assigned DOS 2.0 to three of my sharpest developers: Mark Zbikowski (the group leader), Aaron Reynolds, and Chris Peters. Our goal was to bring several best-of-breed Unix features into the PC and to widen our edge over Digital Research and Apple, whose operating systems were less sophisticated. If we did the job right, it would bolster MS-DOS as the industry standard.

After brainstorming for days on possible improvements, we settled on two major ones. The first was Mark's idea for loadable device drivers, which would allow PC users to add third-party printers or external hard drives without soaking up too much memory. The drivers would be loaded from the PC's hard drive only when the peripheral was actually added to the system, a first step toward today's plug-and-play.

Second, and more important, we were devising a new way to organize files. For stand-alone BASIC, Bill and Marc McDonald had designed a flat, one-level-deep directory called the File Allocation Table, or FAT, which Tim Patterson later reworked for DOS. It functioned well for limited-storage floppy disks but was too limited for a hard disk system, which might contain hundreds of documents. I was impressed by the Unix alternative when I'd first encountered it at Harvard: a hierarchical file system with a root directory and any number of subdirectories underneath it, or folders within folders within folders. It allowed users to organize their data any way they saw fit. What computer maker wouldn't want to provide this improvement if they could?

But it soon became clear that IBM was committed to keeping

DOS 2.0 as close as possible to the eight thousand bytes used by DOS 1.1, so as not to disrupt their existing user base. If our new DOS was too memory hungry, IBM feared that smaller PC systems would run out of room for some popular applications. And they weren't accustomed to contractors going beyond their specs, even if it meant they were getting more for their money. IBM's developers loved our twenty extra features, but management thought we were cramming in arbitrary changes. They weren't pleased that DOS 2.0 was now triple the size of DOS 1.1 or that interim deadlines had slipped.

The day Mark got back from delivering a progress report in Florida, Bill stalked into his office, loaded for bear. He slammed his fist on Mark's desk and started yelling: "I just talked to Boca Raton, and the customer is not happy! You've got to do what the customer wants!" When I overheard the ruckus and walked in, Bill wheeled on me and shouted, "The customer says this is unacceptable! We've got to give them what they asked for!"

It was late in the day, and I was tired and having none of it. "What they asked for is stupid—it doesn't do what we're going to need!" I yelled back.

"All we need is to make the customer happy!"

And I said, "But the customer is an idiot!"

"It doesn't matter, they're the customer!"

"But the next DOS has to push the industry forward!"

By that point we were standing six inches apart, chest to chest and nose to nose. Mark was watching like a horrified teenager whose parents sounded like they wanted to kill each other. (There was no physical contact, but Mark told me later that he saw some spittle fly.)

Bill wasn't reluctant to do technically difficult things if they gave us a competitive advantage. But he worried that I'd get distracted by the chance to do something *cool,* to climb some technology mountain just because it was there. By then, our relationship with IBM—and the PC compatibles—was Microsoft's lifeblood.

Bill was determined to keep our biggest client satisfied, and he probably thought I wasn't giving that enough weight.

After ten minutes of mutual apoplexy and an epic stare-down, Bill finally said, "OK, but your guy better hit the delivery date." Then he left, and I said to Mark, "Make sure you finish getting all those features in."

And Mark and his team somehow satisfied us both.

APPLE WAS MORE than a brand; it aimed to become part of your lifestyle. (*We're cool, we're sleek, we're reliable and easy to use, we think different.*) It wasn't an accident that Steve Jobs had toured Xerox PARC a year ahead of me. At that point, the high-end Apple Lisa was still in development, and the Macintosh was a low-on-the-totem-pole, one-man project. As Bill would say after Apple unsuccessfully sued Microsoft for copyright infringement over Windows' GUI: "Hey, Steve, just because you broke into Xerox's house before I did and took the TV doesn't mean I can't go in later and take the stereo."

Early in 1982, Jobs invited Bill and me down to see a Macintosh trial run. As we sat down, he turned to a young developer named Andy Hertzfeld and said, "OK, let's show them what we've got."

Jobs was already pitching the Macintosh as a computer so simple that even his mother could use it. Unfortunately, the Mac prototype we saw that day was not yet "insanely great," and the display locked up a minute or so after booting. Jobs was disgusted—you could see the contempt on his face. "What the fuck is going on?" he snarled at Hertzfeld, who'd probably been up all night getting things ready and was now trying to shrink under the table. "These guys came all the way down here to see this thing, and this is the best we can do? *This* is the best we can do? We get thirty seconds and a frozen screen? What the fuck is *wrong* with you?" He railed on as Bill and I traded glances and uncomfortably watched the performance. It seemed to me like an exercise in humiliation for its own sake. We couldn't believe that Jobs would attack a subordinate in front of outsiders.

I was reminded of that incident by a 1999 television movie called *Pirates of Silicon Valley*. In reimagining Microsoft in the late seventies and early eighties, the film depicts Bill as an übernerd and Steve Ballmer as a crude cheerleader, while I'm the bearded sidekick who loves gadgets and cracks wise now and then. Jobs, played by Noah Wyle, comes off as a charismatic but ruthless and mean-spirited jerk. The next time I ran into him, I asked him what he thought. And Jobs said, "I thought the guy who played me did a fantastic job." He just didn't care about what people thought of his public persona.

Bill was different; he wanted to be viewed as tough but fair. He could be callous and rude, but he had a warmer, human side, too. And no one doubted that his excesses, for good or ill, were spontaneous. When Bill blew his stack at a meeting, it was never merely for effect. As the late Bob Wallace once said, "The only stuff worth discussing was the stuff you didn't agree about, so you tended mostly to argue with Bill." Microsoft veterans knew the drill, but new employees could be traumatized. Bill would miss the cues from those who reacted with stony silence or cold frustration. He didn't always notice when he pushed too hard.

When someone threatened to quit, Bill took it personally and did all he could to change the person's mind. What he never considered, though, was that he might lose me. Whenever we locked horns, I'd have to raise my intensity and my blood pressure to meet Bill's, and it was taking a toll. Some people can vent their anger, take a breath, and let it go, but I wasn't one of them. My sinking morale sapped my enthusiasm for my work, which in turn could precipitate Bill's next attack.

Top executives like Steve Ballmer and Charles Simonyi had their share of friction with Bill, too, but none shared our long and complex history. I'd known the CEO long before there was a Microsoft, and we'd started the company on an equal footing.

Now my role was diminishing. Bill stopped seeking me out on a regular basis, and I went in to see him less and less. Too angry and proud to make an emotional appeal, I never went in and told Bill, point-blank, "Some days working with you is like being in hell." So my grievances hung in the air, unstated and unresolved. By the time we fought over DOS 2.0, our partnership was living on borrowed time.

On June 1, 1982, to get my point across without getting distracted by counterarguments and rationales, I decided to write Bill a letter. A few excerpts:

> *About two months ago I came to the painful conclusion that the time had come for me to leave Microsoft. Steve convinced me that I should wait to discuss it with you when you were not in the middle of a series of trips. . . .*
>
> *As I'm sure you realize, there is one primary reason that is the basis for my decision. I can no longer tolerate the brow-beating or "tirades" . . . that characterize almost every attempt I make to discuss any subject that is controversial. . . .*
>
> *The kind of personal verbal attacks that you use have cost many hundreds of hours of lost productivity in my case alone. . . . Over the years the result of these and other incidents has been the gradual destruction of both our friendship and our ability to work together. . . . The camaraderie of the early days is long since gone.*

Three weeks later, Bill hired Jim Towne as the company's first president and chief operating officer. Because they'd need to interact so closely, Bill thought it made sense for Towne to take my office. I didn't object, and moved down the hall. Towne inherited the hot seat, with Bill popping in at any moment to grill him about some breaking development. It soon became apparent that the new president lacked the horsepower that Bill demanded. I knew he wouldn't last when Bill said, "I know what he's going to say before he opens his mouth." Towne left the company less than a year later.

As the summer wore on, my twenty-yard move down the corridor put me even further out of the flow. Though neither of us said it, I think we both knew that it couldn't go on this way for long.

# CHAPTER 12

# WAKE-UP CALL

It began that summer with an itch behind my knees at the Oregon Shakespeare Festival, where my parents would take us to see nine plays in seven days when I was in junior high. Not like a rash you got from the wrong soap—this was an agony that had me clawing at myself.

After the itching stopped, the night sweats began. Then, in August, I became aware of a tiny, hard bump on the right side of my neck, near my collarbone. Over the next several weeks, it grew to the size of a pencil eraser tip. It didn't hurt, and I didn't know that any lump near the lymph nodes was a warning sign. I felt as bulletproof as most people under thirty; I took my health for granted.

On September 12, 1982, I left with Bill on a European press tour. We went from London to Munich, where I felt really odd after drinking a beer. By September 20, when we moved on to Paris, I was exhausted and off-kilter—as if I had the flu, except there was no fever. I made it through one press conference, and then I was done. I flew home to see my doctor, who felt my neck and said, "You're going in for a biopsy tomorrow morning."

I checked into Swedish Medical Center in downtown Seattle, my first hospital stay since having my tonsils out as a child. That night I dreamed that a Gumby-like creature was stuck to me. It was made of black tar, and I just couldn't get it off. I awoke in a panic.

On September 25, they performed the biopsy. After I came out of anesthesia, the surgeon entered my room looking grim. "Mr. Allen," he said, "I took out as much as I could, but our initial diagnosis is lymphoma."

I knew that was cancer, but not much else, and as I found out more I got terrified. In those days, even early-stage lymphomas had a fifty-fifty chance of killing you. I tried to make sense of the possibility that I might soon die. I'd had twenty-nine good years, but I couldn't help feeling cheated. I had so much more to explore and experience.

The next morning, the surgeon and oncology team returned, all smiles. "We've got good news," the surgeon said. "You've got Hodgkin's disease." An in-depth look had modified their diagnosis. "The cure rate's in the midnineties, if it's early-stage," he went on. "You're going to be fine. You're going to recover from this."

I wanted to believe him. It sounded good, and everyone's body language seemed positive. But I was still in shock from the day before.

The hospital needed to "stage" my illness to see how far it had progressed, beginning with a more invasive biopsy that drew bone marrow from my hips. I made the mistake of buying a book about Hodgkin's that showed how tumors could metastasize, with charts on survival outcomes, and it scared the heck out of me. The worst part was waiting for test results as the bump on my neck kept growing to the size of a robin's egg. My father, a testicular cancer survivor, told me, "Son, none of this stuff is pleasant, but you have to take it like a man." That might sound cold in print, but knowing that he'd gotten through it was comforting to me. I couldn't give in to panic or despair; I had to tough it out.

Then, good news: They'd caught my disease in Stage 1-A, before it had spread. Early-stage Hodgkin's lymphoma is one of the most curable cancers. I'd drawn a scary card, but hardly the worst.

I began a six-week course of radiation, five days a week. The waiting area was filled with people in hospital gowns, some with conditions that gave them very little chance. The room was eerily quiet as people waited to be called. One day a man wandered in and asked for a cigarette machine. The nurse stood up and said sternly, "Sir, there are no cigarette machines in cancer wards." The man fled.

I was grilled ninety seconds per side with high-energy X-rays. Including setup, the procedure took less than fifteen minutes. The technician said, "Mr. Allen, nobody has ever shown the energy you have to jump on the table and jump off again." I just wanted to get out of there as fast as I could. A month in, after they started targeting my spleen, the nausea came in waves. I'd race home before throwing up for hours. Over two months I lost twenty pounds.

At home I rested and listened to music. I spent time with my parents and sister, but I needed more to distract me. So instead of doing the sane thing and taking a leave, I went into the office a few afternoons a week, just to keep my hand in. That was the no-excuses Microsoft culture: relentless commitment to work. Striving for normalcy, I even took a weekend beginner's ski class when I had barely enough energy to coast down a hill.

Halfway through therapy, my white-cell count dropped so low that they had to stop for several weeks. But by then the tumor was shrinking. There was no guarantee of a cure, and I still felt sick and debilitated, but I began to be encouraged.

After resuming the radiation, I was in Bill's office one day talking about MS-DOS revenues. Our flat-fee strategy had helped establish us in several markets, but I thought we'd held on to it for too long. A case in point: We'd gotten a fee of $21,000 for the license for Applesoft BASIC. After sales of more than a million Apple II's, that amounted to two cents per copy. "If we want to maximize revenue," I said, "we have to start charging royalties for DOS."

Bill replied as though he was speaking to a not-so-bright child:

"How do you think we got the market share we have today?" Then Steve came by to weigh in on Bill's side with his usual intensity. It would have been two on one, except I was approximately half a person at the time. (Microsoft later switched to per-copy licensing, a move that would add billions of dollars in revenue.)

Not long after that incident, I told Steve that I might start my own company. I told Bill that my days as a full-time executive at Microsoft were probably numbered, and that I thought I'd be happier on my own.

I was still undergoing therapy when Bill signed off on my proposal to start a Microsoft Hardware Group, which set about designing a plug-in mouse for Charles Simonyi's GUI applications. We contracted with a Japanese manufacturing firm called ALPS, and soon a Microsoft Mouse prototype took shape: a metal-finish tracking ball and a pair of shafts to read the ball's movement and decode direction and distance. Don Burtis created a card that could interpret those signals for the PC. (It was thirteen years before the advent of Universal Serial Bus connections.) The big question was: How many buttons? I decided on two, a compromise between the three-button mouse on the Alto and the one-button model Steve Jobs was developing for the Lisa.

I visited Jobs in Palo Alto around that time to hear more about his plans for the Macintosh, Apple's cheaper GUI machine then still in development. We had a vested interest in the Mac, which would give our GUI applications—Microsoft Word and Excel—a welcome foothold until the PC platform and our new Windows operating system caught up to them. Jobs launched into a soliloquy about the glories of the graphical user interface, not knowing he was preaching to the choir. After I let it slip that we were planning a mouse for Microsoft Word, Jobs put their one-button mouse through its paces. When I asked him whether two buttons might be better, he passionately lectured me: "You know, Paul, this is all about simplicity versus complexity. And nobody needs more than one button on a mouse."

I said, "But Steve, people have more than one finger, and there's going to be things they might want to do with a right click, too."

Jobs dismissed my point with a shake of his head. He believed in making the entry-level experience as unintimidating as possible—and that there was usually one and only one correct way to do things. At Microsoft, we tried to balance simplicity with power. I considered the trade-off worthwhile if an extra feature made a program or device more functional.

When Word came out before the Mac in 1983, our first-generation mouse didn't sell very well, despite a retail price less than half of our competition's. Jon Shirley, who succeeded Towne as Microsoft's president that year, would complain that we had "mouse-infested warehouses." The main problem was Word 1.0, a dumbed-down, pre-Windows attempt to mimic a graphical user interface. But I wasn't discouraged. Our strategy was geared toward introducing people to a new experience that would pave the way for better versions of our software.

In time, I'd be vindicated. Windows was introduced in 1985, eventually becoming the dominant GUI personal computer platform. The Microsoft Mouse thrived through many incarnations—optical, wireless, laser, Bluetooth—as one of the company's longest-lived products. And every one of those mice had more than one button. People quickly adapted. Today that extra button helps millions of Windows users gain access to context menus and a host of other convenient features.

Postscript: In 2005, after twenty-two years of one-button worship, Apple relented and released the multibutton Mighty Mouse.

ONE EVENING IN late December 1982, I heard Bill and Steve speaking heatedly in Bill's office and paused outside to listen in. It was easy to get the gist of the conversation. They were bemoaning my recent lack of production and discussing how they might dilute my Microsoft equity by issuing options to themselves and other shareholders. It was clear that they'd been thinking about this for some time.

Unable to stand it any longer, I burst in on them and shouted, "This is unbelievable! It shows your true character, once and for all." I was speaking to both of them, but staring straight at Bill. Caught red-handed, they were struck dumb. Before they could respond, I turned on my heel and left.

I replayed their dialogue in my mind while driving home, and it felt more and more heinous to me. I helped start the company and was still an active member of management, though limited by my illness, and now my partner and my colleague were scheming to rip me off. It was mercenary opportunism, plain and simple. That evening, a chastened Steve Ballmer called my house and asked Jody if he could come over. "Look, Paul," he said, after we sat down together, "I'm really sorry about what happened today. We were just letting off steam. We're trying to get so much stuff done, and we just wish you could contribute even more. But that stock thing isn't fair. I wouldn't have anything to do with it, and I'm sure Bill wouldn't, either."

I told Steve that the incident had left a bad taste in my mouth. A few days later, I received a six-page, handwritten letter from Bill. Dated December 31, 1982, the last day of our last full year together at Microsoft, it contained an apology for the conversation I'd overheard. And it offered a revealing, Bill's-eye view of our partnership.

> *During the last 14 years we have had numerous disagreements. However, I doubt any two partners have ever agreed on as much both in terms of specific decisions and their general idea of how to view things.*

True, we were extraordinary partners. Despite our differences, few cofounders had shared such a unified vision—maybe Hewlett and Packard or Google's Sergey Brin and Larry Page, but it was a short list.

> *Sometimes I think that I have more confidence in your abilities than you do. Your strong association with SoftCard always surprises me. . . . Frankly, breakthrough ideas like . . . SoftCard are great, but they are not necessary.*

Bill knew that SoftCard was still a sore point with me. He walked a fine line here, trying to acknowledge my contribution without giving it too much weight.

> *The company is really in great shape by some measures. . . . However, the company is in BAD shape by one measure. We are a lot less unique [than] we were before. . . . Our product spec's and overall approach is [sic] not as unique as they should be.*

Early in the life of Microsoft, nobody else had what we had: a robust yet compact BASIC for microcomputers, plus a proven set of development tools. When we achieved a dominant position with MS-DOS, no other product compared. But as the industry matured, Microsoft's rate of innovation had slowed. The company needed all of the out-of-the-box ideas it could muster, and Bill didn't want mine to slip away.

> *Paul—sometimes I feel like you are telling me I'm a bad guy or that the company is bad. Sometimes I feel like you don't understand all the effort that's gone into the company.*

In fact, I was well aware of the tremendous effort that Bill and others had invested to make Microsoft great. After all, I'd been part of it.

*I know you've thought about this more than I have, but do
you really want to be a solo performer? I understand wanting to take time off but if you really wanted to work solo
why did you come back to Boston and convince me to drop
out of school? Your best work has been helping to plan and
design, not execute.*

Bill was right. Our great string of successes had married my vision to his unmatched aptitude for business. But that was beside
the point. Once I was diagnosed with Hodgkin's, my decision became simpler. If I were to relapse, it would be pointless—if not
hazardous—to return to the stresses at Microsoft. If I continued
to recover, I now understood that life was too short to spend it
unhappily.

Bill's letter was a last-ditch effort to get me to stay, and I knew
he believed he had logic on his side. But it didn't change anything.
My mind was made up.

AS THE NEW Year began, there was much to be done at Microsoft.
The Multi-Tool product line was evolving into what would eventually become Microsoft Office, with Mac versions already under
way. There was excitement over Windows—or "Interface Manager," as it was called, until someone in marketing persuaded Bill
that "Windows" was sexier. The company had plenty of innovative
products in the pipeline. I felt like I was leaving it in good shape.

By the end, Bill and I had diverged in ways that went beyond
our yelling matches. His extreme competitiveness helped make him
a historically successful CEO, but it also destabilized our relationship. One small example came before I left the company, when Bill
was giving me a hard time about everything I hadn't been doing. In
my defense, I said, "The TRS-80 Model 100 math package was a big
job, and it turned out pretty well." A year or so earlier, Tandy had
asked us for a decimal floating point math program for their early

notebook computer, a must for precise financial calculations. I'd never done one before and sweated bullets for months to get it right.

And Bill said, "I wrote all that code."

"Really?" I said. He'd say these things with such conviction that it made me wonder for a moment: *Had* I written it? I went back and found the source code and printed it out, and of course it was mine. Bill hadn't written a single line; in fact, he wasn't even writing code at that point. The next day I went back to his office. I dropped the listing on his desk and said, "OK, Bill, here's the math package. Show me what you wrote."

It was a strange moment. Bill froze in mid rock, glanced down at the code, and muttered, "Yeah, you did write it."

Sometimes it seemed that Bill so utterly identified with Microsoft that he'd get confused about where the company left off and he began. I didn't feel quite the same way. The business was hugely important, but it did not define me. I wasn't sure what the future held, or even how much of it I'd have to enjoy, but I looked forward to a new phase. I had never forgotten my father's advice: "Whatever you do, you should love it." My dad was happy for me when I'd returned to Seattle four years earlier, full of ideas and enthusiasm. It seemed to him that I'd found my calling, and I thought I had, too. But now it was time to go.

In January I met with Bill for one final time as a Microsoft executive. As he sat down with me on the couch in his office, I knew that he'd try to make me feel guilty and obliged to stay. (Months after Vern Raburn had left to go to Lotus Development, Bill wrote to me that he was still "confused and hurt" about what had gone wrong.) But once he saw he couldn't change my mind, Bill tried to cut his losses. When Microsoft incorporated in 1981, our old partnership agreement was nullified, and with it his power to force me to accept a buyout based on "irreconcilable differences." Now he tried a different tack, one he'd hinted at in his letter. "It's not fair that you keep your stake in the company," he said. He made a lowball offer for my stock: five dollars a share.

When Vern left, the Microsoft board voted to buy back his stock at three dollars a share, which ultimately cost him billions of dollars. I knew that Bill hoped to pressure me to sell mine the same way. But I was in a different position than Vern, who'd jumped to Lotus in apparent violation of his employment agreement. I was a cofounder, and I wasn't leaving to join a competitor. "I'm not sure I'm willing to sell," I countered, "but I wouldn't even discuss less than ten dollars a share."

"No *way*," Bill said, as I'd suspected he would. Our talk was over. As it turned out, Bill's conservatism worked to my advantage. If he'd been willing to offer something close to my asking price, I would have sold way too soon.

On February 18, 1983, my resignation became official. I retained my seat on the board and was subsequently voted vice chairman—as a tribute to my contributions, and in the hope that I would continue to add value to the company I'd helped create.

WITH MY HODGKIN'S in remission, I didn't know what to do next; I just knew that I wanted to enjoy life. I would literally stop in my tracks to look at a flower or the sky, or consciously savor a moment with family or friends. Though my Microsoft shares were not yet liquid, I was in decent financial shape. I had a nice house and enough money in the bank to pay my bills for a while and travel.

That spring I went to Hawaii with Marc McDonald and Ric Weiland. As a boy, I'd thrilled to Sean Connery's scuba adventures in James Bond films like *Thunderball*. When I found out that our hotel had a pool where you could try breathing with scuba gear, I jumped at the chance. The next day I did a shore dive among the brilliant fish that swam around the reef, and I was hooked. Diving took me into a different physical realm—something like being an astronaut, I supposed. (I became a certified diver two years later, and have since dived throughout the world, from the Galápagos to the Red Sea. It's my great escape.)

I wasn't home long before I took off again, this time on a road trip to Anadarko, with my father joining me for the home stretch. We saw my Uncle Louis, who took us to a classic barbecue spot and then to his Western Wear store, where I disappointed him by choosing a plain leather pair of boots over snakeskin or alligator. My dad drove back to Seattle with me, and the road got him talking about a subject he'd never broached before: his experience in World War II, when he'd been part of the second wave that landed at Normandy. "It got pretty hot a few times," he said. He told me about the German buzz bombs that rained on the troops as they waited in England before crossing the Channel. At a given point, a cutoff valve sent those early cruise missiles into a dive. If the soldiers heard the buzzing stop overhead, they'd lunge under their card tables for whatever shelter they could find.

There was one last thing my father told me as we drove along, before lapsing back into his typical silence: "If you take care of your men, they'll take care of you."

THOUGH IN REMISSION, I still waited for something bad to happen. My doctors told me I'd be in the clear if I had no recurrence within three years, and that the odds were on my side: a 96 percent chance of a cure. But I couldn't stop thinking about that other 4 percent. I was still recovering from the blow of the first diagnosis, from hearing I might die. I took it harder than some might have. Whenever I caught a bad cold or felt a strange sensation, I got a sinking feeling.

I had a battery of tests every two months, followed by days of anxiety before the results came in. One day in May, I woke up with my chest throbbing. I had blood drawn to check my "sed rate," a measure of inflammation in the body. It came back at 29, about double the norm, a number that might indicate cancer. I was sure that my Hodgkin's had come back. At best, I thought, I'd face the ordeal of chemotherapy. At worst, the end could be near.

On Friday, May 13, I repeated the test, which would take several days to process. Rather than wait at home, I flew to the National

Computer Conference in Anaheim, California. I kept feeling worse and more worried, unable to sleep, and left the convention early for a late-night flight back to Seattle. In the air, at some point after midnight, I was panicked enough to draft a handwritten will. (In distributing my 3.2 million shares of Microsoft stock, I sensibly advised the recipients to hold on to them for a while "to enjoy the maximum return.")

Hours later, my doctor called with the test results: all good. My sed rate had dropped to 16. My chest pain was inconsequential. That was a great day; everything seemed possible again. As I wrote in my journal, "Tonight I walked around Green Lake at sunset. It was a beautiful sight. I even saw a huge catfish swimming by the shore. . . ."

Two weeks after my scare, I traveled with my dad to Twin Lakes, our old family vacation spot. The two of us reverted to our usual interaction style, lots of fishing and reading and not much conversation. One day my father hooked a huge rainbow trout and battled it for half an hour before he could angle it up to our boat. I stood by, net in hand. When the fight was over and the fish safely in the boat, my dad grinned like I'd never seen him grin before. It was as though he'd reconnected with the best days of his youth. He'd caught the biggest trout he would ever catch, and he was content.

Near the end of our stay, out of the blue, my father looked at me and said, "No matter what happens to me, always take care of your mother and your sister." It wasn't like him to be explicit about such things. But perhaps he'd had a premonition.

I'D RARELY BEEN abroad except on business, but now I had all the time in the world for a European tour. I began that July in Scotland and then Ireland, where I met up with my sister and Brian, her fiancé. In Belfast I stayed at a hotel near blocks of rubble; it was the time of the Troubles, and bombings were commonplace. I was on my own the first night and went to the hotel bar. Once the patrons established that I was an American, they bought me drinks and toasted me, one after the next. The next day, Brian's brother picked me up and asked, "Paul, why did you choose this particular hotel?"

My travel agent found it, I said.

"Oh, so you didn't know it's been blown up three times, then?" Now I knew why the Irishmen toasted me. I was the only American crazy enough to stay there.

I'd long wanted to take my father to France, but he had no interest. "I've already seen it," he said. But I'd found another reason to go, a woman I'd met through a friend two years earlier. Francoise was incredibly attractive: dark hair, olive skin, exotic Mediterranean looks. She was a high-level accountant with a wild streak: offbeat, full of energy, always up for adventure. I stayed at her apartment in Villefranche-sur-Mer, and then we drove to Nice and St. Tropez in her Renault Quatrelle with a stick shift in the dashboard and a flip-back plastic roof, the perfect car for the south of France. Francoise was resplendent in her orange or yellow pantsuits and her long hair blowing in the wind. I stopped thinking about past or future; every moment was full.

We spent warm days on the beach, where Francoise got me to wear a Banane bathing suit about two inches high. I felt ridiculous but went along, and gradually I came to see the meaning of the saying that Americans live to work, while Europeans work to live. "Paul," Francoise said in her perfect English, "have you ever experienced wine and cheese together?"

And I said, "I have no idea what you're talking about."

"That's *horrible*, that you Americans don't know these things." She and her friends bought six bottles of wine and six different cheeses, and we spent the evening on the sand tasting the various combinations, each one a distinct explosion of flavor in my mouth. I was a middle-class guy from Seattle who'd been brought up on steaks and potatoes, and suddenly I was eating Vietnamese spring rolls and thin-crust pizza with a splash of spicy olive oil and an over-easy egg in the middle. I was living the good life on the French Riviera, which is a very good life.

AFTER MY FATHER retired from UW, his knee started acting up from an old high school football injury. In the fall of 1983, when it got to the point that he could hardly work in his beloved garden, he arranged to have the knee replaced. The surgery was routine. Afterward, though, he couldn't stop wincing, which was hard for me to watch; he was such a tough man that the pain must have been unbearable. He stayed in the hospital another few days to get his legs back under him, and all went according to plan. When I came to visit him on a Tuesday night, he was looking forward to joining us for the Thanksgiving holiday.

The next day he was up and walking when a blood clot dislodged from his knee, traveled to his lungs, and formed a lethal pulmonary embolism—cardiac arrest, just like that. He was still connected to the EKG machine when we reached the hospital, and it was traumatic to watch the line on that machine get smoother and smoother until it went flat. My father was sixty-one years old. He never got to build that little place on the river that he'd talked about, where you could fish for steelhead whenever you wanted. When my uncles came up to make the arrangements, I could barely speak. I was in utter shock. I couldn't believe that my dad was gone.

We'd left a lot of things unsaid, and now I hadn't had a chance to say good-bye.

Later I'd commemorate him by establishing a library endowment fund in his name at UW, where so many people loved him. In 1990, a new addition was completed that now holds more than a million volumes. The Kenneth S. Allen Library includes the earth and space science collections that absorbed me on many a weekend when I was young. My own memento is much smaller: an oval of turquoise that my father had for years before finding a silver setting in Santa Fe a few months before he died. I have worn that ring ever since, and I think of him each time the stone catches my eye.

\*　　\*　　\*

LOSING THE CAMARADERIE and creative work at Microsoft left a hole in my life. I missed the good times with Bill, when we'd spur each other on to bigger and better ideas, though the occasions had grown fewer toward the end. But I never felt tempted to reconsider my departure. It was like a failed romance. Parts of the relationship had been wonderful, but I remembered the negatives, too. I could not go back.

Microsoft kept an office for me for quite a while. When I came in now and then to brainstorm with my old development guys, I was treated as an elder statesman. I'd get copied on some memos, but I wasn't really in the loop. My guys would tell me that upper management seemed less balanced now that Bill had lost his technical foil-in-chief. As the company kept growing and changing, it wouldn't be long before my legacy became less personal than the stuff of company lore.

One day a big stack of boxes arrived at my home. They were consolidating office space, and they'd packed up my things and sent them to me. That felt like closure of a sort.

For a time I was happy traveling back and forth to France and spending time with Francoise. I thought I'd retire at age thirty and follow my inclinations; once Microsoft went public, I'd never have to worry about money. But after a year and a half of vacationing, I got restless. I saw what happened to my father after he'd traded his librarian's job for fishing and his garden. He seemed diminished, somehow. I didn't want that to happen to me.

Luckily, some new ideas lay in wait.

# HELLHOUNDS

Bill and I kept in touch after I left Microsoft, but it took me a while to get past the bitterness of my last months there. When Bill offered to invest in my new company, Asymetrix, I decided against it. I wanted to see where I could take it on my own, without his help.

Over time, though, the hard feelings faded. In 1990, when Microsoft rolled out Windows 3.0, Bill was generous enough to share the stage with me and ToolBook, an Asymetrix product. After a five-year hiatus, I rejoined the Microsoft board. And when Bill got married in 1995, he included me in his wedding party. After he became a family man, we found a pattern not uncommon among old friends. We saw each other a handful of times a year, took in a movie or went to lunch. We'd fall into old rhythms, that high-bandwidth exchange of ideas—a reminder of our once-powerful bond.

By the late 1990s, Microsoft was the largest and most profitable software company in history, growing at the same rate as the personal computer industry—very rapid growth, indeed. Armageddon seemed unlikely, yet Bill still saw the glass as seven-eighths empty. While Microsoft stock options had created thousands of millionaires, including some long-tenured secretaries, it also led to a gradual exodus as people retired early or went off to try their own start-ups.

Bill had done well too, of course; twenty years after we'd founded the company, he was the richest person in the world. But he felt beset by shareholder and Wall Street expectations for ever-increasing profitability and growth. As the company's chairman and CEO, Bill was never one to hype future earnings. He'd make modest predictions to set the stage for the company to shine when it exceeded projections. But as Microsoft's stock price rose by a multiple of nearly a hundred in the 1990s, he found those victories harder to pull off.

To be fair, he had a tough, tough job. In the high-tech field, there's tremendous pressure even when you're doing well; you have to run incredibly hard just to hold your competitive position. As Bill told Tom Brokaw on an NBC special in 1995, technology was "a very scary business. If you fall behind technically, no matter how much your past success has been, it's no guarantee that you'll keep doing well in the future." Within months of that appearance, in an internal memo that spread swiftly over the Internet, Bill pointed to Netscape Navigator as the main obstacle to Microsoft's ascendance on the Internet "tidal wave," which he now considered the key to the company's future. And because Navigator didn't require a richly endowed operating system, it was also a threat to Windows and Office, Microsoft's core businesses.

Leaders tend to stick with the style that made them successful. In Bill's case, the tried-and-true formula was hyperaggression and supercompetitiveness. When your company becomes the industry leader, though, the game changes, and you need to ease off to avoid too much resentment from the rest of the ecosystem. But Bill couldn't back down; that wasn't in his DNA. He sent the same public message, over and over again: We take on all comers, and we clobber them. Just days before the Brokaw special, when the *New York Times Magazine* portrayed Microsoft on its cover as an eight-hundred-pound gorilla, it signaled something ominous. Bill's hard-nosed approach, on top of Microsoft's run of success, had provoked a backlash from competitors and their allies in the federal government.

The antitrust campaign against Microsoft came to a head in 1997, when the Justice Department demanded a stiff fine against the company for alleged violations. A parallel case was advancing in the European Union. Still on the company's board, I advised Bill to temper his stance: "Look, Microsoft is going to win anyway from the momentum of the market and the position we're in. You don't need to be so aggressive." I questioned Bill's assertion that Internet Explorer had to be embedded within Windows for the operating system to work right, a key point of dispute in the federal lawsuit. There was no technical necessity for the bundling, since Windows could be tied to any competent browser and work just as well. (The company has since acknowledged as much in a settlement with the EU that allows users to choose any browser they wish.)

But Bill insisted, as a matter of legal principle, that a company had the right to add features to a product even when that product monopolized the market. What he failed to grasp, despite warnings from many, was that the government's case wouldn't hinge on its legal merits. The attack on Microsoft was at bottom political. A target had been painted on the company's back.

*United States v. Microsoft* was filed on May 18, 1998. "Microsoft is unlawfully taking advantage of its Windows monopoly . . . to undermine consumer choice," said Attorney General Janet Reno. "The Department of Justice will not tolerate that kind of conduct." That November, in footage that will live forever on YouTube, portions of Bill's three-day deposition were replayed in U.S. District Court. The Justice Department's hired legal gun, David Boies, had pushed all of Bill's buttons, and Bill took it from there. Rather than simply respond to Boies's questions, he belittled them: "What do you mean by Internet software?" *Not only is that question ridiculous, but I'm going to explain just how ridiculous it is—and how clueless you are about the software business.*

Bill was sarcastic, combative, defensive, and contemptuous. I knew those traits well, but they were less than helpful on the stand.

He might as well have told the Department of Justice (and by extension the judge) that the antitrust case was the stupidest thing he had ever heard. Anti-Microsoft sentiment became widespread and intense, and it cut Bill to the core. He'd been the darling of the business press, the crafty entrepreneur and technology genius. Now the media portrayed him as a bully who'd bent the rules and probably broken them. After he called me late one weekend afternoon, I met him in the living room of the lakeside estate I'd helped him choose years before. Bill looked drawn, as though he hadn't slept for days. Redlining from stress, he showed a side of himself that many would have found surprising. He'd been trying to move the company forward all these years, he said, but the strain of expectations had grown too much for him.

"I've been trying to pump air in the balloon," he said, "and now the balloon's popping. I can't keep it going anymore."

NOT EVERYONE SAW Microsoft in a bad light. I was dining alone one night at Il Mulino, the Italian place in New York's West Village, when I noticed a middle-aged man in a double-breasted jacket at a corner table in the back. He had slicked-back hair and a statuesque lady at his side, and he was sitting with his back to the wall, where he could eye the entrance. Toward closing time he sauntered over and said, "Are you Mr. Allen?" He had a thick New Jersey accent, something out of *The Sopranos*. After I confirmed my identity, he said, "Your company's involved in that antitrust trial."

"Yes," I said. I wasn't quite sure where this was going.

"Your Mr. *Ball*-mer said some very critical things about the attorney general."

"Yes," I said. In the events leading up to the antitrust suit, Steve had gotten front-page press by declaring, "To heck with Janet Reno!" Now I was getting a little nervous.

And the man said, "I would like to be able to say the same things, but I'm not in a position to say them. Tell your Mr. *Ball*-mer when you see him that there's someone who appreciates what he's saying."

Relieved, I said, "I'll tell him!"

On April 3, 2000, Judge Thomas Penfield Jackson ruled that Microsoft had violated the Sherman Antitrust Act. Two months later, the other shoe dropped: Jackson ordered the company broken into two, one for operating systems and the second for other software.

I thought the judge had overreached. The remedy seemed draconian, way out of proportion to the violations found by the court. "The judge is out of bounds—he just hates us," Bill said. "This will never stand up on appeal." He was probably right, but what if he wasn't? How much synergy would Microsoft lose if Windows were split off from Microsoft's applications? Would our software be marginalized? Which company would Bill go with, and what would happen to the other?

A few months later, shortly after I ended my second stint on the Microsoft board, a federal appeals court reversed the breakup order. The final settlement imposed relatively mild penalties. But the case's impact on Microsoft was profound because it siphoned so much time and energy, especially from Bill. In a company where tech decisions were still ultracentralized, the repercussions of a distracted CEO had to be damaging. We can only speculate as to how much it affected Microsoft's course in those critical years, and over the difficult decade that followed.

EVEN THOUGH HE'D seemed frayed of late, I was stunned when Bill announced that he was stepping aside to become "chief software architect" in January 2000, with Steve Ballmer succeeding him as CEO. Steve had been best man at Bill's wedding, yet they had a tacit rivalry that went back to Harvard, where they'd vied to see who'd get the better grades. While Steve had long served as Bill's top lieutenant, you got the sense through the nineties that he wasn't necessarily being groomed for Microsoft's top spot. I'd say that Bill viewed him as a very smart executive with less affinity for technology than for the business side—that Steve just wasn't a "product guy." It took a while for Bill to come around to what seemed obvious to the rest of the board. Whatever his strengths and weaknesses, Steve was the only viable successor.

Bill made it clear that he'd still be Microsoft's technical leader. He looked over the new CEO's shoulder at every turn and openly chafed at his own waning influence. Steve called me several times to complain that Bill had challenged him during meetings: "What am I supposed to do?"

"You've got to take him aside," I'd say. "You have to tell him that he can't contradict you in front of your people anymore. You're the CEO now." You had to be direct with Bill. It didn't work any other way.

In 2006, Bill announced that he'd be leaving his managerial role with Microsoft two years later to focus on his health and education work at the Bill & Melinda Gates Foundation. I tried to tell him that things would be different after he left: "Once you're no longer a decision maker, people don't look at you the same way." I remembered what I'd gone through when I tried to keep my hand in after leaving the company. It took me about a year to come to the realization that my advice no longer counted for much.

For Bill, the ground had already begun shifting. At product review meetings, his scathing critiques became a perverse badge of honor. One game was to count how many times Bill confronted a given manager; whoever got tagged for the most "stupidest things" won the contest. "I give my feedback," he grumbled to me, "and it doesn't go anywhere." By the time he finally left the company's day-to-day operations in 2008, it seemed almost anticlimactic.

IN JULY 2010, Microsoft announced record fourth-quarter revenue of more than $16 billion. Quarterly earnings totaled $4.5 billion—a third again as much as Apple, more than twice as much as Google. Yet the company's stock price remained flat, as it has for years. With a price-to-earnings ratio of around 12, it traded at a lower valuation than General Mills or Procter & Gamble. No matter how much money Microsoft mints, Wall Street has declined to price in any future growth beyond the Windows 7 upgrade cycle. Earlier in the year, the company saw its market cap exceeded by Apple's, a development that even recently would have seemed far-fetched.

Microsoft arguably touches more lives on a daily basis than any other corporation on earth. More than a billion copies of Windows are in use around the world. But the company is haunted by a decade and more of missed opportunities in Internet search and smartphones, social networking and digital media sales. Apple, once a niche player in personal computers, is at present the dominant purveyor of the Cool Devices of the future. Google has blown past Microsoft in search and in Internet-based computing, or "the cloud." Facebook is king in social networking, where Microsoft's lone modest success is Xbox LIVE.

Together, these high-tech hellhounds dominate the platforms that people associate with the future. In a breathtaking fall from grace, Microsoft is perceived as yesterday's news. A recent yearlong study by the Pew Research Center found that 15 percent of tech articles were mainly about Apple, 11 percent about Google, and only 3 percent about Microsoft. How did a company once at the forefront of technology and change fall so far behind? It's a thorny question, with roots that go back decades, but I believe it boils down to three broad factors: scale, culture, and leadership.

The obvious answer is that Microsoft got huge and failed to deal with the consequences. When I left the company, it had fewer than five hundred employees. By 1990, there were more than five thousand; by 2000, nearly forty thousand; today, more than ninety thousand. At that scale, cultural changes creep in unless you guard zealously against them. To avoid mediocrity, you need to be rigorous about weeding out underperformers. Microsoft hasn't proven to be good at that. One executive recently told me, "I wish I could shoot every fourth one."

Most of all, an industry leader can never get complacent. It wasn't so long ago that Microsoft stood by the slogan that Bill and I followed at the start: "We set the standards." But there is no one in Redmond, speaking privately and candidly, who would make that claim today.

During 2009 and 2010, I had lunch with more than a dozen people who had recently left the company. They all said the same thing: too many semicompetent managers, too much in-house politics among the fiefdoms and silos of principal product lines. Windows Vista was the dead canary in the coal mine. Released years late in 2007, it became a punch line for pundits and a fat target for a mocking Apple ad campaign. How could Microsoft allow this to happen to its signature commodity?

Like any debacle of this magnitude, Vista was the result of multiple blunders, beginning with its overly ambitious scope. It didn't help that the Windows code base had grown more complex to test and upgrade even as the company lost much of its seasoned leadership. Still, a big part of the problem boiled down to basic oversight. Top management failed to pay enough attention to Vista's development and then allowed it to be shipped when the software was still deeply flawed.

Microsoft bounced back by finding a drill sergeant par excellence, Steven Sinofsky, to manage the development of Vista's successor, Windows 7. But the company's broader cultural issues may be harder to fix. When we began, our mission was narrowly defined as the microprocessor language company. Bill and I were programmers who developed software for other programmers and sold licenses to computer hardware manufacturers. Our DOS deal with IBM marked a departure from that safe home base. Once you start shipping operating systems, and then GUIs and word processors, your products go directly to end users. Microsoft has never stopped hustling in the three decades since to compete in that arena, and continues to make inroads today. But it could be argued that it was never the company's forte to design products that made the consumer's heart beat faster.

That history is currently reflected at Microsoft in the tension between selling to the end user and selling to what's known as "the enterprise," the server-based corporate market. Enterprise software is a cash cow that accounts for a quarter of the company's total revenues and has helped lead it to record profits. (The business division generates another 32 percent of revenues, primarily from corporate sales of Office.) As a result, Microsoft inevitably tilts its energies toward the big clients' IT managers and away from consumers. The company still has strong competitive juices, from its CEO on down. But when you're "the No. 1 wholesale seller of plumbing supplies," as the *New York Times* recently put it, innovation stops being organic. You may *want* to innovate, but it can be like trying to fight gravity.

Today's Microsoft has fingers in dozens of pies, from small-business accounting software to Webcams. But too many efforts can distract from the unwavering focus you need for your core products and strategic initiatives. In the early years, we overlooked databases. Had the IBM opportunity not fallen into our lap, Microsoft might have been a footnote in operating systems; had Charles Simonyi not shown up at our door, we could easily have missed out on word processors, because no one in-house knew how to write one. In these markets and a number of others, Microsoft thrived as a fast follower, the company's MO from MS-DOS through Windows to Word and Excel.

Steve Ballmer forcefully framed the company's strategy in the midnineties: "[The competition] can be taken. But the only way we're going to take them is to study them, know what they know, do what they do, watch them, watch them, watch them. Look for every angle, stay on their shoulders, clone them, take every one of their good ideas and make it one of our good ideas." For a company with a leading market share and a bottomless war chest, it was the ideal approach: minimal risk for maximum return.

Then the world changed (again). As content migrated to the Web, the pace of innovation accelerated. Fast following became more difficult than in the era of disk-based software. Today, for the most part, the best opportunities now lie where your competitors have yet to establish themselves, not where they're already entrenched. Microsoft is struggling to adapt to that new reality. Over time, its Enterprise-leaning culture has calcified; the fast follower became a slower one. Zune came out five years after the original iPod, an established category leader with a potent consumer lock-in called iTunes, and has captured only a sliver of the market. Bing, Microsoft's first credible challenge to Google Search, wasn't launched until 2009. Fourteen months later, the domestic search engine market share for MSN/Windows Live/Bing Search stood at a combined 14 percent, a distant second to Google's 65 percent. It's going to be an uphill battle from here on.

Years before Google became the goliath it is today, I repeatedly asked Bill how Microsoft was going to catch up in search, or whether the company might consider buying Google instead. Bill was unimpressed by his then much smaller rival. "In six months, we'll catch them," he kept saying. Complacency has taken its toll, most tellingly in the newest competitive arenas of smartphones and tablets, like the iPad. Platforms *made* Microsoft. The microprocessors of the midseventies were the nucleus of our early success with BASIC. The PC software platform—created by DOS and cemented by Windows and the PC's symbiotic ties with external software developers—led our young company to dominance. History shows that you ignore emerging platforms at your peril, because one of them might make you irrelevant.

Consider: First there were huge machines called mainframes, and they ruled the world, like the dinosaurs. Then came smaller creatures called minicomputers, offering cheaper access and leading to whole new classes of useful applications. They were followed by the PCs, which elbowed their way into the business world by giving individual users their own computers, with many minicomputers (and companies like DEC and Wang) becoming extinct. The new PC platform sparked killer apps like WordPerfect and Lotus 1-2-3, which owned their respective markets up until they failed to adapt to the next big advance in access, the graphic user interface. When Microsoft's Windows and superior GUI-powered applications evolved, it was game over.

## Important Developments of the Interactive Era

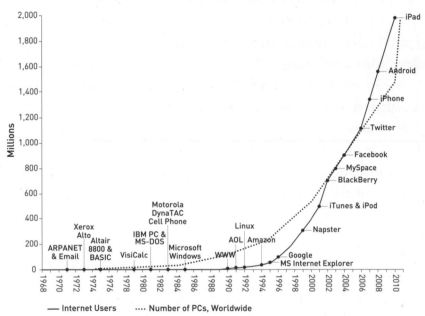

Now we're moving to a new age, and the same pattern keeps recurring. A company jumps out to a big lead and then is late diving into the latest innovation. Before you know it, an adversary has staked its claim and is crowned as the market and technology leader. User inertia makes the new incumbent tough to dislodge, and the one-time alpha dog finds itself trailing.

The new evolutionary species looming in the PC's rear-view mirror are mobile devices, epitomized by the smartphone, a computing platform in your pocket. In technology, the future is promised to no one. *Microsoft cannot afford to be an also-ran in the mobile platforms, which are rapidly becoming the principal delivery point for low- to-medium-intensity computing and Web content consumption.*

Many younger people already spend half their computing time and more on their smartphones and slates. As the phones' displays improve and their network bandwidth expands, mobiles' momentum will only accelerate. Microsoft wasn't blind to this trend. It released its first mobile operating system back in 2000, but the company's early, stylus-driven devices fell flat in the marketplace. Then the iPhone broke through with a seductive touch screen and friendly interface, and Microsoft wound up missing an entire cycle in consumer technology.

Just as the PC carried the day after we persuaded IBM to adopt 16-bit technology, the mobile-platform leaders have thrived by capitalizing on Moore's law. Today's robust iPhones and Droids are the products of high-speed communications, low-cost manufacturing, and superfast microprocessors. Apple and Google have beaten Microsoft to the mobile punch because they've been more

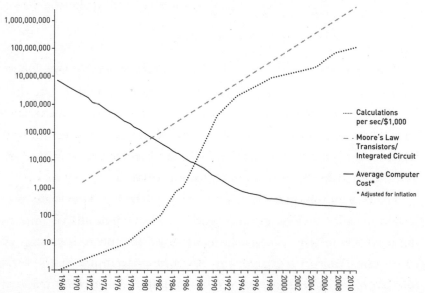

**Increasing Computational Performance and Decreasing Hardware Costs**

alert in developing new and innovative platforms. They've done a better job of following the chips.

As of mid-2010, Microsoft had slipped to fourth in high-end smartphones behind RIM (BlackBerry), Apple, and a hard-charging Google. While advance word on Windows Phone 7 has been positive, the competition is formidable. BlackBerry looks vulnerable, but Apple is the ultimate auteur company with the most fervent cult following in the business. The world of Jobs offers limited options (there's only one basic flavor of iPhone), but everything plugs and plays together and is guaranteed to work. That's a formula that can trump consumers' natural resistance to walled gardens and their predilection for choice. It can even get them to pay a premium price, at least as long as the products remain compelling.

Then there's the nimble, cloud-oriented Google, which takes a different approach: start with limited functionality, copy the leader, bring in apps from everywhere, iterate like mad. In essence, it has mastered Microsoft's old strategy of fast following for the mobile, Web-based era. (As Google elbows and claws for preeminence in the carnivorous tech sector, its new-age motto, "Don't be evil," seems less credible by the day.) The Android mobile operating system is Bill's old bête noire, the open-source version of Unix called Linux. Google essentially gives it away free to manufacturers for the same reason that Microsoft once sold MS-DOS on the cheap: to dominate a market, in this case in smartphone search.

Akin to cameras or TVs, Android follows a product development cycle that runs six months or less or thereabouts, a pace that plays to people's love of the new. By contrast, a major Windows release—slowed by corporate customer demands, backward compatibility, and countless third-party device drivers—has historically required two years or longer. (The last two, Vista and Windows 7, took five and three years, respectively.) The more streamlined Windows Phone operating system could cycle much faster than that, but only if it overcomes the company's cultural drag. Can

Microsoft quicken its pace to compete in the new mobile platforms? I don't think it has a choice.

TOUCH-BASED SMARTPHONES and tablets have obvious limitations, notably for multiuser gamers or typists like me who prefer physical keyboards. A tablet isn't as capable or convenient as a laptop for creating content. But the iPad is unsurpassed for ease of consumption in watching Web videos or reading magazines with a swipe of a finger. Because there are many more consumers than creators in our culture, the Swiss Army–knife strengths of the iPad—and the coming horde of iPad clones—may outweigh its limitations. It appears that tablets are poised to render physical books, magazines, and newspapers obsolete within the next twenty years. As an inveterate book lover, I find the prospect sad but inevitable.

Against this swirl of change, we need to keep in mind that PCs have averaged double-digit growth over the last decade—and as long as there are PCs, there will be a Microsoft. They aren't about to be supplanted by smartphones for intensive office applications like sales reports or spreadsheets. Everywhere else, however, people are shifting from desktops and laptops to more portable mobile devices. As technologies evolve, consumers (especially younger consumers) get pulled along with them. I often hear people saying, "I don't like it personally, but my kids are perfectly happy typing on their iPhone."

New products resonate at first with early adopters, who want the next hot item. But once those products are acknowledged to be more useful than what came before, their consumer net quickly widens, until your grandmother is signing up for her iPhone data plan. Brand loyalties are forgotten as a new platform shoves aside the old. Although the PC still has its place, it is no longer the prime driver of innovation.

Here's what the death knell for the personal computer will sound like: *Mainly I use my phone/pad, but I still use my PC to write long e-mails and documents.* Most people aren't there yet, but that's where we're headed.

If Microsoft fails to catch up in mobile, in other words, it's in for a long, slow slide.

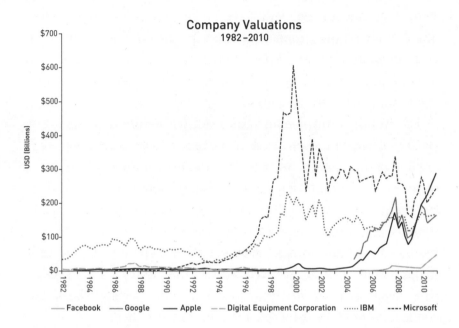

Like the IBM 360, the innovative system of its time, Microsoft Windows has enjoyed an extraordinary run at the top—twenty years and counting, an eon in technology. And like Big Blue in 1980, Microsoft now faces a major threat. For a long time, IBM seemed smug and unassailable, counting money from its corporate client base, and then the behemoth stirred and said, "We've got to have a PC." I was there. I saw how IBM went from nowhere in personal computers to number one in a matter of months, with a fortuitous assist from two young men and their team in Seattle. Still, it's not easy to come from behind once you've ceded momentum; it's so much more challenging to be Avis than Hertz. You need to do more than try harder. You need to be *better,* or at least markedly different in the way you meet people's needs.

If a Microsoft renaissance has grounds for hope, and I believe it does, it's that markets in technology are inherently dynamic—and that my old company has woken up to the challenge. The smartphone market will stay fragmented for the foreseeable future, and it's still relatively cheap and easy for people to switch to something that catches their eye. Five years ago, before anyone had heard of the iPhone, Apple analysts dripped with pessimism about that company's future. Given Microsoft's deep cash reserves and its willingness to use them, it could be in a much stronger position five years from now.

But to take on Apple and Android, whose phones won't stop getting better, Microsoft needs a strategy to *win:* a quicker development cycle, a qualitatively better mobile operating system, and a secret sauce or two to set Windows smartphones apart. Above all, the company needs somehow to return to its cutting-edge roots. In the early days, from the time we squeezed Altair BASIC into four thousand bytes, no core product was released unless Bill and I believed it could be best-of-breed. To win the mobile wars, the company needs first and foremost to produce phones and slates that consumers will love from the moment they use them.

I left Microsoft a quarter century before Bill did, and we've both had our signal triumphs since then. But in certain respects, neither of us has been quite as good alone as we were together. I missed Bill's laser focus on competition in the marketplace, his ability to execute my ideas and keep me from getting too far ahead of what was doable. And I'd like to think that Bill missed my ability to divine where technology was headed and my knack for meeting its trajectory with something big and original.

In my post-Microsoft years, I discovered how challenging it was to operate without a pragmatic partner and business maven. Even so, I have no regrets about taking my own road. It has led me to rich experiences in a great range of pursuits—to the life I'd always dreamed of, even back in the early days, when I was happily chained to my terminal and striving to perfect the next line of code.

# CHAPTER 14

# BLAZERMANIA

On March 13, 1986, Microsoft issued its initial public offering. I sold 200,000 shares and kept the rest, roughly 28 percent of the company. Overnight I was $175 million richer. For some time, I resisted advice to sell stock and diversify. Given how fast computers were improving, I figured that a dominant, well-run technology company like Microsoft would outperform just about anything else. I'd be proven right by the dizzying rise of the company's market cap. By 1990, at age thirty-seven, I'd become a billionaire. By 1996, I'd be one ten times over.

As my attorney, Allen Israel, noted shortly after the IPO: "This wealth should enable you to do whatever you want to do whenever you want to do it. . . ." I made up my mind to exploit my new freedom. Life is short, and there was so much out there to do. I called Bert Kolde, my old Phi Kappa Theta roommate and by then my right-hand man, and said, "I want to buy an NBA team."

I WAS A thin, gangly child with no conspicuous athletic talent. When my peewee church basketball team won the city title, I sat at the end of the bench and played the last few minutes of our blowouts. I have a vague memory of trying to dribble and shoot; the basket seemed way, way up there. I fared better on the playground at four square, where you hand-serve a large rubber ball into quadrants of a court. I liked to compete, but my modest athletic talents didn't flower until high school soccer.

I had little exposure to the NBA before Microsoft moved to Bellevue in 1979, coinciding with the Seattle SuperSonics' stretch run to its first and last championship season. I got caught up in the excitement and became a big fan. In June, after the Sonics finished off the Washington Bullets for the title, I was out among the people thronging the streets and honking their horns.

The next fall I bought my first season tickets. The SuperSonics began trading away their talent, and each year the team got a little worse and my seats got a little better, until I was stationed courtside across from the home bench. Sitting so close deepened my passion for the game. I thought the NBA was the greatest spectacle in sports—equal parts athleticism, ballet, teamwork, and individual grit. The action was almost nonstop, full of vivid moments. Unlike baseball or football, few games were decided with more than five minutes left. And what could match the beauty of a pure jump shot swishing through the net or a tough offensive rebound in traffic?

The Sonics of the early eighties weren't a great team, but they were competitive and entertaining. When I got sick, they became my escape; I went to every game I could and caught the rest on television. I studied box scores in the newspaper while waiting for my radiation treatments, and devoured the *Official NBA Register*. If you asked about Sidney Moncrief's foul-shooting percentage, I could rattle it off within a few percentage points.

The Sonics were a godsend in getting me through that difficult time. No matter how rotten I felt, there was always the next game to look forward to.

IN THE FALL of 1987, I heard that the Portland Trail Blazers might be available. Winners of a championship a decade earlier with Bill Walton, the team was owned by a Los Angeles developer named Larry Weinberg, a gentleman from the old school. I made an overture through Bob Barnett, my old TRW contact. Weinberg's attorney told him that the Blazers were "not for sale, but we might entertain an offer." They insisted that our meeting be private. If word leaked out, our discussions would be over.

That October we met with Harley Frankel, Weinberg's most trusted associate. Going in, I told Bob I had one precondition: a price. I didn't want to bid against myself. Frankel went on about the glories of the NBA, and how the Blazers were a rising franchise with top local TV ratings and sellouts for ten consecutive years. On our way out, I looked at Bob and said, "They didn't give us a price."

I thought the deal was dead, but then in March they called. I still had the itch to own a team, and this time I met with Larry face-to-face. For two hours, he told us his story—how the Blazers won the title the year after he'd become majority owner, but then Walton broke his foot and they'd never recovered. He'd get up in the middle of the night on some overseas business trip and listen over a radio feed for two and a half hours, and the next day was ruined if his team hadn't won. "The losing starts to tear your guts out," he said.

As we wrapped up, Weinberg said he would take $65 million. Ten minutes later, we had a handshake deal. I was thirty-five years old and the youngest owner in major-league sports.

In May 1988, I attended a media conference at the Trail Blazers' office, my first time on the bright red, team-color carpeting. Weinberg said, "I would like to introduce you to the new owner of the team, Paul Allen." Everyone was surprised; we'd been discreet, as promised. This level of public exposure was new to me, and I felt nervous about meeting the press, but Weinberg was extremely gracious. He made it clear that he wouldn't have sold unless he'd found the right person for the team's future success. I was "first of all a fan," Weinberg told the reporters. "Unless you're a fan, nothing else counts in this ownership."

Early on, I met Clyde Drexler, the team's superstar, and we hit it off. Clyde was sharp and candid, a free spirit on the surface but with a calculating edge underneath; I'd heard that he and Kiki Vandeweghe clashed with coach Mike Schuler, a brittle disciplinarian. Before the season started that fall, the two players asked to see me. I had them to my house on Mercer Island, just outside Seattle, and I should have known better. We'd barely sat down when the coach-bashing began: Schuler was a control freak who killed the players' creativity, and so on.

Toward six o'clock, Clyde said, "Hey, Paul, we saw your basketball court on the way down. Do you ever use it?" In fact, I'd been spending a fair amount of time polishing my jump shot—I even had three-point range in those days. We shot around and then Kiki said, "Let's play H-O-R-S-E." I agreed, assuming I'd get creamed. But the players were polite enough to stick mostly to three-pointers, and I hung in there. It began to drizzle, and we turned on the lights. Whenever a stray shot bounced off the court, Clyde and Kiki raced across the slick mesh surface to grab the ball. Maybe this wasn't such a good idea, I thought. What if somebody got hurt?

After I made the game-clinching three-pointer (they'd gone easy on me), Clyde said, "Hey, I want to dunk." Kiki tossed the ball in the air, and Clyde took a flat-footed leap from under the basket. He was twenty-six years old, in his prime, and he met the ball maybe three feet over the ten-foot rim—caught it, dunked it. I've sat courtside at more than a thousand NBA games, but I've never seen anything quite like that soaring slam in the dark, in the rain, on my own outdoor court.

On his way out, Clyde said casually, "Can I call you sometime to talk about the team?"

"Of course," I said. That was my second rookie mistake. It's fine to be friendly with your players and to care about them, but you have to be careful about crossing the line. Get too close, and it may come back to bite you when it's time to renew a contract or weigh a trade. In Clyde's case, I got too close. For years afterward, I'd be awakened by the phone in the middle of the night.

"Paul, it's Clyde."

I'd say, "Who else would be calling me at three A.M.? How's it going, Clyde?"

And he'd say, "We lost again." He'd complain about a team-mate who kept forgetting the plays—like most of us, Clyde was better at seeing others' flaws than his own. We'd chat about the game until he got to the point: "Paul, it's just not fair what I'm being paid."

Shortly before I bought the team, Larry Weinberg had signed Drexler to a six-year contract averaging $1.3 million a year. The deal made him one of the best-paid players in the game, but then salaries escalated sharply and Clyde's had lagged behind. "Paul," he'd say, "I'm only the sixth-best-paid player on the team. You know that isn't right."

And I'd say, "But Clyde, you signed a contract. Nobody forced you to sign the contract." We'd go back and forth, beating each other up until I'd plead exhaustion and hang up the phone. There was no simple resolution. On the one hand, Clyde *did* deserve more money. He had that special extra gear—the turbo, he called it—that you see only in the greatest players, and he'd won a lot of big games for us. On the other hand, I thought a deal was a deal. It seemed both illogical and a terrible precedent to tear up a contract just because a player had my home number.

A year or so after I became owner, my ties to Clyde affected my judgment and changed the course of two franchises. Bucky Buck-walter, an executive under general manager Geoff Petrie, brought me a blockbuster trade. "I think we can get Olajuwon for Clyde," he said. Akeem (later Hakeem) Olajuwon was one of the top two or three centers in the game. I subscribed to the axiom that you always trade a smaller player for a bigger one of like talent, but this time I told Bucky to pass. I had concerns about Olajuwon's long-term health after doctors had found a blood clot in his leg. (The condition turned out to be treatable.) But the other reason I held back was that Clyde was special—to the team and its tradition, but also to me personally. I didn't want to see him go.

*     *     *

THE TRAIL BLAZERS struggled that first year. After word filtered out that the team's black players felt alienated from the coaching staff, we hired Maurice Lucas, a respected star from the Walton years, as an assistant coach. But issues still festered, to the point where *Sports Illustrated* depicted the Blazers as a team rife with turmoil. I sent Bert on a midseason road trip, and he came back with a sobering report. The team was split into "ten and two," with Clyde and Kiki the two. Everyone hated the coach, whom Clyde was doing his level best to undermine. Schuler responded with a bunker mentality. He'd schedule meetings with his staff and "forget" to tell Maurice Lucas. He was freezing Lucas out.

I wasn't keen about disrupting the team with a midseason coaching change, but the divisions seemed irreparable. In February 1989, we fired Schuler and replaced him with Rick Adelman, then a little-known assistant. Kiki asked to be traded, and we packed him off to the Knicks, ending a controversy over playing time with the younger, more dynamic Jerome Kersey. After getting swept out of the first round of the playoffs by the Los Angeles Lakers, the team's needs were obvious. The Blazers were strong on the perimeter with Clyde, Kersey, and point guard Terry Porter, but thin up front. With the oft-injured Sam Bowie missing most of the season, we had a short-armed center in Kevin Duckworth and a hole at power forward. Teams scored on us inside at will.

I've tried to strike a balance as team owner, to be involved and accountable while preserving my executives' freedom to shape the roster. My job is oversight, not execution. While I sign off on trades or free agents, I've rarely overruled my basketball people's decisions. But I'm not shy about steering the discussion or pushing deeper if something doesn't make sense to me.

Shortly before the 1989 NBA draft, my first as a real participant, I attended an all-star game for top college players. My eyes were drawn to Cliff Robinson, a wiry six-ten center from the University of Connecticut with a constant scowl on his face. On tape he looked like a smooth and explosive athlete who could really shoot, my favorite combination. But Cliff had a reputation as a surly kid who didn't play hard. On draft day, I sat in our war room and scanned the board that ranked our top prospects. As the second round began, Cliff was the only one left in the green-room, where projected lottery picks waited to take the stage as their names were called. He was so hurt that he left and went back to his hotel.

By then I was lobbying hard to choose him. Second-round picks are low-risk propositions. Their contracts aren't always guaranteed, and they can be easily cut if they don't pan out. Bucky Buckwalter, who leaned toward long, athletic players, gave his assent. With little to lose, Geoff Petrie agreed to take a flier on Cliff.

That draft taught me how quickly a team's fortunes can change with one or two good decisions. Buck Williams, newly acquired in a trade for Bowie, was the ideal addition to our starting lineup: tough, focused, a pillar of strength against larger players like Utah's Karl Malone. Cliff was rangy, fast, and defense-minded, capable of playing three positions—another perfect fit. (He'd be named the league's top sixth man in 1993 and an all-star the following year.) Together they helped vault the Trail Blazers from a losing record to 59–23, second best in the league. That squad was unselfish and relentless, and it was a privilege to watch them. After we beat the Celtics by thirteen points in Boston Garden, Red Auerbach said, "They just ran us right out of our gym."

There's a special bond in cities with a single major-league franchise. I'd heard about Blazermania coming in, but I didn't know just how rabid the Portland fans could be. Our run that season unleashed a wave of pent-up fervor. We swept Dallas in the first round of the playoffs, and then Cliff set the tone against San Antonio by subbing for the injured Duckworth and holding the great David Robinson to nine points. Then came the Western Conference Finals against the high-scoring Phoenix Suns. Though I'm not demonstrative by nature, I got caught up in the collective emotion of that series, to the point where I was signaling three-point shots and waving the crowd to stand and cheer down the stretch. I'd punctuate a win by pointing to the fans and clapping, to thank them for their support. After we pulled out the clincher on the road, by three points, I got so carried away that I ran out to join the scrum of players on the court. When Buck Williams embraced me, it felt like getting hugged by a brick wall. Our magical ride finally ended in the NBA Finals, when the "Bad Boy" Pistons used their experience and toughness (and the timely shooting of Vinnie "Microwave" Johnson) to defeat us in five games.

We returned to the Finals in 1992, the coming-out party for Michael Jordan's Chicago Bulls. Heading into the showdown, a *Sports Illustrated* cover story featured the players who'd finish one-two in the balloting for Most Valuable Player that year: Jordan and Drexler, who was billed as Jordan's "No. 1 Rival." That only stoked Jordan's competitive fires, which never needed stoking in the first place. Worse yet, Clyde had to guard the league's top scorer without his normal lateral movement. After arthroscopic surgery the previous September, he'd had his right knee drained half a dozen times.

Jordan was a streaky jump shooter at that stage of his career, making only 27 percent of his three-point shots during the season. But in game one in Chicago, he hit six of them in the first half on his way to 39 points. (After the last deep shot, he turned toward the broadcast table and shrugged, as if he'd surprised even himself.) We tried Cliff and Jerome on him, along with Clyde—all solid defenders, but it made no difference. Jordan had his "turbo" on. I've seen just one other person up close who compared to him, who wanted not only to beat you but to crush you if he could. Those two stood apart for raw competitiveness: Michael Jordan and Bill Gates.

We had our moments against the Bulls. Midway through the fourth quarter of a tight game four in Portland, Clyde tapped the ball away from Jordan and converted it into a dunk, setting off a surge that evened the series at two games apiece. Nearly giddy, I went into the locker room afterward and found Clyde slumped in front of his locker, completely exhausted, an ice bag on every joint. And I said, "Clyde that was a brilliant steal. You read Jordan perfectly."

He looked up at me, shook his head, and said, "Stop, stop, you don't understand. Most guys have two or three go-to moves; Jordan has nine. I guessed right, that's all. I got lucky. Sometimes you get the bear, but usually the bear gets you." Clyde knew the score. The Bulls, on the cusp of a dynasty, beat us in six games. Just around that time, to compensate for those years when Clyde was paid below the market, I gave him a $9.8 million, one-season extension, then the biggest yearly paycheck in the history of team sports. I thought he'd earned it.

Though we never won a title in the Drexler era, those were glorious years. I watched up to three hundred games a season, live and on TV; in remote locales like Hawaii, I had a special live satellite feed when the Blazers came on. When I was home in Seattle, I'd invite six or eight people to fly to Portland for each home game. My mother became one of our biggest fans, and she'd bring a friend and drink her tea and eat her cookies en route. Then she'd sit with me on the baseline and scold the referees in her dignified fashion. "You've got to call it the same way on both sides," she'd say, as the nearest official rolled his eyes. For my mom, bad whistles were injustices, and she wasn't going to sit by and not say anything.

One night we were playing the Sonics, and Sam Perkins—six nine and 235 pounds—barreled after a ball that was sailing out of bounds straight over my mother's head. She threw up her hands as Perkins crashed into her, and then I noticed her holding her wrist. "It's broken," she said calmly. At halftime the team doctor iced and taped it, and I asked if she wanted to head home. "No," she said firmly, "we're going to watch the rest of the game."

Over ensuing seasons, Adelman tied our younger players to

the bench and stuck with the tight rotation of veterans who had gotten us to the Finals. But you can't freeze time, and those guys were now on the downside. In 1994, we hired a new coach, P. J. Carlesimo, plus a new team president and general manager who would define the team's next decade.

ARTICULATE, COOL, and deceptively bland, Bob Whitsitt had joined the Seattle SuperSonics in 1986. At age thirty, he was the youngest top executive in the league, known as Trader Bob for his nonstop personnel moves. He built a powerhouse team around Gary Payton, a pugnacious point guard, and Shawn Kemp, a wildly talented big man who'd never played in college. Those Sonics teams were bold, volatile, swaggering, and athletically gifted. In 1993–1994 they posted a record of 63–19, best in the league. Whitsitt was named NBA Executive of the Year, but his owner, Barry Ackerley, became disenchanted after the team got upset in the playoffs. Ackerley disconnected Whitsitt's office phone to encourage him to resign. I jumped to hire him.

Clyde was promptly traded to the Houston Rockets, as he'd requested. I gave my favorite player the news and thanked him for his contribution, and it was an emotional moment for us both. That spring I rooted for him from afar as he helped Olajuwon win a title. I'd always considered Clyde a champion, and now it was official.

Whitsitt proceeded to overhaul our aging roster as he'd done in Seattle, drafting young athletes with upside and adding big-name veterans. A few of his moves were brilliant, like the six-for-one deal that brought us Jordan's all-star sidekick, Scottie Pippen, just one year removed from the last of his six championships with the Bulls. But there were too many times when Whitsitt operated like a rotisserie-league GM, piling up players with gaudy numbers. He openly professed that he cared only about talent, to the exclusion of character and other intangibles. "I didn't take chemistry in college," he told the media. With enough physical ability on the floor, team cohesion would take care of itself. It was a risky assumption for a sport in which five men share one ball.

With hindsight, Whitsitt temporarily staved off decline by using my wallet to load up on pricey long-term contracts—players who were available because they were overpaid or had off-court issues or both. Over a span of seven years, he would draft, sign, or trade for Rasheed Wallace, Isaiah Rider, Damon Stoudamire, Bonzi Wells, Shawn Kemp, Ruben Patterson, Qyntel Woods, and Zach Randolph. Any one of them would have been a handful. Despite the presence of some notable good guys, like Arvydas Sabonis and Steve Smith, they became known as the Portland Jail Blazers.

How could I tolerate this stew of instability? The short answer was that we kept winning. Over the last six years of Whitsitt's tenure, the Blazers won 63 percent of their games, fourth best in the league. We made the playoffs each year and twice reached the conference finals, enough success to give me pause about shaking up the organization. I can be patient to a fault, and Whitsitt had his strengths. He was plugged into the player agent network like nobody else, and I counted on his connections to get deals done. He was also a great rationalizer. When I'd ask why a draft pick fizzled or a trade backfired, he'd respond, "Just watch. Next year he's going to be so much better."

When you come so close to winning a championship, as we had in the early nineties, it makes you that much hungrier because you know what the Finals taste like. It was the same for Whitsitt, who was desperate to validate his approach with a title. We were perpetually one big-salaried veteran away from contention, and our payroll ballooned. Deep down I knew that something was wrong. In the playoffs, when the pressure peaks and higher-caliber opponents target your weaknesses, a player's makeup is revealed in performance. In the 2000 Western Conference Finals against the Lakers, we fell behind three games to one and then fought back to earn a deciding seventh game. Up fifteen points in the final quarter, it looked as though we were headed to the NBA Finals against Indiana, whom I thought we could beat. When I watch my team in the playoffs, I get superstitious; I try not to think about how much I want to win. *Whatever happens, I'll be fine with it. The players tried their best.* But in that fourth quarter, I succumbed. I couldn't deny it. I really wanted to beat the Lakers.

Within minutes, the Blazers unraveled. We missed thirteen consecutive shots. Our players suddenly looked as though they'd met for the first time that morning. The coup de grâce came when Shaquille O'Neal dunked an alley-oop from Kobe Bryant with forty seconds left.

That seventh game exposed us as a team without leadership or discipline. I'll never forget the feeling I had when we boarded our plane—still festooned with BEAT LA stickers—and headed home, our season done. It was a crushing defeat, and it took me a long, long time to get over it.

IN 2002, EIGHT years after Whitsitt's arrival, we fell into the abyss. We led the league in payroll at $106 million, $44 million more than the championship Lakers. We were $65 million over the salary cap and $50 million over the league's new luxury tax threshold, which had been designed to level the playing field for small-market teams like ours. Our player salaries cost us an outrageous $156 million, all for a medium-to-good fifty-win team that would lose yet again in the first round of the playoffs.

Off the court, it was worse, as the Trail Blazers became exhibit A for all that was wrong with professional sports. I found myself reeling from one lowlight to the next.

November 9, 2002: Bonzi Wells is suspended for spitting on the Spurs' Danny Ferry.

November 22: Co-captains Damon Stoudamire and Rasheed Wallace, on their way home from a game in Seattle, are pulled over and cited for possession of marijuana. To settle the case, both agree to attend drug counseling sessions.

November 25: Ruben Patterson is arrested for felony domestic abuse. His wife later asks prosecutors not to pursue charges.

January 15, 2003: Rasheed is suspended for threatening a referee.

April 3: Zach Randolph is suspended after sucker punching Ruben in the face during practice and fracturing his eye socket.

The fans who felt so close to the Drexler-Kersey-Porter Blazers were disenchanted. Our attendance suffered, and our TV ratings fell by half. The wayward players showed little remorse. Bonzi Wells told *Sports Illustrated:* "We're not really going to worry about what the hell [the fans] think about us." You could see why parents weren't rushing out to buy Bonzi or Rasheed jerseys for their kids.

One day I said to Whitsitt, "What's it like in the locker room? How is the team reacting to the latest incident?"

And he said, "Well, Paul, half our guys are normal and half our guys are crazy. The good guys are all freaked out, but the crazy guys are crazy, so they're fine."

I'd heard enough. A team might be able to absorb one erratic personality, but who could win with a group that was half crazy? Three days after our season ended, I fired Whitsitt and gave his successor, Steve Patterson, a mandate to clean house. We traded established starters like Rasheed and Bonzi for forty cents on the dollar while letting bad contracts expire. The win-now regime had stunted younger talents like Jermaine O'Neal (who blossomed into a six-time all-star after being moved to Indiana), and our cupboard was bare. In 2004, the Blazers missed the playoffs for the first time in twenty-one years.

And then we sank even lower. An internal investigator came to me with a report on Qyntel Woods: "We think there may be dogfighting at Qyntel's house."

*Dogfighting?* I couldn't believe what I was hearing.

A few days later: "We think there may be some dogs buried in his yard."

*Buried in his yard?*

And a day or two after that: "There's a room in his house where we hear the walls are covered with blood."

*Blood on the walls?*

I was shocked and mortified. Qyntel eventually pleaded guilty to animal abuse and got eighty hours of community service. We suspended and then released him three months later.

The next year we touched bottom. With a record of 21–61, the Trail Blazers were indisputably the worst team in the league. Though things were quieter off the court, I had a new challenge: how to pay for my team's home court.

The old Memorial Coliseum, with our fans seated nearly on the floor, was famously intimidating for visiting teams. It was also the smallest arena in the NBA, with no signage, luxury suites, or big-screen replays. In 1993, at a cost of $262 million, we built the Rose Garden. I put in $46 million to Portland's $34 million, with most of the balance covered by bonds from a group led by a teachers' pension fund. The interest rate was a stiff 8.99 percent, with no option for prepayment or refinancing.

As we discovered too late, the financial formula was fatally flawed. Add a local downturn and an unpopular losing team, and we had a perfect storm of red ink and disaffection. The Blazers were getting booed at home, once unthinkable in Portland. Our season ticket holders were canceling in waves amid calls for a boy-cott, despite our explicit efforts to rebuild and start over. All told, I'd invested more than half a billion dollars in the franchise, at a huge net loss. Something had to give.

In February 2004, my Oregon Arena Corporation filed for bankruptcy to push our creditors to restructure the Rose Garden loan. When we failed to reach a compromise, the bankruptcy court conveyed the arena to the lenders, with its sagging revenues to continue to be split among us. In 2006, as our deficit mounted, we announced that we'd entertain bids on the team. I was banking on the creditors' reluctance to kill the golden goose or possibly shove it out of town. No one wanted to see the Blazers leave Portland, least of all their owner.

\*     \*     \*

THE NBA DRAFT is one of my favorite days of the year. I begin preparing weeks ahead of time, poring over our five-hundred-page draft book and watching hours of college game highlights. The day before the big event, I convene with our personnel guys in Portland to watch more film and hear from our international scout. Then we head to a restaurant to hash out player rankings over dinner.

In the 2006 draft lottery, we started with some bad luck; despite our NBA-worst record, we were picking fourth. By then we'd handed the operation's reins to Kevin Pritchard, who had a good gut for gauging young talent. Meanwhile, we got word about a rangy UW guard named Brandon Roy who didn't look all that impressive on videotape. But in a private workout, he was bigger, quicker, and more explosive than we'd expected. After some draft-day maneuvers, we wound up with both Brandon and LaMarcus Aldridge, the skilled big man out of Texas that I coveted: two young men of unquestioned character. That was a banner night for us, a turning point for the franchise.

Shortly after the draft, I pulled the Blazers off the market. The next February, literally minutes before the case was set to be filed in court, the bondholders agreed to a restructuring and I bought back the Rose Garden. In June, a month after Brandon Roy was named Rookie of the Year, we traded Zach Randolph to the Knicks, ending an era that none of us would miss. The following season, we had the youngest team in the league and not a single arrest or suspension. The culture had changed, and it was my pleasure to invite the Blazers to Mercer Island for practice on Easter Sunday, 2008. After a light run-through, Coach Nate McMillan said he would end practice early if I could make a foul shot. The pressure was on. I walked to the line, took two dribbles, and banked the ball in. The players cheered.

The next year, with strong play from Brandon and LaMarcus and unselfish teamwork all around, the Trail Blazers shared a division title and returned to the NBA playoffs for the first time in six years. We lost a tough first-round series to Houston, but you wouldn't have known it from the thousands who jammed Pioneer Courthouse Square to celebrate. Like me, the fans had never stopped loving their team. They'd been through rocky times with us, but Blazermania was alive and well.

Today we're building a contender the old-fashioned way, the way it was done in the Walton-Lucas era or with the Drexler editions. Before we add a new player, we ask ourselves: How would he fit? Does he work hard? Will he balance his ego with the needs of the team? If we can't answer yes to all of the above, we don't do the deal.

AS OF THIS writing, at the start of the 2010–2011 season, the Trail Blazers are working on a new streak of sellouts, 124 and counting. After replacing Kevin Pritchard (who struggled in the managerial parts of his job) with Rich Cho, we believe that we've found a leadership team that can get us back to the Finals. Under team president Larry Miller, our season ticket base has tripled since the Whitsitt era, and local TV ratings are among the league's highest.

That's the good news. The bad is that we're doing just about everything right, but we're still losing money. With Brandon and LaMarcus now signed to contract extensions, we won't be turning a profit anytime soon, a fact that speaks volumes about the plight of smaller-market franchises in the NBA. Team ownership can be very satisfying, but nobody enjoys losing money. As in any business venture, the bottom line is the ultimate measure of success.

According to *Forbes,* twelve of thirty teams were in the red in 2008–2009. A recent study showed that a team's net income had more than twice as strong a correlation with market size than with winning percentage. Teams in larger markets have built-in advantages: higher ticket prices (based simply on supply and demand), more lucrative local cable TV deals. Their deeper stables of Fortune 1000 companies generate sponsorship dollars and luxury-suite sales.

Whatever the outcome of our ongoing collective bargaining

agreement negotiations with the players' union (the current deal expires on June 30, 2011), the NBA has yet to address this big market/small market discrepancy. Sports economist Andrew Zimbalist has noted that in the NBA less than 30 percent of revenue comes from shared revenue. In the National Football League, he has said, it's as much as 75 percent.

Every owner *wants* to win, and the free-spending Whitsitt mentality is alive and well in some quarters. But then it's February, you're at .500, free agent X has misplaced his jump shot, and you're staring at another eight-figure loss. It can get demoralizing. Before long, the league may become stratified into haves and have-nots, with small-market teams shaving player payrolls just to stay afloat and large-grossing teams having "huge economic disparities to utilize to make them better," as NBA Commissioner David Stern said recently. At that point, only four or five franchises will have a legitimate shot at a championship. You'll see more half-empty arenas as people weary of watching their lovable losers get hammered. Top free agents will focus on fewer cities, typically those with the best media and promotional opportunities. National interest and TV ratings can't help but suffer.

Or as Stern put it, the NBA "is viable as long as you have owners who want to continue funding losses. But it's not on the long term a sustainable business model. . . ."

During the throes of the Rose Garden's bankruptcy, I met with Stern in New York. When I asked him what alternatives he saw for me, the commissioner told me, "Well, you can always sell your team." But I wasn't looking to bail out; I wanted to fix things. And even had I sold, the next owner would have faced the same predicament.

In my perfect world, the most successful NBA teams wouldn't necessarily be those with the biggest local television markets or corporate-suite bases. They'd be the ones with the best talent judges, management, and coaching, big market or small.

# CHAPTER 15

# 12TH MAN

If I entered the NBA out of passion, I was called to the National Football League out of civic duty. The Seattle Seahawks had been mired in mediocrity even before Ken Behring bought the franchise in 1988. By the midnineties, the team was losing more than $5 million a year. It had an absentee owner and a lackluster coach. The Kingdome, which it shared with the Seattle Mariners, was falling apart. The roof leaked, and four heavy ceiling tiles had dropped into the stands just before a baseball game.

In February 1996, Behring declared that he was moving the team to Southern California. The NFL refused to sanction the move. King County sued Behring for trying to break his Kingdome lease, and the owner countersued. With the Seahawks' future so precarious, I was approached by a contingent of local politicians on the hunt for a buyer to keep the team in Seattle.

I liked football, but I didn't plant myself in front of the TV all day Sunday. And I wasn't on a quest to take on a second major-league team and all the responsibilities that came with it. Still, I was sympathetic. I went to four or five Seahawks games a year. I thought of Seattle as a three-sport city, and I knew how hard it was to retrieve a major-league franchise once a community lost one. In April, I agreed to a $20 million option to buy the team within fifteen months for approximately $200 million. I had one stipulation: I would exercise my option only if we could get a new stadium. Based on my experience with the Blazers, it made no sense to get involved unless revenues could cover the costs of re-signing top players and pursuing the best free agents. You needed a first-class facility to generate that kind of money, and the King-dome was grossly inadequate.

A new stadium would run $430 million, and I was willing to chip in close to a third of it. But the rest had to come from public funding*—not just to give me a fighting chance to make a modest profit, but to forge a public-private partnership that would keep the franchise in Seattle for the long haul, regardless of who owned it. My hometown had asked for help, and I wanted to respond, but I wasn't about to go it alone.

The day after I negotiated my purchase option, the *Seattle Times* ran a story headlined "Allen's Rescue Makes Him City's Latest, Greatest Sports Superhero." I guessed that it wouldn't be long before the media changed its tune.

IN A DECEMBER 1996 *Seattle Times* poll, opponents of a new Seahawks stadium outnumbered supporters by eight percentage points. The one bright spot: Among ten local figures involved in the issue, I was the only one rated favorably. Unlike the politicians, I had no legacy of unpopular decisions. People knew me as a low-profile guy who'd cofounded Microsoft and who now might save the franchise.

As the six-week campaign over Referendum 48 unfolded, I was surprised by how many people still liked the Kingdome. While cit-ies like New York constantly tear down and revitalize, Seattle-ites cherish their architectural icons, even the unsightly ones. To expand our constituency beyond hardcore football fans, we

---

*The public contribution would come from the interests who stood to benefit most, via an extended county hotel tax and increased parking and admission taxes at the stadium, along with new lottery games and a state sales tax credit that reflected the team's economic value to Seattle.

emphasized the new stadium's potential to lure a major-league soccer team. We were making headway in the polls and had pulled almost even when opposing groups found traction with a superficially convincing argument. There was no need to vote yes on the stadium, they maintained, because I'd never walk away and let the Seahawks leave town. Political cartoons struck the same theme: *Why doesn't Paul just pay for all of it, since he can?* Our poll numbers dropped. It looked like my wealth was working against me. As a *Seattle Times* columnist wrote, "Mr. Allen is a splendid fellow whose only drawback may be that he has too much money."

I knew about voter resistance firsthand from the Seattle Commons project, where we'd pushed for a sixty-one-acre waterfront park to anchor industrial and biotech development in the South Lake Union neighborhood. Despite my pledge of $20 million, the voters twice defeated our proposal. (We've continued to revitalize South Lake Union, but without the park.) Now I put aside my aversion to TV appearances and took my case for a new football stadium directly to the voters. On June 2, two weeks before the referendum, I sat in a staged living room backdrop and taped a thirty-second spot:

> When I said yes to help save the Seahawks, I meant that I'd do my part in building something for the future—personally and financially. . . . I stand by that commitment. But if you say no, that means no for me, too, because I'm not going to do this without you.

The ad seemed to work. By Election Day, polls showed us with a narrow lead, but it was less than their margin of error and nothing was assured. When I arrived at our headquarters that night, I could feel the worry. Early returns from eastern Washington, where the case for a Seattle stadium was least persuasive, were worse than we'd projected. We were down thirty thousand votes.

If the ballot failed, I knew there was a good chance the Seahawks would leave town. The Kingdome would become a white elephant (actually a brownish gray elephant), hosting the occasional truck or home show. It was a glum prospect all around.

We were banking on late returns from King County and the suburbs to put us over. As Senator Warren Magnuson once said about Washington's statewide elections, "You can see every vote that matters from the top of the Space Needle." Every few minutes, I checked in—we were still behind, but gaining. By ten o'clock, it was clear that the suburban soccer moms had turned out in droves. By eleven, we knew that the referendum would pass in a squeaker. Months of tension drained away. I joined a local band in a celebration jam, and Bert Kolde jumped up to sing "Wild Thing." I could see how people got addicted to electioneering.

And on top of it all, I was about to join the small and special club of NFL owners.

THE NEW STADIUM would be built in the footprint of the old one in Seattle's International District, a transportation hub with restaurants and hotels within walking distance. The Kingdome's destruction was slated for March 2000. As I watched from three hundred yards away, fifty thousand tons of concrete would be demolished by a rapid-fire series of 5,800 gelatin dynamite charges, the largest implosion in history. ESPN Classic covered the event live, and I was asked if I wanted to push the button that would set the whole thing off. I wasn't sure about that, so they offered plan B. At the end of the countdown, I would give the high sign to the demolition man, and *he* would push the button. "OK," I said. "That sounds like fun."

I got my instructions. There would be an audible count over a PA from ten down to six, then a silent count to zero. (The logic was that if anybody happened to be inside the Kingdome and ran out yelling, we needed to be able to hear them and abort the blast.) I followed the audible count and continued it in my head. There was an awkward pause. The demolition man looked at me expectantly, his hand over the button.

And I froze. I can't explain why. Maybe I had a flash of nostalgia for all the SuperSonics and NCAA Final Four games I'd seen at the Kingdome. At that pregnant moment, my brain just locked up.

The poor demolition guy was raising his eyebrows at me: *Can we blow it up now?* I finally snapped out of it and gave my thumbs-up. We heard what sounded like gigantic firecrackers going off in a timed sequence, with streaks of light flashing across the dome. Then the building imploded as people cheered from nearby office towers. Within seconds, all that remained was a tight mound of rubble and—moving toward us at highway speed—a billowing cloud of dust. On cue, we jumped into a van until it passed.

MY FORMATIVE EXPERIENCE with big-time football was at the University of Washington, where my father and I sat in the stands and stomped on the risers as we cheered on the smashmouth teams of the early sixties. Later we went to see Sonny Sixkiller, the dynamic Cherokee quarterback who led the nation in passing in 1970. Win or lose, there was a special feeling to those games in the open air. When I met with the stadium architects, I talked about creating a twenty-first-century version of the experience I loved as a boy. Instead of an insulated bowl in a parking lot, I wanted an open-ended design and seats with a view. Husky Stadium looked out on Union Bay; Seahawks Stadium would have expansive vistas of downtown, Elliott Bay, and Mount Rainier. Because our winter weather is rainy, I asked for an overhang that would cantilever over the lower deck to keep fans dry and bring them as close to the action as possible.

Qwest Field would be the first NFL facility with field-level luxury suites. Behind our north end zone, we installed a "Hawks' Nest" of budget-priced bleachers for some of our most fanatical supporters. The stadium's architects managed to recreate the Kingdome's acoustics and deafening crowd noise, so much so that the Seahawks are perennially among the league leaders in false-start penalties against the opposition.

\*     \*     \*

IN 1999, Bob Whitsitt signed a new head coach and general manager: Mike Holmgren, the charismatic "Walrus" who'd taken Green Bay to two conference championships and a victory in Super Bowl XXXI. In Holmgren's first season, the Seahawks ended a ten-year playoff drought and won a division title, but then we hit a plateau. For reasons that seemed to make sense at the time, I kept Whitsitt on as the football team's president after forcing him out of the Trail Blazers. I had a thin management bench in Seattle, with no one else strong enough to counterbalance Holmgren.

The shakeup began in June 2003, when I brought in Tod Leiweke as the Seahawks' first CEO. A great communicator and savvy marketer, he had a proven track record with the National Hockey League's Minnesota Wild. With Tod reporting to me directly, Whitsitt was no longer my sole conduit to the organization.

The 2004 Seahawks blew a number of late leads and ended with a frustrating wild-card loss at home to St. Louis. The franchise had gone twenty-one straight seasons without a playoff win, eight of them on my watch, and was living down to its cynical moniker: "Same Old Seahawks." I kept asking why we were underachieving—what needed to change? I wondered about Holmgren's conservative game plans. Wedded to the West Coast offense that had won him a Super Bowl, Mike refused to try the shotgun formation that had become the NFL's standard third-down call. Was the game passing him by?

Bob Whitsitt had played a big role in helping me acquire the Seahawks and had brought in a successful coach. But the issues that had tripped him up in Portland also became his undoing in Seattle. He overpaid middle-of-the-road performers and failed to re-sign our top talent in a timely fashion. After the 2004 season, he inexplicably allowed sixteen players to enter unrestricted free agency, including quarterback Matt Hasselbeck and star running back Shaun Alexander, squandering our leverage in negotiations and costing me tens of millions of dollars.

Tod Leiweke and others reported that the organization was dysfunctional. Whitsitt and Holmgren weren't speaking to each other, and the coach was on the verge of walking away from his contract. The only front-office solidarity came out of people's shared dislike of Whitsitt, who seemed too casual about building our revenue base despite a first-class venue and ample on-field talent.

On January 14, 2005, six days after our season ended, I fired Whitsitt. I'd previously relieved Holmgren of his duties as general manager, where he was spread too thin, but kept him on as coach. Whatever his shortcomings as a personnel man, the Walrus was a strong and experienced on-field leader who commanded his players' respect.

This time my patience would pay off.

HEADING INTO THE 2005 season, we were underdogs rated eighth most likely to represent the NFC in the Super Bowl. But our turnaround had already been set in motion at the NFL Draft that April. Tim Ruskell, our new GM, moved us up nine spots in the second round to choose an undersize linebacker named Lofa Tatupu, who would lead the team in tackles and make the Pro Bowl in his rookie season. Hasselbeck was in top form, and Alexander was unstoppable; he set an NFL record for rushing touchdowns and finished as the league's MVP.

Everything clicked. Holmgren called great games; the Hawks' Nest was appropriately out of control; the ball bounced our way. The team won eleven games in a row and finished at 13–3, the best record in franchise history. After beating Washington in a divisional playoff, we prepared to host the NFC championship game at Qwest Field against the Carolina Panthers.

In a tribute to our fans' support of the eleven players on the field, Tod had revived our Twelfth Man tradition. Minutes before kickoff at each home game, we played the Verve's "Bitter Sweet Symphony" as the video board told a thirty-second story about a former Seahawk great or a local like Huston Riley, the soldier

Top: My parents, Faye and Kenneth, moved to Seattle from Anadarko, Oklahoma. (© Paul Allen)

Left: My father holds me on the front step of our first home in Seattle. (© Paul Allen)

I was a sports fan from an early age. My father and I watched University of Washington football games together. Here, I'm wearing his leather football helmet from the 1930s. (© Paul Allen)

I met Bill Gates at Lakeside. We became friends in the computer room, above, where we could dial in to a mainframe computer.

(© Jane Carlson Williams '60 Archives, Lakeside School)

My parents had to scrimp to send me, above in 1971, and later my sister, Jody, to the private Lakeside School.

(© Jane Carlson Williams '60 Archives, Lakeside School)

Rita and I went to my high school prom. We continued dating after graduation and we moved together to Boston. (© Paul Allen)

Here I am in the Phi Kappa Theta house at Washington State University. The fraternity was an eclectic mix of students. (© Paul Allen)

In 1979, we took our first business trip to Japan. Above, from left, are me, Bill, Junichi Okada, and Kay Nishi. (© Paul Allen)

Bill and I formed Micro-Soft in 1975 in Albuquerque, New Mexico. By 1982, above, we were featured in the *Seattle Times* for having "turned a pivotal idea into a multimillion-dollar business in the explosively growing personal-computer field." (© Barry Wong/*The Seattle Times*)

Jan 2, 1975

Sirs:

We have available a BASIC language interpreter which runs on MCS-8080 series microcomputers. We are interested in selling copies of this software to hobbyists thru you. It could be supplied on cassettes or floppy disks to users of your ALTAIR series microcomputers. We would anticipate charging you $50 a copy which you would then sell for somewhere between $75 to $100. If you are interested, please contact us

Sincerely,

Paul G. Allen
President

On January 2, 1975, I wrote a letter on Traf-o-Data letterhead to MITS offering BASIC to the fledgling personal computer company for $50 a copy. When we got no response, we followed up with a phone call. (© Paul Allen 2011. Courtesy of Dr. Eddie Currie)

Poster made for Microsoft's tenth anniversary showing Bill and me and, right below Bill, the MITS Altair 8800. (Courtesy of the Microsoft Archives)

The Faye G. Allen Center for Visual Arts was named after my mother, above in 1990, and built at the University of Washington with the help of a $5 million donation from my family. (© Richard S. Heyza/*The Seattle Times*)

Steve Ballmer, above, in 2003, was hired by Microsoft in 1980 after being recruited by Bill, his former Harvard classmate. (© Paul Allen)

When I bought the NBA's Portland Trail Blazers, I became the youngest owner in major league sports. Above, at the Rose Garden with former Blazer greats, from left to right, Clifford Robinson, Jerome Kersey, Clyde Drexler, and the late Kevin Duckworth. (© Sam Forencich/Getty Images)

Some of my favorite friends to play music with are, at left, Robbie Robertson and, far right, Dave Stewart. At this 2004 party for the release of the *Ladder 49* movie, also playing are Joe Kara on bass and Michael Jerome on drums. (© Paul Allen)

In 1999 I was lucky enough to jam with Mick Jagger at his birthday party. Jonny Lang is the other guitarist, along with an unidentified bass player. (© Paul Allen)

Bono and I pose for a snapshot on the way to St. Tropez. When I was ill, Bono and The Edge accepted an award on my behalf from the Thelonious Monk Institute. (© Paul Allen)

My sister, Jody, spearheaded construction of the Experience Music Project in Seattle. Here we sit outside the EMP building designed by Frank Gehry.

(© Vulcan Inc.)

I bought the NFL's Seattle Seahawks in 1997 to save the team from being moved to Los Angeles. In 2006, the team won the NFC Championship and a trip to the Super Bowl.

(© Seattle Seahawks)

In the background is *Octopus,* my yacht that was delivered in 2003. In the foreground is the eight-person submarine *Pagoo,* which launches from an internal lagoon on *Octopus.* (© Vulcan Inc.)

In 2003, my film company, Vulcan Productions, coproduced with Martin Scorsese *The Blues,* an Emmy Award–winning PBS series. With me here are Scorsese and B.B. King. (© KMazur/Getty Images)

Allan Jones, PhD, CEO of the Allen Institute for Brain Science, is pointing to the cerebellum in this thin section of a human brain that has been stained for analysis. (© Kevin Cruff, courtesy of Vulcan Inc.)

In northern Namibia in 2009, from left to right, Bert Kolde, guide Chris Bakkes, and me in front of a giant baobab tree. (© Vulcan Inc.)

Burt Rutan and I went to Washington, D.C., for the installation of SpaceShipOne alongside Charles Lindbergh's *Spirit of St. Louis* in the National Air and Space Museum. (© Win McNamee/Getty Images)

In Magadi, Kenya, with Shompole Mountain in the distance. From left to right, driver and guide James Lakalali, my cousin and tech support man Tom Grubbs, me, and Dan Aykroyd, whose family joined mine on safari. (© Paul Allen)

Jody and I on safari in Botswana, 2010, with Jabu, an elephant we spent the morning with on our sightseeing trip. (© Vulcan Inc.)

At the Experience Music Project in October 2010 I joined an all-star guitar jam to honor Billy Cox, Jimi Hendrix's collaborator and last bass player, with the 2010 Founder's Award. I'm at the far left, with Andy Aledort, Scott Nelson, Noah Hunt, Chris Layton, Kenny Wayne Shepherd, Billy Cox, and Orianthi Panagaris. (© Bryce Covey for Team Photogenic NW Inc. 2010)

who made the cover of *Life* magazine storming Omaha Beach on D-Day. Then the camera trained on the upper deck, as the celebrity raised a flag that bore the number 12. The ritual became the talk of the town. Nobody outside the organization knew who Sunday's flag raiser would be.

A few days before the conference championship, Tod said to me, "You're raising the Twelfth Man flag on Sunday." At first I was unconvinced. I wasn't sure how people would react, and I wanted the crowd's energy to stay high. But Tod insisted, and I made my way to the flagpole that afternoon in time for the scoreboard narrative: "His dad took him to Husky games. A passion was born. He saved our Seahawks, built the NFL's most beautiful stadium. Now the NFL's loudest stadium. Welcome, Paul Allen."

As I read those words on the mammoth screen, my eyes were wet. I thought about my father, the man who'd taught me how to throw a tight spiral, and I wished he could have been at my side. As I pulled on the rope, the intensity of the crowd's response amazed me. I lost count of how many people around the flagpole thanked me for keeping their team in town. I waved a white towel in the air to help boost the frenzy, not my usual style. It was the most passionate public celebration I've ever been part of.

Back up in my suite, I hopped on and off my chair, pacing throughout the game. Holmgren had told me that he'd be calling one of his rare trick plays with backup quarterback Seneca Wallace as wide receiver. The coach's tricks often backfired, but this time Seneca made an over-the-shoulder catch for twenty-eight yards midway through the first quarter, setting up our first touchdown.

The Seahawks never looked back. Hasselbeck was near perfect, and Alexander ran roughshod. Tatupu made an early interception and knocked the Panthers' running back out of the game. Steve Smith, Carolina's star receiver, was stopped cold with double and triple teams. With the score mounting to a twenty-point blowout, I could hardly contain myself as I descended to the field for the last few minutes. At the postgame ceremony, Holmgren, Hasselbeck, and I stood under the lights, raising the NFC championship trophy over our heads.

I appreciated what the coach told the press afterward: "I was fortunate enough to have an owner who has been patient with me. In this business, that's not always the case. . . . If you believe in something, and you stay the course, and you get people who believe in you, it gives you a chance."

WE CAME INTO Super Bowl XL as four-point underdogs to the Pittsburgh Steelers. We had a three-point lead early but were hurt by some questionable officiating. (That isn't sour grapes on my part. More than four years after the fact, the game's referee acknowledged that he blew two pivotal calls in the fourth quarter.) We also had too many penalties and dropped passes and missed field goals. In the end, Pittsburgh was tougher and more poised that day. They outplayed us when it counted.

You're always sorely disappointed to lose a Super Bowl, because who knows when you'll be back? It may not happen in my lifetime, but we're sure going to try—to me, that's the point of owning a major-league franchise. The Seahawks don't play in the largest market, but we spend what we need to spend to compete at the highest level. In 2010, after two sad seasons, I hired Pete Carroll away from USC to help get us back there, along with a new front office team in Peter McLoughlin and John Schneider. (Tod Leiweke returned to his first love, the National Hockey League.)

Football is much more than a civic chore for me now. I've gotten hooked on the weeklong buildup to Sunday, to the point where I can't tell you which I enjoy more, the Seahawks or the Blazers. Every football playoff game is like a game seven in basketball, sudden death. And the sport pulls a community together in amazing ways. During our run to the Super Bowl in 2005, I'd look out my office window and see Twelfth Man flags flying from buildings all around the city. Those are moments you savor in life.

Along with the Mariners' Safeco Field, Qwest Field has established a vibrant stadium district in Seattle. Our team helped revive the adjacent Pioneer Square, the original downtown that dates from the Klondike gold rush of the 1890s. We've also played a role in the largest United Way campaign in the country, matching funds for every game program sold and raising half a million dollars during a climb of Mount Rainier, where we planted the Twelfth Man flag.

In 2009, with the debut of Major League Soccer's Seattle Sounders FC, we made good on the final piece of our promise to Washington's voters. After one year, the Sounders had a season ticket base of thirty-two thousand and had sold out the team's eighteen-game season. The majority owner is Hollywood producer Joe Roth; I'm a minority owner, along with Adrian Hanauer and comedian Drew Carey. We're proud that our team has helped to raise the bar for community support for soccer in North America. And it feels all the sweeter that it's happening in my hometown.

# CHAPTER 16

# SPACE

In the library, when I was young, I'd head straight to the science and science fiction sections. I got hooked on sci-fi by Robert Heinlein's *Rocket Ship Galileo,* the story of teenage boys who build a rocket in the desert and blast off to the moon. But I also loved nonfiction like Willy Ley's *Rockets, Missiles and Space Travel,* the story of the birth of German rocketry.

Novels were hard-pressed to keep up with reality in those days. On April 12, 1961, Yuri Gagarin became the first man in space—a riveting event, even for a second-grader. That night I went out on our front porch, where my mother had taught me the constellations. I looked up and wondered, *Can we see him up there?* I didn't know that Gagarin's one-orbit trip had lasted less than two hours and that he'd already parachuted safely to earth.

I knew by heart the names of the Mercury 7 astronauts, our country's original space heroes. Three weeks after Gagarin, I watched a grainy TV picture of Alan Shepard, the first of them to lift off. Nine months later, when John Glenn became the first American to reach orbit, his name was on everyone's lips. Space science was a national crusade, with JFK pushing for an American on the moon before the end of the decade. Like countless other boys, I planned to become an astronaut when I grew up. For sheer adventure, you couldn't beat outer space.

That was also the year of the Seattle World's Fair, and my cousin Tommy came up from Oklahoma to stay the whole summer. I remember how we thrilled to the movie *Moon Pilot,* with Dany Saval, an exotic French actress who played an alien. Our headquarters—the closest thing I had to a tree house—was my bedroom closet, under a sloping roofline. We'd take out my hangers of clothes and sit on cushions on the floor, and the fantasy was on (with occasional intermissions for my mother's tuna fish sandwiches).

"It's T minus five minutes to launch. Are you ready?"

"Yes, ready. All systems go."

My drawings from that time were elaborate: a spaceman with a full complement of tools and supplies, including a backpack that converted carbon dioxide to water; a spherical spacecraft that featured a space taxi landing pod and an "ion engine." Beneath a rocket ship being readied for takeoff, I scrawled a message to my cousin, whose copiloting I'd missed: "Dear Tommy, this big rocket is called the Eagle Thunderbolt. It was designed by me. It is a rocket to be used to explore Mars. I wish you were here to help me make the plans, because this job is too big for me to do alone. So hurry back and we will get started. Love, Paul Allen."

Then I got jerked back to earth. In fifth grade, I kept changing seats to get closer to the blackboard, until my teacher noticed me squinting from the front row. My parents got my eyes checked, with tragic results for an aspiring space pioneer: 20/400. I'd never make the cut at NASA or even a commercial airline.

Still, I kept reading. After exhausting the public library's catalog, I went with my father to the university stacks and browsed in the rocket and aviation section, shelf upon shelf. What could be more fun than that? I can still remember those musty pages and illustrations. My favorites were the *Jane's All the World's Aircraft* books. I memorized the specs of World War II planes and their engines, like the German Junkers Ju-88. I began to sort out how a rocket motor worked.

With its mix of technology and adventure, science fiction holds a natural appeal for adolescent boys. In my early Lakeside years, I'd spend my weekend mornings lying in bed, making my way through the Ace Double genre novels. I moved on to more sophisticated writers: Arthur C. Clarke and Isaac Asimov, and that wonderful stylist and personal favorite, Jack Vance. I especially liked Heinlein's "hard" science fiction, which paired authentic scientific theories with ray-gun battles. And I'd get irked by authors whose characters traveled faster than the speed of light, which I knew was theoretically impossible.

(A quarter-century after I'd left home, I went up to my old room to hunt for a book and found them all missing. "I sold them," my mother explained. "And would you believe it, Paul, a man gave me seventy-five dollars!" It was hard to forgive her for that, but an old photograph saved the day. After enlarging the picture, I was able to make out the titles on my old collection's spines. I had copies tracked down and retrieved almost all of them.)

Science fiction led me to wonder about parallel universes and how the wildest ideas might be possible. Some of those notions are now seen as scientifically unattainable (antigravity, warp drive) or financially and logistically impractical (flying cars). But others, from videoconferencing to communications satellites, turned out to be sneak previews of the future. Either way, those paperbacks got me thinking about where technology might be headed. I've tried to repay my debt by opening the Science Fiction Museum and Hall of Fame in Seattle, the only facility of its kind in the world.

My hands-on rocket experiments began with old-fashioned kitchen matches wrapped in foil, perched on bent paperclip launch pads. I played with Jetex glider kits powered by guanidine nitrate pellets: minimal thrust, lots of hissing exhaust. For more excitement, Doug Fullmer and I strung a string across the street and fixed a bottle rocket to one end with a lit cherry bomb attached. If we timed it just right, the cherry bomb would explode over a passing car, startling the motorist and sending us diving into the bushes.

I had less success when I tried to launch the arm of an aluminum lawn chair by stuffing it with powdered zinc and sulfur and setting it atop a coffee pot. With my cousin Chris in rapt attendance, I lit the fuel. My rocket sputtered and shuddered before toppling over and melting. My ultimate Wernher von Braun moment came in Doug's basement, when we tried to make a rocket fuel called Grandma's Fiery Molasses. We heated potassium nitrate and sugar into a slurry, using Doug's father's blowtorch instead of a Bunsen burner. That might have been too hot, because the slurry ignited until the flames licked the ceiling. To our relief, the fuel burned itself out without torching Doug's house. We kept it a secret and didn't repeat the experiment.

Other enthusiasms came and went, but my obsession with rocketry endured. At age sixteen, I sat with my mother and sister to watch Apollo 11's lunar module land in the Sea of Tranquility. Six hours later, we saw Neil Armstrong walk on the moon. That night I went outside as I had when Yuri Gagarin flew, my eyes fixed on the pale disk above. In wonderment I mused, *There are people from earth up there, walking around.*

After Apollo, NASA shifted to unmanned probes. Space lost its cachet, but it never lost my interest. In the spring of 1981, in the middle of Microsoft's frenetic work on Project Chess, Charles Simonyi suggested that we fly to Florida for the maiden launch of the space shuttle *Columbia*. Neither of us had seen a live liftoff; Charles had missed Apollo 8 by half an hour after making a wrong turn in Georgia. I was all for going until we realized that the launch was set for Friday, April 10, the date for Microsoft's first-ever companywide meeting. Instead of joining the throng at the Kennedy Space Center, we'd be stuck in a Red Lion Inn in Bellevue.

Then some kismet: The launch was postponed to Sunday *because of a software glitch*. We reached the NASA causeway before dawn. At seven, there began a deep rumbling that became more than sound, until the air was literally vibrating. We could see the orange glow as the rocket fired, and then I could feel its heat on my face. As the *Columbia* headed straight up, and the crowd chanted "Go!" I got a lump in my throat. (Rocket takeoffs get me every time, even on television.)

Bill wasn't happy that we'd taken the weekend off with IBM's deadlines still pending. But I didn't second-guess going. I had seen a rare thing; I'd seen history.

IN SEPTEMBER 1996, I flew to Mojave, California, to meet Burt Rutan, president of Scaled Composites and the renegade genius of modern aerospace engineering. Burt was tall and thick-chested, dressed in denim. He had a mane of silvery hair, muttonchop side-burns, a desert tan, and a fanatic's glint in his eye. He'd designed more than thirty unorthodox experimental aircraft, mostly with lightweight carbon composites, and had set a raft of world distance and duration records. In 1986, his *Voyager* became the first plane to be flown around the world without landing or refueling.

Burt had already begun thinking about a supersonic plane that could fly above the atmosphere. Two years later, over lunch in Se-attle, he floated his plan for a manned rocket flight into suborbital space. Burt wanted to demonstrate that you didn't need NASA-level resources to create a commercial space tourism industry and bring ordinary people to the same black sky that once greeted Alan Shepard.

I had a narrower goal. I wanted to do something in rocketry that no one had done before. I wanted to do it with Burt because none of his designs had crashed during testing. In government-funded spaceflight, there was a historical 4 percent fatality rate. For space tourism to succeed, that risk needed to be cut to no more than one in five thousand, comparable to the early airline industry.

Burt had a lot going for him: a crack engineering team and a brilliant body of work, plus the aura of confidence that marks great innovators. But the right design still eluded him, and so our project was tabled.

\* \* \*

IN 1965, Burt was hired as a flight-test project engineer at Edwards Air Force Base just south of Mojave, the place where Chuck Yeager first broke the sound barrier. Burt's stay overlapped with the government's research program for the X-15, the only winged aircraft to fly into space. It was launched not from the ground, but from a B-52 mother ship, high in the atmosphere. The idea was to avoid the most dangerous phase of a ground launch, the first seconds, when there's no way to abort after liftoff without creating a fireball. (If a rocket starts instead at 50,000 feet, and then something goes wrong, you can dump propellant and still have time to glide down for a safe landing.) Beyond being safer, the two-plane concept avoided the conventional one-and-done missiles that would have made the rocket's price prohibitive. Yet another plus: In thinner atmosphere, you use less fuel, which allows for a smaller rocket.

But if the going up seemed relatively straightforward, the coming down was something else again. In 1967, during Burt's stint at Edwards, an X-15 test pilot named Mike Adams was killed during reentry after a spin at Mach 5 (five times the speed of sound) broke his plane into pieces. Burt was committed to finding a more dependable design—something at least as safe as NASA's Mercury model, where the astronaut sat inside a capsule at the tip of a missile and parachuted back to earth. His first big idea, which he called a "carefree reentry," was to "feather" the capsule like a badminton shuttlecock. The resulting drag would decelerate the craft faster and minimize heat buildup as it returned to the atmosphere.

But the capsule-shuttlecock approach had drawbacks. You couldn't land the spacecraft without a parachute. And you couldn't market flights for tourists if you needed search-and-rescue missions to find errant capsules. Besides, parachute mishaps were all too common; a Russian cosmonaut died in the first Soyuz flight in 1967 after his chutes failed. Burt needed a craft that could reliably survive reentry and yet enable a pilot-controlled, horizontal landing on a runway. Which brought him back to square one: a winged airplane.

One morning in 1999, Burt had his eureka moment: The wings themselves could act as the feather! SpaceShipOne was effectively two planes in one. During the boost phase and ascent, the wings would be configured normally. But for the supersonic phase of the descent, their rear halves would fold upward along a hinge at a 65-degree angle, creating the high drag needed for a carefree re-entry. Back in the atmosphere, the plane would revert to its original configuration and become a pilot-controlled glider, along the lines of the X-15. From a safety perspective, this was the best of both worlds.

Burt tested several feathered-wing designs by tossing Styrofoam and balsa-wood models off the Mojave control tower. In the summer of 2000, after he found one that passed his tests, we reached an agreement. Under its terms, Burt would develop the design and build the two planes in return for a minority equity stake. He'd later call me the perfect customer because I deferred to him on all mission-critical decisions. That's a core element of my management philosophy: find the best people and give them room to operate, as long as they can accept my periodic high-intensity kibitzing.

At the start, my goal was to get the first privately supported astronauts to space and back, thereby kicking off a new era of commercial spaceflight. Though the X Prize for this feat had been announced four years earlier, its financing seemed shaky and we weren't counting on it. But in 2002, not long after Burt and I signed our contract to form Mojave Aerospace Ventures (MAV), the Ansari family purchased a "hole-in-one" insurance policy to guarantee the $10 million prize. To meet its criteria, Burt modified his design from a solo pilot craft to a pilot plus two passengers. The cost estimate more than doubled, from $9 million to $19 million, and I knew it was unlikely to stop there. Based on what I'd heard about bleeding-edge aircraft, I expected SpaceShipOne to come in overweight, underpowered, over budget, and behind schedule.

The remarkable thing about MAV was that it built a manned space program from scratch with a staff that averaged around thirty people. And they didn't just engineer a spacecraft; they also built the launch airplane, flight simulator, avionics system, and rocket motor test facility. I flew down periodically for project reviews as *White Knight*, the mother ship, was prepped for its first go in August 2002. Looking like a catamaran with wings, *White Knight* was both launch vehicle and pilot training platform. All of its control systems, down to the pattern of porthole windows in the cockpit, were identical to those on our rocket ship.

My anticipation grew as SpaceShipOne's carbon-fiber design took shape like something out an old sci-fi magazine. With a mere twenty-seven-foot wingspan, it weighed less than a Honda Civic. As X Prize Chairman Peter Diamandis would say, it was "a spaceship that could fit in a two-car garage." Unlike the space shuttle (but like the X-15), SpaceShipOne would fly through the sound barrier without active computer assistance. Early on in his career, Burt couldn't afford wind-tunnel testing, and so he relied on carefully designed flight test programs, computational analyses, and supremely skilled pilots. Although SpaceShipOne's avionics would monitor trajectory and projected altitude and warn about potential problems, the pilot commanded the controls: the manual stick and rudder pedals, the gas jets that adjusted attitude in space, even the rocket boost cutoff. "This," Burt said, "is really out there."

Scaled Composites' first effort to build a rocket was a tricky proposition. For safety and flexibility, Burt employed a hybrid rocket engine, the first ever used in a manned spacecraft. At ignition, liquid nitrous oxide would flow from a tank into a motor filled with synthetic rubber, causing a controlled burn. As the rubber was consumed, high-speed gases would spurt out of the motor's nozzle and propel the ship. If the pilot needed to shut down the motor, he could simply cut off the nitrous flow and dump what was left.

On February 1, 2003, five months before our first flight test, the space shuttle *Columbia* broke up on reentry over Texas. All seven people aboard were killed, a harsh reminder of the risks we faced.

GREAT LEAPS IN aviation have long been spurred by cash incentives, going back to the $25,000 Orteig Prize won by Charles Lindbergh in 1927. Competitions tend to invigorate people's ambitions. They're also laced with cautionary tales like Admiral Byrd, the Orteig favorite, who spent a then extravagant $100,000 on his entry. He crashed during a practice takeoff, giving Lindbergh the opening he needed.

The X Prize rules were strict. We needed to reach 100 kilometers (or about 62 miles) above the earth, the edge of space—not once but twice within a two-week period, and no later than December 31, 2004. No more than 10 percent of the craft could be replaced between the two flights, and it had to return from the second one intact. Finally, no government aid was permitted.

The contest attracted twenty-seven teams from seven countries, though Burt took none of them seriously. The Canadian da Vinci Project, which counted on a gigantic helium balloon to carry their rocket plane, seemed especially far-fetched. We had some concern about rumored covert efforts in Eastern Europe, but our main adversaries were the clock and the unpredictability of Mach 3 flight.

AS A RULE, test pilots have a rare combination of intelligence, motivation, and emotional stability. As I came to know the men chosen to fly SpaceShipOne, I was impressed by their fearlessness but also their attention to detail. All three were in the Lindbergh tradition, exceptional people.

Brian Binnie was a lanky military test pilot with degrees from Brown and Princeton. A veteran of more than thirty combat missions during Desert Storm, he left the navy after they tried to make him a desk jockey. He was thoughtful and highly organized, a quiet guy whose intensity burned beneath the surface.

Pete Siebold was a young aeronautical engineer who'd designed the avionics for the planes and the flight simulator, which he operated like a pinball wizard. He knew every line of the software's code and brought tremendous authority to the pre- and postmortems for each flight. Round-faced and curly-haired, he also had impressive cockpit skills. In his one powered flight, his trajectory was absolutely on point.

Mike Melvill was the outlier, a high school dropout and balding grandfather who wore baseball caps and wire-rim glasses. At sixty-three, Mike was three years past the retirement age for commercial pilots. But he was incredibly fit, a world-class kayaker who biked a hundred miles a week. Since hiring on in 1978, he'd twice been Burt's best man. He believed in Burt's planes without question and would do anything not to let his friend down.

Mike could struggle in the simulator. But for seat-of-the-pants improvisation and that mysterious quality called *feel,* there was no one you'd rather have in a critical test flight. Burt would call him "the best stick-and-rudder pilot I've ever seen." In a project with more than its share of calculated risks, Mike's makeup would be a key to our success.

A WELL-DESIGNED FLIGHT test program expands the envelope cautiously, incrementally. Burt was a master at moving forward in baby steps. First, SpaceShipOne would be tethered to the belly of *White Knight* in captive-carry flights. If all went well, the ship would progress to independent glides and finally to a series of six rocket-powered boost flights. Each step presented tougher g-forces or airspeeds or altitudes, or some mix of the three.

On December 17, 2003, the hundredth anniversary of the Wright brothers' first flight, SpaceShipOne was set for its first powered outing—and the first privately funded flight to break the sound barrier. After consulting with Burt, Doug Shane, the director of flight operations, tapped the one pilot who had previously flown at supersonic speeds, Brian Binnie. Having managed the project's rocket development program, Brian was also more familiar with the rocket's motor. He was the obvious choice.

I flew to Mojave early that morning to join the five A.M. pre-flight meeting in Burt's hangar. After SpaceShipOne was wheeled out on a dolly and secured beneath *White Knight*, I followed Burt and Doug to the control room, where team members donned headsets and sat before their networked desktop or laptop computers. (I got a kick out of seeing how modern PCs were being put to use.) As they scanned their screens, Doug ran them through a checkoff.

"Aerodynamics."

"Go."

"Propulsion."

"Go."

"Systems."

"Go."

This flight was new territory for Burt, with his first plane designed to go faster than Mach 0.7. The thrust of a rocket motor is basically a controlled explosion. If a leak led to some structural failure, it was a good bet that we'd lose our pilot. The other nightmare scenario was that the motor might not light at all, which happened several times in early ground testing: a puff of smoke, then nothing. With eight hundred pounds of rubber molded into the rocket casing, a lot of it needed to burn away before the pilot could land SpaceShipOne in anything close to its normal center-of-gravity envelope. If too much rubber remained, he'd come in so hard and fast that he might have to divert to a longer runway at the air force base, and even then there was no telling whether the spaceship's small tires could handle the weight. As *White Knight* climbed into the sky, with the spaceship strapped beneath it, I had plenty of time to wonder, *Is it really going to work?*

Nearly an hour after departure, more than eight miles high, SpaceShipOne was released. A moment or two later, Brian lit the motor. It felt, he'd say later, "like a tsunami" coming through the cabin. Unlike a jet, a rocket accelerates to full power instantaneously, like a slam in the back. Back at mission control, I peered at the video monitor. To me, nothing can compete with a rocket boost for pure exhilaration: the bright orange glow, the vertical contrail of ice crystals like an arrow reaching for space. I was awed and grateful to be a part of it.

Then came something unforeseen, a wave of dread. I'd been deeply affected when the Apollo 1 crew lost their lives in a preflight fire; I'd felt sick watching *Challenger* disintegrate a minute into its flight. I knew intellectually that someone might die in SpaceShipOne, but that was Burt's familiar territory, not mine. (In the software business, after all, your worst outcome is an error message.) Now I *knew* the person whose life hung in the balance, and I found that hard to handle.

A fifteen-second burn got Brian twelve miles high at a maximum speed of Mach 1.2, and we had made our first bit of history. All systems were in order, so I went outside to watch the landing with Dave Moore, my liaison to MAV, where he served as managing director. (Along with his deputy, Jeff Johnson, he was instrumental in keeping the project on track.) Dave briefed me as I followed Brian's final descent. Then he stopped, because my face had gone white.

Navy pilots are notorious for hard landings, a product of their aircraft-carrier training. Their heavy-handed style is a running joke among test pilots, but today it wasn't funny. Brian hit the runway so hard that one of his landing struts snapped, and his plane careened off the pavement in a cloud of red desert dust. As we raced to the site, my heart was in my throat. Was Brian hurt? When they opened the cockpit, I was thankful to see that he was safe, visibly cursing himself out. My attention turned to SpaceShipOne—how badly was it damaged, and how much time would we lose? Our plan had been to complete the X Prize flights by the following summer. Any delay could push us up uncomfortably against our deadline.

Burt was consoling Brian, stressing the positives. He'd flown a good boost, gone supersonic, feathered and defeathered, had a nice glide. As for the plane, Burt said, "All we've got there is real minor stuff." He came over to me: "I think we can get it back." Once the craft was towed back to the hangar, we had a clearer picture. The ship's hull was scraped but not damaged; the nitrous oxide tank was intact; the landing gear was fine, just ripped out of the ship. The accident would set us back about two months. There was still time to get in the three remaining powered flights on our test schedule.

The postmortem pointed to a newly installed vibration damper with an unfortunate side effect. It had made the flight controls less responsive when they got "cold-soaked" in the frigid temperatures of high altitudes. As Brian approached the runway, he found himself wrestling with his stick. Fearing a stall, he dropped his nose and came in too fast. (For future flights, the damper would be wrapped in electric blankets and cut to one-third power.)

Though it wasn't all his fault, I could tell that Brian's mishap had shaken the team's confidence in him, and he dropped a notch on the depth chart. He'd have to redeem himself to get back in the mix for another shot.

BURT HAD FOLLOWED a cardinal rule since founding his business in the mid-1970s: no press or public at any test flight when the envelope was expanding. On June 21, 2004, six months after Brian's misadventure, he broke his own protocol for SpaceShipOne's trial to become the first privately funded craft to pierce the boundary of space. For Burt, this was more than a dress rehearsal for the X Prize. It was a chance to make history, and he wanted the public to be part of it. Spectators began arriving Saturday morning, two days before the launch. By early Monday, while it was still dark, tens of thousands of people had mobbed the grounds around the newly renamed Mojave Air and Space Port. There were children, dogs, bicycles, telescopes, lawn chairs, barbecues—a spaceflight tailgate party.

In the weeks leading to the launch, the pilots had worked as a team in the simulator, taking turns and critiquing one another. As it came time to decide who would fly, Doug Shane argued that Pete Siebold would find the optimal trajectory and give us the best chance to reach 100 kilometers. "Yeah," Burt replied, "but Pete might quit." He was referring to an earlier flight, the first with a full load of nitrous oxide, when Pete had considered aborting after an early stall. They finally settled on Mike, a gutsy call. Despite Mike's 6,400 hours of flight time, this would be well beyond anything he had done.

When I watched the pilots in the minutes before takeoff, it felt as though they were on their way to war. Brian Binnie's wife handed him a lucky ring. For Mike's wife, Sally, it was a silver horseshoe pin that Mike had given her when they were teenagers in South Africa, engraved with their names and the date they'd met. Sally fixed it to the left side of her husband's flight suit, and it hit me that no one knew for sure if Mike would return. As I shook his hand and wished him a safe flight, Sally was plainly terrified. A pilot herself, she knew the hazards too well.

Mike squeezed into his five-foot-diameter cabin and waved a thumbs-up. At 6:47 A.M., he was in the air. Inside mission control, tension built as the time approached for the drop and separation, and the violent boost phase that would follow within seconds.

Lacking a NASA-style centrifuge, our pilots couldn't fully simulate a rocket boost. Their aerobatic practice plane could roughly simulate the four g's (four times earth's gravity) produced when they pulled back on the spaceship's stick to go vertical, or "eyeballs down," in pilots' parlance. But it couldn't begin to mimic the initial three g's of forward thrust, or "eyeballs back"; only a rocket motor could do that. Together, those forces were so disorienting that a pilot had to trust his instruments over his body.

Mike lit the rocket. Within ten seconds, he had nearly hit Mach 1, and that's when his first problem arose. In designing SpaceShipOne, Burt had set the wings high over the fuselage to optimize the feather's supersonic performance when it folded. The trade-off was poor lateral stability when the plane was "transonic," or moving from subsonic to supersonic speeds. While the pilots were trained to compensate, there was no way to prepare for wind shear, a sudden change in wind speed as a plane climbed through the atmosphere—which is just what Mike encountered at 60,000 feet. SpaceShipOne rolled 90 degrees to the left. Mike stamped on the rudder and overcorrected. The plane rolled to the right.

Watching on a monitor linked to a camera on the plane's tail, I jumped off my chair. I'm a pacer when I get wired up, a habit from the days when Bill and I walked in circles while talking about our software. Now I was wearing a path in Burt's thin carpet as I waited for Mike to abort the boost and live to fly another day. But Mike hated to quit. In his previous powered flight, after his avionics screen blacked out, he'd amazingly kept his craft aligned by sighting the horizon. I knew that Mike wouldn't shut down a mission unless his life seemed in danger, and even then he might think twice.

With the atmosphere thinning and his stick and rudder useless, Mike tried to correct the plane's orientation by angling the horizontal stabilizers, the electronic control surfaces on the craft's tails. They promptly froze, a potential catastrophe for reentry, but came back on seconds later. Mike got the plane straightened out and quickly pulled up its nose, but the delay had squandered energy and thrown him off trajectory.

Still pacing behind Burt and his team, I kept an eye on the digital altimeter as the plane climbed straight up and the simulated needle spun in a blur. I thought about Mike, that warm-hearted guy inside a very small projectile at close to Mach 3. I can honestly say that all thoughts of the X Prize vanished. I kept repeating to myself: *I just want him safe on the ground again.*

Then I heard Burt remark that Mike hadn't cut the motor. He didn't shut it down until his "energy altitude"—his predicted apogee, reading out in thousands of feet—blinked once at 328, the official threshold for space. When he finally cut off the engine, the plane was actually at 180,000 feet, barely halfway there; it coasted up the rest of the way and then down again on a ballistic arc. Our eyes stayed glued to the altimeter as it edged toward 100 kilometers. The needle slowed, then barely crossed the line before stopping and reversing. We were jubilant but a little uncertain. Had he really made it? I shook hands with Burt, who was glowing.

On his way into work that morning, Mike had stopped at a convenience store and on impulse bought a bag of M&M's. As he began his descent and entered three minutes of weightlessness, he opened the bag and watched the colored candies float and sparkle about his cabin. (I have a few of those M&M's encased in plastic, along with a pine tree growing outside my house that was hauled in the ship as a seedling, my "space tree.") Peering through the portholes, he marveled at the view: the jet-black sky, the blue curve of the earth, the white fog over Los Angeles, the red Mojave Desert.

SpaceShipOne kept gaining speed on the way down, reaching Mach 2.9, or 2,150 miles per hour. The feather did its work upon reentry, quickly slowing the craft to subsonic speeds. At 57,000 feet, as Mike defeathered into the glide phase, I couldn't help but notice that he was nearly thirty miles off course. When I asked if he'd have to land at another airport, Burt assured me that the plane was well within its glide range.

Moving outside for Mike's approach, I saw him land on the runway ("like falling into a feather bed," he'd tell us) to huge roars from the crowd. SpaceShipOne's entire flight, from drop to landing, lasted barely twenty-four minutes. I felt like I had aged several years.

As *White Knight* and the chase planes buzzed over our heads, Sally Melvill ran to the little spacecraft and leaned into the cockpit to embrace her husband. Mike emerged, hands raised. He hugged Burt and then flung his arms out wide for me. There are moments in life that deserve a hug, and that was one of them.

Mike was towed up and down the runway for twenty minutes, standing atop his plane as he waved to his fans. Then Burt and I brought him back to the hangar and to Sally. He completed their ritual by unpinning the horseshoe and returning it to her. "Thanks for coming home," she told him. "We'll get old together in rocking chairs."

We still weren't certain that SpaceShipOne had gotten to space. Mike told Sally that he didn't think he'd made it; Burt was more confident but still had concerns. According to the low end of our in-house calculations, we'd cleared it by an infinitesimal sixteen feet. At last we received word from the Naval Air Weapons Station at China Lake, which had tracked us on radar. SpaceShipOne's apogee was officially 328,491 feet, barely a tenth of a percent over the threshold. After flying sixty-two miles straight up, Mike had passed the magic line by the length of a 5-iron to the green. If the plane had been eight ounces heavier, Burt said, we'd have come up short.

We set lots of records that day. The 433rd person to make it into space, Mike was the first commercial pilot to do so. He earned his astronaut wings from the FAA, the first ever awarded for a nongovernment space program. SpaceShipOne was the first privately built plane to exceed Mach 2 and the *only* U.S. craft to leave the atmosphere that year, NASA's space shuttles having been grounded in the wake of the *Columbia* disaster.

The world took notice. On June 21, 2004, a color photograph of SpaceShipOne sat above the fold on page one of nearly every newspaper around the globe.

A MONTH BEFORE Mike's historic flight, Richard Branson had come to see me. When we met years before, I'd found him very sharp and very restless, one of those people who can't stop moving. Now he said he wanted to license our patented technology and take our program to the next level: full-fledged space tourism. In September 2004, three months after Mike's flight, we signed a contract with Branson's Virgin Galactic that could net me up to $25 million over the next fifteen years. A master of branding, Branson was eager to close the deal to get his lipstick-red Virgin logo painted on SpaceShipOne for the first X Prize flight, which was scheduled three days later.

Burt's early assessment of our competition was on target. On a single day in August, unmanned test vehicles from both Space Transport and Armadillo Aerospace crashed beyond repair. Rumor had it that the da Vinci Project would launch their balloon in a prize-eligible flight on October 2, but I didn't believe it. They hadn't done a single test flight, and there was no historical example of going from zero to a launch of that magnitude in one shot. No one else had given the required sixty-day notice for a prize-qualifying flight. It was up to us.

Our biggest concern was that SpaceShipOne would be carrying an additional four hundred pounds, in line with the X Prize rule that stipulated a three-person vehicle. Fiberglass boxes filled with wrenches and other ballast would be strapped into the plane's two rear seats. (We wouldn't put three people in the plane, I was told, "because if something goes wrong, you'd rather have one fatality than three.") The extra weight was a legitimate worry. Would our rocket motor have enough juice to make it back into space?

In fact, SpaceShipOne hadn't been pushed as close to its limit in June as it had seemed. Mike's shutdown time had been pre-set as a precaution; he could have run the motor at least another five seconds. (Burt chose to limit the burn because too much altitude would make reentry more hazardous.) With a cleaner run, the plane might have made it into space with ten thousand feet to spare. Even so, we knew we couldn't afford a flawed trajectory on the X Prize flight.

To minimize the risk, Burt exploited the ship's robust design. NASA's unmanned rockets are built to withstand 25 percent more than the maximum aerodynamic loads, which translates to a safety margin of 1.25. In the space shuttle, the margin is 1.4; on commercial airliners, it's 1.6. But in SpaceShipOne, the wings were built with a margin of 2.1 and the cabin, 3.0. (Burt wanted higher margins in the cabin because his pilots would be flying without pressurized spacesuits.) Both the nitrous oxide tank and the rocket motor, the components most vulnerable to catastrophe, were also overengineered by a factor of 3.0, which now gave Burt crucial leeway.

For Mike's spaceflight in June, up to 15 percent of the rocket's nitrous oxide tank had been reserved for ullage, the empty space that allows heated fuel to expand and prevents a tank from cracking. That was standard. But with *White Knight* scheduled for takeoff just a half hour after sunrise, when it would quickly climb into cold air, Burt realized that he could safely top off the tank for a longer burn and extra boost. It was a typical MAV solution, simple and clean. For insurance, Burt wrapped an insulating ring around the tank, to be removed just before takeoff.

For more of a margin, the team reduced the craft's weight; for every pound removed, it would go 150 feet higher with the same amount of thrust. Small holes were carved out of overbuilt parts. And when the X Prize lawyers decided that optional safety items, like parachutes, could be counted toward the required payload weight, we saved thirty-six pounds.

One issue remained. Which pilot would get us halfway to the $10 million prize? Mike having earned his wings, Doug and Burt chose Pete Siebold for the first prize flight and held Brian in reserve for the second. Believing his job was done, Mike cut back on his simulator training to give more time to the other two. But less than a week before the launch date, Pete pulled out. In the previous month, he'd experienced a health scare and the birth of his second child. The health issue was a false alarm, but Pete felt unprepared to be the man in the cockpit.

We were left with one obvious choice. Doug went to Mike's office and said, "I hate to tell you this, but we need you to fly." Mike quickly said he'd do it. He went to see Sally, who took one look at her husband and burst into tears. She'd been assured that Mike wouldn't be asked to go again, and was beside herself that he'd have to push his luck one more time.

Mike flew sixty simulator runs a day over the next several days, with a focus on getting the plane's nose up aggressively to convert the rocket's thrust into pure altitude. He made a series of runway approaches in *White Knight* and in his own homebuilt Long-EZ, another Rutan design. And he used the aerobatic plane to condition himself for forces that would exceed 5 g's. By September 29, he was ready.

Peter Diamandis told the assembled crowd that morning, "Ladies and gentlemen, we are at the start of the personal spaceflight revolution—right here, right now. What is happening here in Mojave today is not about technology. It is about a willingness to take risk, to dream, and possibly to fail."

Takeoff was on schedule at 7:12 A.M. Seated behind Burt in mission control, I watched the video monitor as *White Knight* reached the release point. Mike fired the rocket motor and abruptly "turned the corner" from horizontal to vertical. His trajectory and contrail looked perfect. I watched the altimeter whiz around: 100,000 feet, 110,000, 120,000 . . .

By that point, I'd learned to read the team's body language. Normally they sat relaxed in their chairs, checking their computers and following the exchanges between Doug and Mike on their headsets. But a minute into the burn, when Mike was at Mach 2.6, I saw them all lean forward and hunch over. I did a double take at the monitor, which showed what the team had picked up on their displays. The straight-line contrail was now an ominous corkscrew. SpaceShipOne was spinning rightward like a top on its longitudinal axis, in uncontrollable supersonic rolls. Erik Lindbergh, Charles's grandson and an X Prize Foundation trustee, said he was convinced that "the craft was going to break up and [Mike] was done."

For a brief and awful time, I feared the same thing. Then I saw Burt calmly polling the room without a hint of panic. He'd seen similar rates of roll in the flight simulator, and had every confidence that the ship could handle the dynamic loads and make a safe reentry. "We should be able to ride this thing out," he said after a bit. "We should be able to control it once we get out of the atmosphere."

Test pilots feel fear like the rest of us, but the best of them don't let it affect them. Inside SpaceShipOne, whirling at nearly one revolution per second, Mike's left hand came off the trim control and poised over two toggle switches beneath red plastic guards, the motor shut-off. (In the flight video, you can actually see his hand shaking.) He knew there was no easy way out of the jam. True, SpaceShipOne had an emergency exit route. The pilot could crank a handle, push out the nose plug, and parachute down. But a parachute does you no good much above 50,000 feet, where the atmospheric pressure is so low that air in the lungs expands until the organs rupture. Mike was at 220,000 feet. He withdrew his hand from the toggle switches. He would see the flight through.

Battling vertigo, Mike kept his eyes fixed on his avionics display. As the sun strobed in and out of the cabin's portholes, he worked his stick and rudder against the direction of the roll. After eight or ten revolutions, he stopped feeling dizzy. By around 300,000 feet, where the atmosphere was so thin that his manual controls no longer functioned, the roll had slowed to a manageable half a revolution per second. With SpaceShipOne's GPS disrupted, Mike's altitude predictor lagged behind Doug Shane's at mission control. After Doug called out, "Three-twenty-eight, shut down," Mike stayed with the burn another second or two, until his predictor read 334,000 feet. He didn't want another close call. The spaceship actually topped out at 338,000.

Mike feathered the wings just before apogee and activated his gas jets to damp out what was left of the spin, which stopped after twenty-nine full rotations. His trajectory was perfect; the rolls had effectively stabilized the plane's course, like a bullet's spin out of a rifle. He retracted the feather at 61,000 feet and began his glide back to earth. At 40,000 feet he added a signature to his performance, in the style of a World War II pilot returning from a combat raid. He did a victory roll, to make it an even thirty.

In the conference-room postmortem, we learned that Mike had been hurt by his own success. He'd flown exactly as he'd been trained, pointing SpaceShipOne dead vertical as he turned the corner. No one had realized that a straight-up, 90-degree angle of attack would result in rotational instability. Once the rolls started, there wasn't enough air left to resist them with the rudder and ailerons.

Burt was delighted. Mike's flight had certified SpaceShipOne's structural integrity; the little craft was tougher than it looked. What's more, the plane would need no adjustments for its next try. Pete Siebold and Jim Tighe, the team's aerodynamicist, quickly determined that a more gradual pull-up, stopping a couple degrees short of vertical, would avert the rolls the next time.

BURT SET THE second X Prize flight five days later, on October 4, 2004. Beyond commemorating the forty-seventh anniversary of *Sputnik 1*, the first man-made satellite to orbit the earth, the schedule would give us room for another try within the two-week limit if something were to go wrong. The team was ready ahead of time. On Sunday night, the eve of the flight, Burt invited everyone to his home to watch the Discovery Channel premiere of *Black Sky*, our own Vulcan Productions film about SpaceShipOne. (The two-part documentary later won the Peabody Award for distinguished achievement and meritorious public service.)

A lot rode on Monday morning: the $10 million prize, plus a critical jump start for Branson's SpaceShipTwo. An unsuccessful flight, let alone a disaster, would jeopardize all that we'd worked for. I assumed that Mike would be in the cockpit again, but I didn't know that Doug had asked him to take Brian Binnie under his wing. Starting in late August, Mike took Brian up in his Long-EZ to simulate runway approaches at the optimal speed and sink rate for SpaceShipOne. To replicate the spaceship's portholes, an engineer lined the canopy of Mike's plane with a black cardboard cutout mask. Two days before the flight, after the two pilots went up one last time together, Mike told Doug and Burt, "Brian can do this."

I arrived early at Mojave on Monday, but not before the crowds and camera crews. For the next several hours, the world's attention would be on this remote corner of the desert. Despite my confidence in the team, I couldn't quite block out a little voice inside my head. With each powered flight, something unexpected had occurred. The voice said, *What's going to happen this time? Different pilot, different day, different angle of attack—will it all work?*

There was one unscripted moment just after separation, when Brian ignited the rocket motor especially quickly. Sound carries poorly at 47,000 feet, and the people piloting *White Knight*, including flight engineer Matt Stinemetze, hadn't heard the rocket's roar on the earlier runs. This time Matt picked it up loud and clear, and he shouted, "Holy crap, that was close!" But he wasn't really worried. Given SpaceShipOne's higher rate of acceleration, the two ships couldn't have collided if their pilots had tried.

Brian followed the flight plan to the letter. He pushed SpaceShipOne's nose up to 88 degrees and ascended with minimal roll. In the control room, all eyes were on the altimeter. As I watched and paced, Richard Branson sat down near me and said, "Paul, isn't this better than the best sex you ever had?"

And I thought, *If I was this anxious during any kind of interpersonal activity, I couldn't enjoy it very much.*

"Three hundred thousand," Doug called out on the radio, based on his altitude predictor. And just eight seconds later:

"Radar is three twenty-eight."

"Copy that," Brian replied. Edwards Air Force Base confirmed that we'd made it to space. A cheer went up in the room.

Seven seconds after that: "Three fifty, suggest shutdown," Doug said.

"Roger. Shutdown." In fact, Brian let the motor burn another few moments, eighty-four seconds in all.

The feather was up by 7:52 A.M., but Brian climbed higher still. "X-15 record!" Burt broke in. SpaceShipOne had surpassed 354,200 feet, the X-15's forty-one-year-old mark. It had gone higher than any airplane in history.

"X-15," Doug echoed.

And Brian said, "Outstanding!"

Getting that record meant a lot to Burt, and I was happy for him. The flight's official apogee would be 367,500 feet, nearly 70 miles straight up—7 miles more than we needed.

On the way down, Brian reached Mach 3.25, another record for a civilian craft. After he retracted the feather and began his glide, I drove out with Burt to watch the landing. It's hard to see a ship as small as SpaceShipOne from a distance, especially without a contrail to guide the eye. Most of the crowd wouldn't spot the plane until it was almost overhead. But Burt picked it up early, and he brought Richard Branson and me close to see where he was pointing. There's a great candid photograph of us standing side by side with our left arms raised high and index fingers extended, shading our eyes as we looked to the east to see that little white speck coming home.

Twenty-four minutes after the drop from *White Knight*, Brian's plane touched down: a spotless landing. We finally had our perfect flight, start to end.

After popping champagne on the tarmac, Burt and Richard and I sat on the tailgate of a pickup truck that slowly towed the stubby, homebuilt spaceship back to Burt's hangar, or what I called the world's greatest garage. There was something wonderfully unpretentious and non-NASA about that scene. SpaceShipOne was a small plane built by a modest operation, but it had been to space and back with a person inside. And no one had been hurt; I felt a huge burden lifted. As we made our way down the taxiway to the roars of the crowd, it struck me that SpaceShipOne was more than some momentary spectacle. It offered hope to everyone who aspired to journeys beyond the earth.

There was a reception in the hangar and a call from President Bush, who congratulated Burt and me for "opening up the space frontier." I stammered out a thank-you. Burt's biggest thrill had come in June, with the first private manned spaceflight. For me, though, nothing could top the X Prize. When the pressure and scrutiny were most intense, our team had come through.

One month later, I flew everyone out to the X Prize award ceremony in St. Louis, where Burt and I held aloft a gigantic check for $10 million. Based on an incentive clause I'd put in our contract years earlier, half the money went to Scaled Composites. Burt distributed bonuses to every person in his company, including the guys who swept the floors.

I could have happily closed the book right there, content with the X Prize and the 2004 Collier Trophy for "the greatest achievement in aeronautics or astronautics in America." But an even greater honor was in store. Before Branson came on board, Burt's original plan was to launch SpaceShipOne once a week for five months to lure investors and strengthen the public's confidence in commercial space flight. But after Mike made history in June, we received a letter from the Smithsonian's National Air and Space Museum. They wanted to add SpaceShipOne to the Milestones of Flight gallery, home to the 1903 Wright Flyer and the Apollo 11 command module. With nothing left to prove and a legacy to preserve, Burt and I canceled all further flights.

In July 2005, with SpaceShipOne strapped underneath, Mike Melvill piloted *White Knight* to Dulles Airport in Washington. As he dropped below the clouds, the pilot of a nearby airliner said, "What's that hanging under that airplane?" The air traffic controller, who hadn't gotten the memo, ordered Mike to descend to 6,000 feet, make a 180-degree turn, and leave the area. At that point, a supervisor intervened and directed Mike to go ahead and land. Our craft was lifted onto a truck and hauled to the Smithsonian.

That October, SpaceShipOne was hung between Charles Lindbergh's *Spirit of St. Louis* and Chuck Yeager's Bell X-1. To comply with the museum's guidelines, our craft was repainted to look exactly as it had for Mike's first trip into space. There was the name of the maker (Scaled Composites), the name and number of the airplane, and in small black letters on the fuselage: "A Paul G. Allen Project."

I haven't had any days prouder than that one.

AS PREDICTED, SpaceShipOne wound up taking longer and costing more than we'd planned. The final price tag was $28 million, money well spent. Adding up the X Prize, the tax credit from our Smithsonian donation, and the Virgin licensing revenues, we achieved a net positive return by 2006.

For a time I was tempted to stay involved in the effort to commercialize space tourism. Burt and I had worked together well, and he asked me to continue. But I stepped back some months before we won the X Prize and watched from afar as Branson began development for SpaceShipTwo, a craft designed to take two pilots and six passengers beyond the atmosphere. While the plane's feathered design is similar to our original, accommodations will be a lot plusher: reclining seats to mitigate the g-forces, bigger windows for a better view. By early 2006, Virgin Galactic had $13 million in deposits for rides on the VSS *Enterprise* at $200,000 per head.

On July 26, 2007, during a routine nitrous oxide flow test for SpaceShipTwo's engine, an explosion killed three Scaled employees and injured three others. It was the kind of accident that could happen in any space program, at any time.

Burt has since semiretired from day-to-day operations at Scaled, passing the baton to Doug Shane. In October 2010, the *Enterprise* completed its first glide flight. Its test program is slated to continue through 2011, and I'm betting it will succeed. There's a real chance for large-scale orbital space tourism within a decade, though it's hard to predict the cost of a ticket. The Russians currently charge as much for one ride to the Space Station as we spent altogether on SpaceShipOne. (In the spirit of competition, Elon Musk's SpaceX operation is working to lower that price.)

More than forty years ago, Neil Armstrong changed the way we looked at the moon, and voyages to other planets suddenly seemed within our grasp. Since then our aspirations seem to have contracted. I'm well aware of other urgent social priorities, from health care to global warming. But I also believe that the drive toward new frontiers is integral to our humanity. A Mars program would demand billions of dollars, decades of development, and a willingness to accept failure and tragedy. If our government steps back from the challenge of planetary exploration, private initiatives will face a hard road.

I'm reminded of what Wernher von Braun replied when someone asked him, "What's the hardest thing about going to the moon?"

And von Braun said, "The will to do it."

IN MARCH 2009, I traveled to Kazakhstan to wish Charles Simonyi bon voyage on his two-week holiday: a Soyuz flight to the International Space Station. (In characteristic style, Charles carried takeout from Alain Ducasse and Martha Stewart into orbit with him.) As the rocket took off from the very same pad that launched Yuri Gagarin in 1961, I revisited the rush and trepidation that I'd known at Mojave.

There was a time when I thought I'd be in Charles's place. But seeing up close what's involved in spaceflight gave me pause. I'm not an edge walker. I've never done a parachute jump, for example, because it just doesn't seem worth the downside. Yet when I peered into the sky that October day to track our spaceship's homeward glide, I recaptured my boyhood sense of wonder when I'd looked up at the starry night. I never really lost that feeling, but in the whirl of life, I'd almost forgotten it. It was good to get it back.

While I may never be an astronaut, a part of me is up there nonetheless. A small piece of SpaceShipOne was placed inside the New Horizons robotic probe to the outer reaches of our solar system. In 2007 it passed Jupiter en route to Pluto, the Kuiper belt of asteroids, and beyond.

# CHAPTER 17

# JIMI

I grew up with music. Our family never missed the visiting Romanian dancers or Spanish flamenco troupes at the Seattle Opera House. Our record collection was mostly classical, heavy on Beethoven. By age seven, I was air conducting the Fifth Symphony with bravura.

My parents rarely splurged on presents, but they never passed up opportunities for us to learn. My sister was a great lesson taker: ballet, piano, clarinet, flute. I started violin in the second grade, with mixed results. A nice minuet was heaven, but my teacher was big on scales. Major scales, minor scales—I hated them all. I practiced sporadically, never got past first position, and my tone was awful for some time. As I sawed away, our dog Jett would start howling. "It's good that you're practicing," my mother would say, backing out of the room. "You have to keep at it."

I didn't quite want to quit, but I understood the deal: My parents would pay for the lessons as long as I applied myself. At age nine I wrote:

*Dear Father,*
*I wish to continue the study of violin for one year for the following reasons: It gives me pleasure sometimes, I can*

*hardly wait to play a Mozart, etc. I will try my best to prac-*
*tice every day.*

*Your son,*
*Paul Allen*

In fact, my parents were disinclined to let me stop until I got beyond grade school and was "old enough" to decide if I wanted to continue. My swan song was a chamber music performance at our sixth-grade graduation, which I might have enjoyed if I hadn't been so nervous that I lost my place in the score.

IN 1964, walking home from Ravenna School and fiddling with my transistor radio, I came across the Beatles' "I Want to Hold Your Hand": my earliest memory of popular music. I watched the Supremes and other Motown groups on *The Ed Sullivan Show* and thought they were fabulous. When I first heard live rock at a seventh-grade dance, loud enough to reverberate under my skin, it made a lasting impression.

Every August my parents took a vacation and left Jody and me with the Catania family up the block. In 1966, when I was going into eighth grade, Terry Catania—one year older—knew the Top 40 cold. I'd listened to some of her prized 45s, like Neil Diamond's "Cherry, Cherry," and now she had something new. "You know the Monkees?" she asked.

I shook my head. I hadn't heard about the prefab band whose hit single had taken the charts by storm. "Listen to this," Terry said, and soon I was bopping to the beat of "Last Train to Clarksville." I bought the Monkees' album and played the heck out of it. Then I started watching their sitcom. I'd been too young for Beatlemania when the Fab Four invaded North America two years earlier. (I was with my family in Vancouver, Canada, just after the Beatles played there, and was amazed to hear that someone had bought the hotel sheets they'd slept on.) But my timing was right for the Monkees.

The following August, Terry was wild about a new album that

had broken out in Britain that spring but was still little known in the United States. "Paul, you've got to hear this!" she exclaimed. I stared at the cover as she slid out the vinyl. A swerve of psychedelic purple letters ran together against a yellow background:

*areyouexperienced*

*Was I experienced?* I wasn't sure what that meant, but I guessed the answer was no. Even the group's name was strange: the Jimi Hendrix Experience. A fish-eye photo showed a black musician in an orange scarf flanked by two white sidemen, in itself unusual. The back cover was equally arresting, a black-and-white backlit photo of the group that showed off their big, glowing Afros. I knew then and there that you could not get cooler than Jimi.

Once Terry dropped the needle on the first cut, "Purple Haze," I wouldn't have cared if that record had come in a plain brown wrapper. I was floored by the introduction, a back-and-forth "devil's interval" between Hendrix and his bass player, Noel Redding, weird and dissonant. This was Jimi with a sledgehammer: *Here's what I'm about, check it out.* Then he set up his vocal with a swooping guitar riff. Jimi's playing was funky and aggressive, but smoothly inflected. No one else sounded anything like him. (As Carlos Santana once said, "Most people play fast and shallow. But Coltrane played fast and deep, and so did Charlie Parker, and so did Jimi.")

The sound itself blew me away. "Purple Haze" was heavy with deliberate distortion and feedback, a swirling stereo soundscape, yet the guitar runs were like lace, clear and distinct even with so much going on. And what to make of those lyrics, thrown out there in that husky voice?

*Purple haze all in my brain*
*Lately things just don't seem the same*
*Actin' funny, but I don't know why*
*'Scuse me while I kiss the sky*

*Whoa,* what was he talking about? What kind of poetry was that? The singing was even stranger because the deep reverb on Jimi's voice made him sound as though he was in the next room. There were African-inspired grunts and clicks, à la Miriam Makeba, and a stop-and-start phrasing that kept you off balance. At the end, he used his customized Octavia pedal to boost his notes by an octave and fly off into the stratosphere with a shimmering guitar solo.

I didn't have the background to dissect "Purple Haze" back then, but I knew it felt fresh and wonderful. While Eric Clapton and Mick Jagger were also bending old blues forms, Hendrix took those same root elements (along with R & B and jazz, a little flamenco, and George Frideric Handel) to go faster, deeper, right out of the solar system. *Are You Experienced* spoke to me in a new language. (And with *Electric Ladyland,* his masterpiece released a year later, he would go further still.)

I got off the last train to Clarksville; once I heard Hendrix, I was hooked. He wasn't for everyone, which made him even more special. I remember another neighbor, Paulette Cotton, a protohippie at the time, who wore funky clothes and burned incense and liked Hendrix almost as much as I did. I felt avant-garde, even if I still looked like a conventional middle-class kid from Seattle. (I wasn't ready to emulate the flower children and hippies in the University District, though I did have a buddy at Lakeside who wore a paisley scarf.)

I bought *Are You Experienced* and played it nonstop on our living room stereo. My mother was dismayed: "How can you stand that, Paul? It's just noise!"

And like generations of teenagers before me, I'd respond, "But mom, *listen* to it. Give it a chance." But when I tried to explain why I loved it, she shook her head and left the room.

My tastes were changing. I bought records by bluesmen like Buddy Guy and B.B. King, and I switched to a progressive FM station that played Hendrix and the Velvet Underground and Cream.

Lakeside had a stereo reel-to-reel setup in the basement of what used to be the school chapel. Whenever I had the chance, I'd use it to record Hendrix songs off the radio: "Like a Rolling Stone" from the Monterey Pop Festival or the feedback-laden national anthem that had astonished people at Woodstock. I was playing the latter back one day when the music department chairman rushed in and said, "Turn that off—stop it! Those are the most awful sounds I have ever heard from an instrument!"

I was embarrassed but defiant. I knew he was wrong. How could anyone who loved music not *get* it? How could they miss what I was hearing?

MY DREAM INSTRUMENT was a Fender Stratocaster like Jimi's. I'd walk past the First Avenue pawnshops that Hendrix himself once haunted and stare at the rows of guitars, so close yet so far. I was sure they'd help me play five times better, but even a used Strat cost several hundred dollars, way beyond my allowance. When I was sixteen, my mother gave me my first electric guitar. She found it at the Wise Penny thrift store and paid five dollars, knowing full well what she'd be in for. The guitar was a bright red Japanese copy of a hollow-body Gibson, with crummy tone and noisy pickups, and I was thrilled to have it.

I tried to crib from Doug Fullmer, who took guitar lessons, but mostly I taught myself. Though I could read a bit from my time with the violin, there was no sheet music for what I wanted to learn. Mostly I just listened to the same records over and over, straining to absorb what I heard as I played along. Looking back, I wish that I'd gotten a teacher, joined a band, laid a firmer foundation in fundamentals and music theory. There is something to be said for the methodical. But Jimi was addictive and I forged on alone with him, making slow but steady progress.

I started with "Hey Joe," a relatively simple song. Then I moved on to "Purple Haze," which Hendrix wrote when first making his name in London. It has a rawness that's missing from his later, studio-oriented compositions, but make no mistake: "Purple Haze" is the work of a fully formed artist. It's a steep challenge for any disciple, and it became my white whale. It took me countless hearings to fumble around and find the chords with Jimi's extra notes hammered on. Hendrix played with otherworldly speed when he soloed, and I was usually overmatched. I'd be absurdly happy when I captured even 25 percent of a riff. I felt like I was slowly cracking the code.

Though I might never be technically polished, I strove to find my own style and put emotion into each note, as Jimi did. Even in songs like "Machine Gun," full of fireworks and special effects, Hendrix was all about expression. When I jammed on "Hey Joe" after school with friends, I'd try to get inside the chord sequences and add a little soulfulness to my solos. I loved the freedom of improvisation, when you could make a song your own.

Now put yourself in my parents' place. Your teenage son is struggling to play along with some really loud music, over and over again, and it's so bad that your dog howls along. With my mother's tolerance nearing its limits, I hooked my instrument into our stereo so I could mute the sound and listen to both record and guitar through my headphones. But whenever I was home alone or just with Jody, I'd crank it up and wail away. That led to my own first brush with feedback, which I thought was pretty cool, though I couldn't even begin to control it the way Jimi did.

IN MAY 1969, when I was in tenth grade, a Lakeside classmate named Jeff Wedgwood clued me in to a Jimi Hendrix Experience show at Seattle Center Coliseum, my first rock concert. With blind dates in tow, we sneaked down close and center for the first three songs before getting kicked back to our real seats behind the stacks of speakers, where you could barely see Jimi unless he was on the apron of the stage. Even so, I was dazzled. Hendrix was a magnetic virtuoso, in total control; I'd come with high expectations, and he blew right past them. The four of us got so high on the music that one of the girls invited us afterward to her house to listen to *Are You Experienced*. Jeff and I buzzed for days.

By the summer of 1970, I was obsessed with all things Hendrix. On weekends I sported button-fly purple bell-bottoms, a medallion around my neck, and a Mississippi River gambler's hat—sort of a poor man's Hendrix hat. In my bedroom I put up a black-and-white poster of Jimi playing with his eyes closed. He wore a dark band jacket and a gold medallion on his bare chest, and his arm shot off in one direction and his upside-down guitar—a leftie, he used a right-handed instrument—in another.

A Seattle native, Hendrix returned that July to play at Sicks' Stadium, a baseball park. This time the seating was open, and my date and I got there early enough to score spots twenty feet from the stage. The weather was dry when Jimi came out, but then it began to drizzle, and soon we had a good Seattle rain. They had prepared a plastic awning to shield him, but Hendrix ignored it. He stood at the edge of the stage with his eyes closed as the rain soaked through his orange velour jumpsuit and water streamed off his Stratocaster. Up close he was a powerful presence, and so mind-crushingly loud that you couldn't always be sure what the song was.

Hendrix looked wiped out that evening, and he didn't play as well as he had at the Coliseum. But Jimi at 60 percent was still something special, especially if you could watch his hands up close. Playing "Voodoo Child" and "Red House" and a few of his newer songs, he'd sail into gorgeously fluid runs with lightning moves along the neck of the guitar and never a wrong note. Hendrix was on the slight side, but his hands were huge and his fingers freakishly long. He could make his Stratocaster "talk" like human speech, fluttering his wrist for a deep vibrato that made the notes sing. There were stretches where he'd play the bass part with his thumb and the lead chords with his fingers, or the rhythm against the lead. It sounded like two guitars coming out of one.

Jimi improvised for much of the concert; his solos were different each night. When great artists play live, they take what's inside them and offer it to the audience. It's both a gift and an invitation: *I'm going way out there, come with me. But after I do some crazy stuff, I'll bring it all the way home.*

Sicks' Stadium was Jimi's last appearance in Seattle. One day after school, two months later, I heard the shocking news: Hendrix had choked to death in his sleep in London after mixing alcohol and barbiturates. I went home that day and played *Electric Ladyland* for hours. My parents took one look at my face and were kind enough not to protest.

My sadness took a while to fade. Jimi had written and recorded so many great songs in just three years, and I couldn't stop thinking about all the music he'd never get a chance to create. He was buried in Renton, just southeast of Seattle, but I never could quite bring myself to visit his grave.

ONE OF MY first major acquisitions as a Hendrix collector was the white Woodstock Stratocaster whose feedback had so appalled the Lakeside music director. I bought it in 1991 for $750,000, a record price for a guitar but not too much, I thought, for a touchstone of rock and guitar history. As I fingered its rusted strings or its headstock, it struck me that it was a tool of Jimi's trade, no more and no less, one of dozens of guitars he went through in his career. The Woodstock Strat wasn't in playing condition, but I did plug another guitar into Jimi's Uni-Vibe, the pedal that created his watery reverb. It felt like I was touching his sound, just a little.

At a Sotheby's auction, I bought a wide-brimmed black felt hat that Hendrix had worn for his *Smash Hits* cover photo. When I opened the box and pulled off the tissue paper, it felt strange to hold that hat in my hands—there was something of Jimi in it. The power of that moment helped spark the idea of creating a public venue to honor his art. I figured that other people would get a kick out of the artifacts, too.

At the time, Hendrix was officially remembered in Seattle by a brass star on an artificial rock at Woodland Park Zoo, nothing more. (Though after our project was under way, the city installed a bronze statue in Capitol Hill of Jimi playing on his knees.) I thought he deserved better. As Jody and I originally conceived it, the Jimi Hendrix Museum would be a ten-thousand-square-foot gallery at the Flag Pavilion, a building from the 1962 World's Fair. I met Al Hendrix, Jimi's father, a gardener who owned the rights to his son's music and legacy. He was a sweet-tempered man and seemed enthused about our idea.

A few months later, Al and Janie Hendrix, Jimi's stepsister, came to my office. "Look," Janie said, "we found out that we're getting ripped off." As Al later claimed in litigation, he'd signed papers on the advice of his then lawyer, Leo Branton, thinking they were licensing deals. But gradually, he said, he came to believe that he'd been deceived into transferring Jimi's legacy to a complex web of companies, all linked to his attorney. Al said he was getting $50,000 a year for intellectual property worth tens of millions of dollars. The family lacked the resources to pursue an all-out lawsuit, so they came to me.

Wanting to help level the playing field, I agreed to cover the family's legal expenses in their effort to recover Jimi's legacy. If the action was successful, they'd repay me out of revenue from the recovered catalog; if it failed, they'd owe me nothing. In April 1993, Al Hendrix filed suit, charging Branton with fraud. Meanwhile, we went ahead with our plans for a nonprofit Jimi Hendrix Museum. We asked the family for the rights to use Jimi's name, likeness, and image, and to display some family memorabilia, making clear that this wasn't a quid pro quo for our support. A memorandum of understanding was drawn.

By mid-1994, I'd advanced $5.9 million for the litigation and chose to stop there. The family had made good progress, and it looked as though they could finish the job without more help. Around that time, licensing negotiations stalled between the family and our museum. I was surprised, but I understood. Losing control of Jimi's legacy had been traumatic for Al and Janie. They were being extra cautious to prevent it from happening again.

In May 1995, a month before the case was to go to trial, the parties agreed to a settlement that conveyed to Al Hendrix "all rights, claims and interests in and to any and all parts of the properties described generally as the Jimi Hendrix legacy. . . ." Though the defendants admitted no wrongdoing, it was a big victory for the Hendrix clan, and I felt good that justice had been done—for the family and for Jimi's music as well.

AFTER A WELL-ATTENDED public hearing back in 1992, we realized that it "wasn't enough to just lay out some clothes and guitars and say this represents creativity," as Jody told a local magazine writer. "We had to have substantial programs to connect the memorabilia with the ideas we were trying to get across." In short, our museum had to tell a story. It needed to place Jimi in the context of his musical heritage in Seattle and the Pacific Northwest. Along the way, I hoped that we might investigate one of the great questions: Where does creativity come from?

This more ambitious institution deserved a new name. I came up with Experience Music Project to imply a place that would always be dynamic, a work in progress. ("Experience," of course, was a tip of the hat to Jimi and his band.) In February 1995, Jody announced that EMP would be sited on a parcel leased from the city near the Space Needle. The museum would expand to 140,000 square feet and end up costing $250 million. My sister is that rare manager who can foster collaboration while injecting direction and urgency. As president and CEO of Vulcan Inc., the holding company we co-founded in 1986 to manage my business affairs and investments, she'd led a wide range of corporate and philanthropic operations on my behalf, including the raising of the Rose Garden and Qwest Field. EMP was a big challenge, but Jody was up to it.

We kept scouring the country for artifacts that fit the museum's mission, like the shard of the guitar that Hendrix had burned and smashed to pieces as a "sacrifice" at the Monterey Pop Festival. Jimi's journal from *Electric Ladyland,* his ultimate studio album, contained song lyrics and girls' phone numbers. His personal record collection, acquired at another Sotheby's auction, leaned heaviest toward Bob Dylan (nine albums), the Beatles (five), and blues great Lightnin' Hopkins (five). Disks showing the most wear included *The Immortal Otis Redding, Crying Time* (Ray Charles), *Bookends* (Simon & Garfunkel), and excerpts from Handel's *Messiah.* The collection was all over the map, like Jimi's imagination.

A BIG FRANK Gehry fan, Jody approached him in 1996, when his Guggenheim Museum in Bilbao, Spain, was still a year from completion. Gehry's own tastes in music were strictly classical, but he had a playful, maverick quality that seemed apt for EMP. Like Jimi, he was fearless. He took on our project, he said, "because it's unique. It's a mountain I haven't climbed." In a meeting at his office in Santa Monica, the start of a multiyear design process, he asked me point-blank: What kind of building did I want?

It was a tough question. I knew that I wanted colors, because Jimi's music—like his painted guitars and wild stage outfits—was anything but monochromatic. Much of Gehry's past work had been rough-edged and angular, but I preferred something more flowing and organic, like the Guggenheim Bilbao. What I wanted most of all, a certain freeness of spirit, wasn't easy to distill into words.

Gehry asked what I liked about Jimi's music, and I reflected on the hundreds of hours I'd spent listening to it. I thought about the way it soared into the stratosphere and then swooped down again. And I said, "I want something swoopy."

The architect steered me to a table packed with models of his work and asked me to choose the "swoopiest." I picked an undulating silver shell, the "horse's head" conference center at Gehry's DG Bank in Berlin. It had powerful curves, even in miniature, and a nonlinear form that reminded me of an improvised Hendrix riff. And Gehry said, "That's just where I wanted to go." His first

three-dimensional model for EMP was an asymmetrical group-
ing of rounded shapes in bright metallic colors, with broken wires
connoting guitar strings along the top. (I fear that I might have
offended Gehry when I said they reminded me of linguine.) Two
tweaks later, with the broken wires morphing into colored glass
strips, I was happy.

With not a single straight line or right angle, EMP had to be
one of the most complicated buildings ever designed. It had a free-
form quality that evoked music, just what I'd been after. We could
have made it square and gray and monochromatic, but wouldn't
that have been boring? EMP is rock-'n'-roll architecture: in your
face, rebellious, larger than life. It's exuberant and fearless, like the
man who inspired it.

We set the tone for EMP's grand opening in June 2000 with
a red-carpet charity fund-raiser the night before. I've hosted my
share of eclectic gatherings, but none more so than this one. Guests
included Grace Slick and Sheryl Crow, Annie Lennox and Gina
Gershon, Bill and Melinda Gates, Jeffrey Katzenberg and Steven
Spielberg. Inside EMP's "On Stage," they all became virtual rock
stars, complete with colored lights, a fog machine, and a digital
crowd screaming adoration.

The night capped eight years of planning and construction. I
celebrated by jamming with Herbie Hancock, Robbie Robertson,
and Dave Stewart in EMP's Sky Church, an open space eighty-five
feet high with a 2,800-square-foot LED screen. It was named after
Jimi's conception of a gathering spot where people of every color
and nationality could make music and set spirits soaring. As we
riffed together, Herbie used chords I didn't know existed, but no
matter. My own spirit flew high that night.

The next morning, at the ribbon-cutting ceremony, I said:

*To create a world-class institution—one which expresses the
dynamic, engaging, rebellious nature of something as powerful and ever-changing as popular music—was no small*

*undertaking. EMP is a unique combination of breathtaking architecture, exhibit design, technology, and, not least, a love for the music itself. . . .*

As I finished, I was handed a Dale Chihuly glass replica of a Fender Stratocaster. In homage to Hendrix, I held it above my head and shouted, "Let the experience begin!" before hopping into the air and smashing it at my feet. It worked almost too well; I hadn't realized that Chihuly's "sugar glass" would shatter into a zillion pieces.

Dale made several other guitar casts in various hues, and I stowed them on one of my boats. Whenever I walk past them, I can't help but smile.

MUSIC MUSEUMS FACE a special challenge, which became clearer to me when I used EMP for "Double Take: From Monet to Lichtenstein," an exhibition of twenty-eight paintings from my collection. Fine art museums celebrate direct experience with the art itself, but you don't need to go to EMP to hear "Purple Haze." And so we didn't conceive our museum as a one-way gallery of worshipful viewers and static objects. Our Sound Lab allows visitors to make their own music and even record their own CD when they are ready. A real guitar is harder to play than *Guitar Hero*, but they may also find that it's more accessible than they suspected. For younger visitors, Sound Lab can lead to one of our teen artist workshops or summer camps, or into our mentoring and scholarship program for those aiming at a music career. Each year we host a pop music conference and a battle of the bands for regional musicians twenty-one and under.

I know how important these opportunities are. The computer room at Lakeside gave me a creative outlet and changed my life. If we can do something similar for other young people through EMP, we'll be honoring Jimi Hendrix in the best way possible: with life-changing experiences for all who are open to them.

\*      \*      \*

I'VE RARELY GONE a week without picking up a guitar. It's more than a hobby; it gives me balance and keeps me in the moment, which can be a challenge with all the projects I'm pursuing at any one time.

I became more serious about playing after Microsoft moved to Bellevue, when I formed my first real band with a group of programmers. We jammed on blues and rock tunes, an ear-opening experience. I'd played along mostly to records up till then, and I had a lot to learn. My technique improved because you need to be more precise when playing with others. We got some gigs at birthdays and wedding receptions at twenty-five dollars a head, which technically made me a professional musician.

In 1996 I formed a band called Grown Men, with Terry Davison, who plays almost every instrument known to humankind. I play rhythm and lead, and write or cowrite most of our original songs. I'm still moved by the power of live music, and I seek it out every chance I get. I've been fortunate to play with many musicians I've admired—including one inspirational session at an EMP Founders Award ceremony, with inductee Billy Cox, Jimi's last bass player and musical partner. Amateur actors could never improvise onstage with a top Shakespearean thespian, but musicians are a welcoming brotherhood. They'll invite you in if you can play even a little bit.

Jams are special times for me. There is nothing like really listening to other players as we feel our way forward together to cover a standard tune or to create something out of thin air. Only a small percentage of these musical ideas become fully realized songs, but the joy is in the process. For someone like me, who tilts toward the analytical, jamming taps into my creative, intuitive, more emotional side. (Dave Stewart put me on to a National Institutes of Health study on how jazz improvisation shuts down the brain's "monitor," encouraging the flow of new ideas.)

When I'm jamming, my shoulders drop and my mind slows. I'm

loose and relaxed. After a good session, I feel physically drained yet wired with nervous energy. I'm refreshed.

ROBBIE ROBERTSON, the songwriter and guitarist who first made history with the Band, is a superb storyteller and music historian. Back in the midsixties, he knew Hendrix in Greenwich Village when they both were young artists. During a visit to Jimi's hotel, Robbie discovered how Hendrix kept his guitars in tune despite the abuse he dished out. When Jimi strung his instrument, Robbie said, he would massage each string in his hands, pulling it tighter and tighter until it was stretched to the point where it had no more give and couldn't possibly go out of tune. The process took a full forty minutes. "Jimi Hendrix," Robbie said, "just *oozed* music."

Another time, after a jam in New York's Meatpacking District, the two of them didn't emerge until morning. A construction worker outside the club said, "You guys are pretty good. Keep playing, you're going to be famous one day."

YOU NEVER KNOW what you'll talk about the first time you meet someone. Mick Jagger is a history buff and a serious student of different cultures. But when we first met, he asked me, "What do you know about garden design?" He was landscaping his place in France and wanted to do it right.

Jean Pigozzi, the Italian businessman and photographer, invited me to Mick's fifty-sixth birthday party at his waterfront estate during the Cannes Film Festival. I brought some equipment from my boat—guitars, amplifiers, drum set—and found plenty of co-conspirators to jam with, including Jonny Lang (only eighteen at the time) and Ronnie Wood, the Stones' guitarist. That night gave me a taste of what it's like to make music with a world-class sideman. Whatever I played, Ronnie instantly added the perfect rhythmic counterpart. It was as though he knew what I would do before my fingers touched the strings.

I kept nudging Mick to join us, but he was reluctant. Later in the evening, I asked Bono for help. And Bono said, "I know what'll work. I'll get up and start singing his song really slowly. Then he'll have to sing."

We went up together, and I dove into that famous, driving guitar riff as Bono launched into a soulful "Satisfaction" at about half-speed. I saw Jagger looking surprised—*What the hell is going on here?* By the end of the first verse, he could hold back no longer; he grabbed the microphone and picked up the song in the same slow groove. I was playing "Satisfaction" behind Mick Jagger, an insane proposition for an amateur guitar player. And Bono looked at me and nodded: *I told you so.*

I take music with me wherever I go. My boats carry a full complement of instruments, and each has a recording studio. My musician friends periodically make use of them—often for fun, on occasion to work on their next albums. Last year, Dave Stewart brought his new world-music supergroup on board: Mick Jagger; A. R. Rahman, the Indian composer and instrumentalist; and Joss Stone, the young English soul singer. (Reggae artist Damian Marley stayed home for the imminent birth of his first child.)

I first met Dave more than fifteen years ago at a dinner in New York, not long after he and Annie Lennox disbanded the Eurythmics, and we hit it off. He's full of energy and genuinely curious about all sorts of things, including the latest trends in technology. When he's not on stage, you wouldn't know he's a rock star.

Dave visited me in Seattle a few years ago and had his hair bleached blond. Then he came with me while I got a haircut at a place on University Avenue, where he began running his video camera—for Dave, life is a documentary. I was still in the chair when two beefy bikers entered the shop to get their beards trimmed. They had tattoos up and down their arms and across their necks, and Dave asked if he could film them.

*Oh no,* I thought. The bikers were bound to take offense at this nosy guy with long yellow hair and a camera, and then all bets would be off. But Dave has such a sweet way about him that the bikers happily explained the origins of each tattoo: "I got this one in Iraq. . . ."

I used to call Dave "Mr. Permission" because he's like a pied piper, spurring you to follow your muse. He encouraged me to write the lyrics for *Grown Men,* the album I produced in 2000. It was the sort of thing I'd dreamed of doing, as I like to say, before getting sidetracked by technology. I dug down and put my deepest feelings into those lyrics, and the results surprised even me. (When I played the cuts for my mom, she said, "But all the songs are so sad. I wanted you to write happy songs.")

Another time Dave joined Grown Men at a battle of the bands for charity in Las Vegas. After our sound check, I noticed a stack of animal carriers and a bored-looking person standing next to them.

"What are they for?" I asked.

The guy said, "They're for the armadillo race tonight."

"The race? What time is that?"

"They're going off at nine o'clock."

My band was scheduled for 7:30. Dave took it all in and said dryly, "Paul, this is what my career has come to. I'm opening for an armadillo race."

PETER GABRIEL IS the kind of person who always asks if you'd like a cup of afternoon tea. He's a Renaissance man who can speak with equal authority about Senegalese drumbeats and modern art. The tiny hotel he keeps in Sardinia is his oasis of relaxation.

In 2005, the hot news from the Live 8 benefit concerts was the reunion of Pink Floyd, twenty-four years after their last show together. At a lunch with Peter, I talked with the band's drummer, Nick Mason, and asked him about the experience. I said, "You guys must have had a real lovefest backstage after the concert."

Nick paused and said, "Actually, Paul, we shook hands. And for Englishmen, that's a lovefest."

I first met Nick after Peter remarried and we celebrated on my boat with a jam. We played some Beatles songs and then a Pink

Floyd number, and everyone was loose and having a great time. I was enthusing about it afterward with Terry Davison, who said, "Yeah, that drummer played really well on the Pink Floyd tune."

"You thought so?" I said.

"Yeah," he said, "he really seemed to know it."

And I said, "Terry, he *is* the drummer for Pink Floyd."

DAVE WAS WRITING a song with Paul McCartney in the late nineties when he invited me to join him at McCartney's studio outside London. As I watched them record, it was surreal to hear the ex-Beatle—that unmistakable voice I'd known since grade school—over a studio monitor a few feet away.

When Dave called a break, Paul showed me around the studio, which could have provided the core exhibit for a very good music museum. Here was the Mellotron that the Beatles used for their haunting string sound in "Strawberry Fields Forever" and "Lucy in the Sky with Diamonds." There was McCartney's bass guitar from Shea Stadium in 1966, one of the band's last live performances. When Paul flipped it over, I saw something taped to its back: a yellowing set list.

Paul said, "I'm supposed to look at some pictures for a Beatles anthology. Would you like to come?" We crossed to a shed lined with photographs of the Beatles from every period of their career. As Paul considered which ones he liked best, he became pensive. Then he said, "Everyone wants to talk about John, John, John. You know, I wrote some songs, too."

I was taken aback, but I had to say something: "You've written some of the most amazing songs ever." Which was true, but it felt strange trying to cheer up a Beatle who was still trying to compete with a fallen bandmate.

McCartney cast his own shadow, of course. As Bono once told me, "Every day I wake up with the Beatles." Bono's longtime ambition was to lead the biggest band in the world, which he's pretty much accomplished with U2. But he's still striving to write songs that stand up to the great Beatles tunes, and it ain't easy, even for the most talented musicians.

I met Paul again with Dave a few years later at the Abbey Road Studios in London, where the Beatles had so many historic recording sessions. They were working on another song, this one in connection with the "46664" project, which Dave named after Nelson Mandela's prison number. Paul's band smoothly cranked through the material. For really good studio musicians, playing is like breathing; those guys polished off four-part harmonies in three takes. I got so caught up in the process that I overcame my reticence and said to Dave, "On that last chorus, where everything builds, it would be great to have some piano."

Dave said, "Let me ask Paul." A minute or two later they rolled out a little upright piano that they'd used on many Beatles songs. Paul warmed up with some honky-tonk, and then he said, "OK, let's roll it." Just like that, he recorded a piano overdub on the out chorus, and that's the way "Whole Life" was released.

I'VE LISTENED TO "Purple Haze" literally thousands of times. I still find new things in it, particularly in the rhythms and the guitars' interplay. (One phenomenal aspect of Hendrix is that the greatest lead guitarist of all time, as ranked by *Rolling Stone*, was also peerless on rhythm guitar.) It wasn't until the late 1980s that I found the song's charts in a French magazine, with Jimi's solos transcribed note-for-note, exactly what I needed to master the unconventional fingering patterns. Twenty years after I'd started, playing along with a cassette, I finally got through "Purple Haze" at tempo. Though it had been all I could do to keep up, I was euphoric.

Through Dan Aykroyd, my band has been invited to open House of Blues franchises in Las Vegas, Dallas, and New Jersey. As with many musicians, my self-consciousness recedes in performance. When it all clicks, and I can feel the audience with me on my solo, I play that much better. Our band did well enough in

Dallas to take an encore, and I damned the torpedoes and went with "Purple Haze." Over the next three minutes, all those years of listening and absorbing and practicing came together. I'm still not the most technically accomplished guitarist, but I always try to go for a few "killer moments," as Jimi called them, where I dig in and reach for a note that has some real soul and power to it. With Hendrix, just playing the notes isn't nearly enough. You have to feel them, too.

That night, I hit everything I went for. The solo built and built, and then I caught my breath and took it in a different direction, and it built again to a great finish. The audience was on their feet and cheering, even singing along with the third chorus. It was probably my best live performance, a more than decent version of an incredibly challenging song.

I knew I'd never play it the way Jimi did, but I was satisfied.

# CHAPTER 18

# WIRED WORLD

It all began for me in the late 1980s with a small company based south of Seattle: SkyPix, the world's first direct digital broadcast satellite system. According to its business plan, a one-time customer fee of $699 would buy pay-per-view Hollywood releases with none of the ghosting or snow that plagued analog cable TV reception of the day. Less than two feet in diameter, the SkyPix dish was much smaller and cheaper than the C-Band (known colloquially as BUD, for "big ugly dish") that I'd been using on Mercer Island. And I was impressed by satellite's potential. With a signal that could be beamed nationally from day one, SkyPix wouldn't be burdened by cable's capital-intensive, dig-a-trench-to-the-home infrastructure.

In 1991, three years before the launch of DirecTV, I took a flier and invested $10 million. A year later, amid an SEC investigation alleging securities fraud, SkyPix collapsed into bankruptcy without selling a single dish. It was a bloodbath, but it opened my eyes to the potential of new digital delivery technologies. If my experience with computers had taught me anything, it was never to underestimate how quickly a new platform could bring a wave of change. How would a fire hose of digital bits, blasted into the home, affect our consumption of video, or data, or music? What were the opportunities?

By November 1992, months before the first graphical Web browser, I was telling *Business Week* that we were on the cusp of a "Wired World" with vast ramifications. "At some point," I said, "everybody in the industrialized world will have access to computers, and they'll all be wired together." My vision dated back to the earliest days of Microsoft, when I'd talk Bill's ear off about a connected future in which services and information would be accessible—anytime, anywhere. In my 1977 interview with *Microcomputer Interface,* I predicted that the personal computer would far outstrip the social impact of the pocket calculator.

> *. . . the computer—and I'm talking about the home information retrieval system—I think that's a much more powerful concept than a machine that just adds, subtracts, multiplies, and divides. Definitely. If you take [the computer to] its limit, perhaps you could have groceries delivered, take care of all your bills and, if you're a programmer, you could do your work at home, never leaving the house. That's a dramatic change.*

As of the early 1990s, social applications were just beginning to take root. Our human drive for connectivity had spurred the recent development of CompuServe and America Online, and it wouldn't stop there. Like the personal computer, the Wired World fit my criterion for a big idea, the marriage of two powerful elements. On March 31, 1992, I told the *New York Times*:

> *If you look down the road, what you see is the pervasiveness of high-bandwidth data communications and completely inexpensive computing power. If you combine those two things, there are many interesting things you can do.*

At the time, digital fiber-optic technology and new compression techniques held the promise of lightning-fast, two-way multimedia networks, a global platform for new families of products and applications. High-speed data delivery—the so-called information superhighway—would redefine how we talked and learned and experienced entertainment. The computer would evolve from a tool for work into a medium for content of all sorts.

These developments weren't speculative, in my view. A high-bandwidth network would be built, and people would use it—I was sure of that. Less easy to foresee was who would do the connecting. Satellite or cable? Telecom or wireless, or something yet unimagined? But regardless of how the delivery system played out, I was determined to be part of it. I invested in more than a hundred Internet, media, and communications companies, expecting some to pan out and some not. It seemed wise to spread out my bets as the Wired World took shape.

I FIRST NOTICED America Online in the late eighties, when there was no Internet consumer presence to speak of. Entrée to the embryonic online network required special software for access to a rudimentary bulletin board system—or, for a friendlier graphical user interface, one of the new network service providers. The genius of America Online (in its pre-acronym days) was its accessible online experience for computer novices. Simple to install, it was the Internet with training wheels: one-stop shopping for proprietary content (news, weather, games, stock quotes), plus embedded links to other companies' "storefronts" before the dawn of modern Web sites. As the engine for the public's early embrace of e-mail, America Online also helped introduce chat rooms and instant messaging. A budding powerhouse of interactivity, it was a natural partner for my Wired World, and in 1992 I bought fifty thousand shares. Convinced that the stock market had underestimated the value of connecting tens of millions of users, I began building my position in earnest that summer. Ten months later, I owned 15 percent of the company.

My hope was for America Online to move from a low-bandwidth, dial-up network to the inevitable high-speed future. In the spring of 1993, I traveled to Virginia to meet with CEO and chairman Steve Case and his team. As I laid out my ideas for a broadband network, I could feel the chill in the air. Case and I were oil and water. He was wedded to his dial-up walled garden, even if it meant limiting content to what an analog network could handle, and found my ideas about broadband too far ahead of his game plan. It probably didn't help that I was still Microsoft's second biggest stockholder and a member of its board. Though Microsoft had yet to do much of anything online, Case perceived it as his greatest threat.

Actually, he had it backward. I wanted to use my stake in America Online as a hedge *against* my holdings in Microsoft and other Wired World investments. As I kept snapping up shares, Case's board adopted a poison-pill threshold, first at 20 percent (which I'd already passed) and then at 25 percent. Once triggered, the provision would dilute my ownership percentage and make it next to impossible to mount a hostile takeover. That was never my intent, since takeovers rarely work in tech companies. But I took the hint that my active collaboration wasn't welcome.

I held on to my piece of the company until the summer of 1994, when Bert Kolde attended an open house at Bill Gates's home on Lake Washington. Microsoft had recently targeted the network services business with an initiative called Blackbird, a precursor to the Microsoft Network. Bill approached Bert in a buffet line on the lawn, and the conversation turned to my interest in America Online. Bill said, "Why would Paul want to compete with us? I'm just going to tell Russ Siegelman [the Microsoft Network leader] to keep losing money every year until we have the number-one market share in online. How does it make sense to compete with that?"

When Bert relayed Bill's remarks to me, they had the intended effect. A year earlier, I'd attended a meeting at Microsoft where Bill had told Case that he was thinking about buying all or part of America Online—or, à la Khrushchev, that he might decide to "bury" the smaller company. Now it sounded like Bill had settled on a burial. I could see Steve Case trapped in a two-front war, besieged on one flank by Microsoft and on the other by the emerging World Wide Web. Suddenly my stake seemed less attractive, especially without any synergy between America Online and my other ventures. I dumped my stock and took a $75 million profit.

Within a year, as online traffic exploded, Bill realized that the threat wasn't America Online, after all. It was Netscape Navigator, the newly hatched Web browser that became the centerpiece of the Internet. Blackbird was aborted. In May 1995, Bill issued his famous memo, "The Internet Tidal Wave," and fast-tracked the release of Internet Explorer. The browser wars were on.

Out of Bill's crosshairs, AOL thrived through the go-go years of the late nineties. The company had obvious points of vulnerability, from its slow adoption of broadband to the growing migration of content to the Web. But the tech boom masked AOL's weaknesses, and sometimes scale alone carries the day, at least until something a lot better comes along. In January 2000, five years after I'd sold my stock, AOL announced the acquisition of Time Warner. When I first heard the rumors, I thought that AOL's market cap (an outlandish $163 billion) was wildly overvalued. Just three years later, the *New York Times* would call the merger "the greatest enduring monument to the folly of the Internet boom."

Still, one hard fact remains. Had I held on to my 24.9 percent of America Online, I would have been sitting on a $40 billion bonanza, more than all the money I'd make from my stake in Microsoft.

AS I LOOKED for more commercial opportunities in the Wired World, the ticket business seemed like a natural fit. It had a mass clientele, and I could add value with a range of interactive features: search functions, preorders, seat location graphics. In November 1993, after Microsoft backed off from a last-minute bid, I paid over $300 million for 80 percent of Ticketmaster. Thrown into the deal were the services of the company's tough-talking president and CEO, Fred Rosen. Since joining Ticketmaster in 1982, Fred had built it from a group of straggling regional ticketing services into a billion-dollar behemoth that dominated the industry. He cut deals with venues and paid preemptive fees for exclusive rights. Nobody dared cross him.

I thought that Fred and I should get to know each other, so I flew to Los Angeles to join him for dinner and then Steely Dan's reunion tour at the Hollywood Bowl. We got great Ticketmaster seats, tenth row center, and Fred slept through most of the concert. He wasn't much of a music fan.

Ticketmaster had built its dominance via two modes of customer service. Say you wanted to go to a U2 concert. You could: (a) stand in line at one of Fred's retail outlets at a record store or (b) call a Ticketmaster phone bank and hope you wouldn't be on hold for too long. My solution was to move the operation online. We could create a Web site and link our service to sites in the sports and entertainment fields, from the Super Bowl to the Rolling Stones' next U.S. tour. These were fresh ideas; Amazon.com was two years away, and e-commerce still in its infancy. A few people made airline and hotel reservations online with AOL or Prodigy, but the Web had yet to catch on as a way of selling entertainment.

It definitely hadn't caught on with Fred Rosen. Though his business had been computerized for years, he fought me tooth and nail over taking it online. Every so often, I'd ask him how development of the new ticketing system was going, and Fred would metamorphose into a high-decibel, old-school promoter. "I'm not selling tickets online," he'd roar, "because the banks won't take the credit cards and the customers won't trust the security! You have to go with me on this, Paul!"

I'd hold the phone three feet from my ear as I tried to get a word in: "But Fred . . ."

"You don't understand this business, Paul! I've been doing this forever, and people aren't going to print out their tickets at home—it ain't gonna work, Paul! I'm not going to do it! And the tickets can be forged or stolen, and then what do we do?"

"But Fred . . ."

"My customer isn't the guy who buys the ticket. My customer is the venue, and they're not going to go for this! It's just not gonna fly!" Finally, after twenty minutes of bluster, he'd run down and mutter, "It's OK, we're making progress. It's coming along."

Two years later, Fred grudgingly gave his blessing to our ticketing Web site. It was a complex piece of software engineering that tackled credit-card clearance, user authentication, and real-time database updates. At last all was at the ready. When customer number one had completed the first transaction, our Web people called him and said, "Congratulations, you just bought the first concert ticket in the history of the Internet! Can you tell us why you decided to buy online?"

The man said, "Because I don't like talking to people, and I don't like talking to you." And he hung up.

Rosen fatigue took its toll. In 1997 I sold my stake in Ticketmaster to Barry Diller's Home Shopping Network, receiving equity in return in Diller's USA Networks, Inc. I sold that stock in 2002 and doubled my original investment. Barry parted company with Fred, and before long Ticketmaster was conducting 90 percent of its business online.

AROUND THE TIME I bought Ticketmaster, I was addressing a central question for the Wired World: What kind of content would people want most from a broadband network? To find an answer, I founded a start-up called Starwave as a new-medium software publishing company and hired an ambitious president, a former Microsoft executive named Mike Slade. We brainstormed as a test market of two. We were both obsessive sports fans, and our first idea was probably our best: to develop the world's most comprehensive sports information source.

Sports is intrinsically data driven, the natural raw material for computer software. A fair portion of the population tracks it on a daily basis. Mike and I wanted more in-depth coverage than we could get in the *Seattle Times,* whose sports section could barely hold all of the box scores. We wanted to keep up with games inning by inning, even pitch by pitch. Most of all, we wanted stats, *lots* of stats, that people could sort as they pleased.

Existing Internet services were simply dumping the Associated Press sports wire online, which meant their products wouldn't be hard to beat. After flirting with a pair of AOL competitors, who quickly went belly up, our new plan was to partner with a recognized sports brand and publish directly to the Internet. The Web was sparsely populated, and page downloads slower than slow; Mike's staff was building a Web site for an infrastructure that didn't yet exist. But our strategy turned out to be correct. An independent site, with hyperlinks to many others, could deliver richer, more imaginative content than any walled garden. And, as we'd discover, it could make a lot more money.

*Sports Illustrated* passed, but we found a warmer reception at ESPN, the young TV network then owned by Cap Cities. After making a splash with a half-hour national broadcast called *SportsCenter,* ESPN was eager to expand online. Under a five-year licensing deal we signed in 1995, Starwave would generate original content and operate the Web site. ESPN would lend its on-air muscle to promote the site with twice-hourly address crawls. Revenues would be divided.

We turned on the site that spring, and SportsZone reinvented sports coverage on the fly. It combined the local focus of newspapers with the depth of magazines, the immediacy of TV, and the real-time power of the Internet. The site debuted during the NCAA's Final Four weekend, which happened to be held in Seattle that year, and we seized the opportunity to post the first online sports video clip: Bryant "Big Country" Reeves shattering a backboard at a Kingdome practice session. Though the clip was the size of a postage stamp and wouldn't work without a high-speed connection, it caused a sensation.

SportsZone pioneered real-time game stats. (Our NBA scores were updated three times a quarter, which was unheard of.) We were the first to organize wire-service copy into interactive hierarchies (sports/baseball/clubhouse/Giants/Barry Bonds), the first to offer an interactive database of statistics. We had the original sports fantasy games, online polling, and live sports chats. By Labor Day, we were supplementing SportsZone's free "front porch" with a paid premium area, which demonstrated that strong online content could sell ads and win subscribers.

We quickly built a massive content base of 60,000 text pages, 6,000 photos, 2,500 audio clips, 1,000 video clips. SportsZone became the world's biggest sports section, hands down. But only 7 percent of American households were online in 1995, almost all of them on dial-up modems. Low bandwidth rendered much of our site too slow to be practical. We had the best product of its kind, but how would it reach the public?

Fortunately, we hadn't reckoned with the size of the "goof off at work" market. People might not feel comfortable cracking open a newspaper at their desk, but they could steal two minutes to check on a fantasy team on their computer screen. SportsZone traffic spiked highest on Monday mornings, when young men used Ethernet hookups at their offices to peruse the weekend scores and recaps. We had another surge at noon, as people headed out to lunch and the West Coast folks were sitting down, and another at five, as people prepared to head home. By mid-1996, the site was recording 7.5 million hits a day, up to 12 million during the summer Olympics in Atlanta. Our core demographic, affluent males under thirty-five, would maximize dollars per click. SportsZone didn't merely change the pattern of sports news consumption. It set the standard for commercial, content-based Web sites.

Encouraged, Starwave developed sponsored sites for the NBA, the NFL, and NASCAR, and also branched into entertainment.

Another Starwave site, Outside Online, broke the Mount Everest story by Jon Krakauer that later became the bestselling book *Into Thin Air.* The *New York Times* rewrote our posts and credited Outside Online, one of the first uses of the Internet as a real-time news medium.

In 1998, shortly before our licensing contract was set to expire, I sold my interest in Starwave for $350 million to Disney, ESPN's new owner. SportsZone's legacy survives today as ESPN.com, still the leading sports content Web site.

I NEVER FORGOT my sneak peek into the future at Xerox PARC, one of a long line of seminal think tanks that dreamed up the electric light, the phonograph, and the transistor. By the early 1990s, it seemed to me that we needed a similar wellspring for digital technology and media. Most R & D in the field was skewed to short-term development, with an eye to that year's profits. Who would take a longer view and bring home the next wave of breakthroughs?

In 1992 I founded Interval Research in Palo Alto, California, just a short walk from PARC. To direct it, I hired David Liddle, a former PARC scientist who'd led the development team for the Xerox Star, the commercialized version of the Alto. In announcing Interval, I said:

> There are a number of interesting technologies just over the horizon, but they aren't ready for a typical two-year product cycle. . . . David and I have a vision of future computing that is far from anything we see today. We intend Interval to pursue that vision.

Interval was designed as a for-profit venture with an exploratory approach, what *Wired* would call "an unusual hybrid between an industrial research lab and a venture capital fund." Or as Liddle put it, "a PARC without a Xerox." Like PARC, Interval had a mandate to incubate next-generation applications. Unlike PARC, it aimed to turn those innovations into licensed products or spin them off as new companies. The plan was for it to become self-sustaining within ten years.

At full strength, Interval employed more than a hundred scientists and researchers, recruited from top institutions like Stanford, MIT, and Bell Labs. We had stars like Lee Felsenstein, designer of the Osborne 1, the first portable computer; Jim Boyden, a father of the inkjet printer; and David Reed, inventor of the communications protocols that made the Internet possible. The staff was nothing if not eclectic. Liddle hired journalists and virtual-reality artists, anthropologists and musicians, even a parapsychologist. Artists were essential, as Liddle told *Fortune*, to push new technology "to the edge of what's possible. . . . You need unreasonable people doing things for reasons they can't verbalize."

On paper, Interval had it all: talent, resources, and the time to pursue the frontiers of technology. Its leader was ferociously smart, articulate, and unafraid of risk. In the end, though, the lab was a case study of good intentions gone wrong. My heart sank when David told me that he relied on the researchers to decide when to discontinue their own projects, a prescription for what I call the running-man syndrome. Picture a man running uphill toward a goal. He gets tired and thirsty, but he'll keep running until management applies a fitness test and winnows out ideas without promise. "When Interval began, we just did cool things," one of our video artists told *Wired*. "It was 100 percent research, 0 percent development." Lacking focus on the marketplace, Interval got sidetracked into paranormal phenomena, interactive robots, and alternative art installations—or "sidelines and weirdness," as one of the scientists put it. In our effort to buffer people from bottom-line pressures, we went too far the other way.

The Wired World was a wide-ranging vision, and Bill Savoy, the point man for my private investment firm, Vulcan Capital, was a compulsive dealmaker. I should have slowed him down. By the midnineties, involved in 140 companies, I wasn't able to give

Interval sufficient direction or keep it focused on the Internet. Over its eight-year life span, Interval spun off seven start-ups. They were generally ill-conceived or premature, and all but one or two foundered in the marketplace. None made real money.

Among the lab's more tantalizing, ahead-of-its-time ideas was the Mouse of Life, a "magic wand" that could be waved at any barcode for instant product information, from the supermarket price of a can of corn to the ownership history of a used Buick. (This concept is now reemerging as a cell-phone application.) Then there was WebPad, an experimental touch-screen platform—an amalgam of a Web browser, e-mail terminal, GPS mapping display, PDA, and home television remote control. With a 10.7-inch display and a weight of less than two pounds, WebPad was a conceptual forerunner of the iPad. But it would have cost at least a thousand dollars to retail, a major obstacle to consumer acceptance back then.

In 1999, I made a last-ditch stab to redirect Interval toward interactive video and broadband cable television projects. After a foray into three-dimensional cameras, a progenitor of 3-D TV and movies, I conceded defeat. Though Interval developed several potentially groundbreaking ideas and registered about three hundred patents (some of which may turn out to be quite valuable), the lab and its spin-offs had proven ineffective in exploiting them. In April 2000, after investing $300 million, I shut it down. Like others who have tried to walk the same path, I concluded that Xerox PARC was probably unique to its time and place. It would not be easily replicated.

These days, I'm disinclined to invest in completely open-ended research. I've learned that creativity needs tangible goals and hard choices to have a chance to flourish.

IN THE EARLY nineties, the Ticketmaster business had me flying to Los Angeles twice a month and into the Hollywood orbit. My higher profile brought an invitation to the Sun Valley summer retreat hosted by Herb Allen, the financier with deep ties to the entertainment industry. I met David Geffen there and found that we had common passions, notably art and music. Geffen was smart, charming, and full of advice on how to run your business and your life.

He was a great persuader. One day he called me with the news that he was starting a new film studio called DreamWorks SKG with Steven Spielberg and Jeffrey Katzenberg. It was a masterful soft sell. "I don't know if you're interested," he told me, "but you can have your financial guys contact my guys. We'd love to have you be part of our team."

I didn't need much coaxing; I was flattered that he'd asked and intrigued by the venture. I'd been a passionate movie buff since growing up with genre triple-features at Seattle's Colonial Theater. (Sometime later, when Seattle's classic movie palace, the Cinerama, was about to be torn down, I stepped in to buy it and restored it to its former glory.) I'd already been scouting movie studios as possible investments before Geffen called.

DreamWorks represented something special, the first new major Hollywood studio in decades. It was a chance to get involved with some of the most creative minds in the business: Spielberg, the genius auteur; Katzenberg, the razor-sharp perfectionist; Geffen, the consummate dealmaker. Together they seemed ready to join me in creating a new convergence of entertainment and digital technology. Maybe we'd use content from the studio to enrich the value of the broadband pipe. Or we might form a strategic partnership with Starwave. It was the beginning of the dot-com bubble, and anything seemed possible.

In March 1995, I put up $500 million, the single biggest investment I'd made to that point. In hindsight, it wasn't such a great deal. While my half-billion dollars bought an 18.5 percent stake, the three principals put up a total of $100 million for two thirds; I paid eighteen times more per point of equity. Worse, I was taking the lion's share of the risk without equivalent voting rights.

The principals' pitch was that they'd be putting in valuable sweat equity. But as Tom King wrote in *The Operator*, the deal was structured according to Geffen's MO:

> *In his previous businesses, Geffen had proven to be a risk-averse executive, masterful at limiting overhead. But with such capital intensive plans as building an animation company from the ground up, Geffen realized that staggering overhead would be unavoidable for DreamWorks. Thus, he brilliantly employed another tactic that had worked so well for him in the past: Use other people's money.*

I didn't plan to be a passive investor in DreamWorks. While I wouldn't have dreamed of intruding on the moviemaking, I was given to believe that I'd have a say in the company's broad direction. A press release described me as a member of the studio's board of directors who would "also have input on DreamWorks' strategy, particularly in the areas of multimedia and interactive development." The three principals went on to say:

> *We are excited about our partnership with Paul because his vision and technology expertise complement our interests in film, animation, music and television. Paul Allen was one of the first people in the world to realize technology would bring about a fundamental, positive change in the way people live and work—he's the perfect partner for a company that is committed to building the digital studio of the 21st century.*

I have no way of telling whether their professed enthusiasm was authentic, but one thing is certain. My creative opportunity would fall short of my expectation.

The studio took three years to release its first movie, and the television and record departments lagged as well. In 1999, I took a

50 percent stake in a joint venture by DreamWorks and Ron Howard's Imagine Entertainment. It was called Pop.com, a short-film production company for the Internet, what initially seemed like the perfect Wired World application. The problem was that we overestimated both the adoption curve for broadband and the appetite for short-form videos. Millions were entering AOL chat rooms or downloading songs from Napster, but less than one in ten households had high-speed connections. Without one, a six-minute short could take up to an hour to load. Pop.com closed a year after it opened. Like SkyPix, it was hatched before its time.

I had great moments with DreamWorks. When *American Beauty* won the Academy Award for best picture and I met Kevin Spacey at an after-party, he was over the moon, clutching his Oscar as though he'd never let it go. Then there was the time Spielberg invited me onto the set of *The Lost World,* the *Jurassic Park* sequel. For hours I observed a laborious sequence of takes and retakes and camera setups. For someone uninvolved in the process, it was like watching beautiful paint dry.

Katzenberg periodically ushered board members to dog-and-pony shows at the studio, but he seemed resistant when I suggested that he shift completely from cel-based animation to the computer-generated format used in *Shrek*. (He got there a few years later. Today, all DreamWorks animated films are made in 3-D computer-generated imagery, or CGI.) I did make one aesthetic contribution, however. At a *Shrek* screening, I had the nagging sense that something was wrong. Then it came to me that the title character's footsteps weren't disturbing the ground. I pointed it out to Katzenberg, who told me later that he'd gotten it fixed.

Its thoroughly modern image notwithstanding, DreamWorks treated investors in the Old Hollywood tradition: *Give us your money, and we'll introduce you to some interesting people. But we really don't want your input.* The board's input was minimal. Katzenberg would outline the company's plans and tell us that everything was good, and tomorrow would be even better. DreamWorks was 180 degrees from the self-flagellating culture I'd known at Microsoft.

By 2003, with record companies devalued by file sharing, the studio's music division had been sold. Plans for interactive computer games and other Internet ventures were shelved with the dotcom crash, and the live-action division continued to falter. The studio came back to me periodically for cash, more than $200 million in all, and my stake grew to 24 percent. After a series of bombs, notably *Sinbad: Legend of the Seven Seas,* my investment was under water. By the terms of our agreement, I could soon exercise my option to start cashing out. It no longer seemed prudent to wait.

In 2004, after hammer-and-tongs negotiations, DreamWorks agreed to spin off its animation division—its one consistent source of profit—in an initial public offering. I divested slowly to avoid destabilizing the stock, and got another chunk of my investment back when the live-action division was sold off to Viacom in 2006. The following year I resigned from the board.

When the smoke cleared, I wound up more or less doubling my money. After a dozen years in the glamorous, high-wire world of film production, I would have done about as well with a certificate of deposit. I just didn't mesh well with Hollywood. I could never tell how much of what people told me was real.

Even so, DreamWorks failed to sour me on the art of moviemaking. I continued to work with Richard Hutton on my own film company, Vulcan Productions. We followed a distinctly non-Hollywood formula of bare-bones budgets (as little as $1 million or less for live-action releases), creative freedom for directors, and generous revenue-sharing deals. Our documentaries (notably *Evolution* and *Rx for Survival: A Global Health Challenge*) won three Peabody awards, as well as an Emmy for Outstanding Informational Programming. The U.S. Defense Department will be distributing 200,000 tool kits with *This Emotional Life,* our series on human psychology, for returning servicemen and their families.

Among our feature films, *Hard Candy* and *Where God Left His Shoes* won outstanding reviews, while *Far from Heaven,* with Julianne Moore and Dennis Quaid, earned four Oscar nominations. Films like those reminded me of the magic of great acting and directing and screenwriting. And how much I enjoy sitting in a dark room, watching a great story unfold.

CHAPTER 19

# FAT PIPE

Prescience is a double-edged sword. If you're a little early, you might hit the jackpot with Altair BASIC or Starwave. But if you're too far ahead of technology or the market, you can wind up with something like Metricom.

With the advent of digital cellular technology in the early 1990s, it occurred to me that the Wired World "pipe" for the global network of the future might not be wired, after all. The appeal of wireless technology, named untethered access, was obvious. Because most people move from home to work to shops and restaurants in their daily lives, I thought the Internet should travel with them. Who *wouldn't* want to surf the Web when riding in a car, or check e-mail in the shoe department at Nordstrom's?

In 1993, I bought my first shares in Metricom, a broadband mobile data provider with national aspirations. At the time, it was the one reliable wireless avenue to the Web. A Metricom customer could Velcro a modem to a laptop and get consistent digital service throughout a wide area network, or WAN, from the corner coffee shop to the airport gate. It was a grand idea, and soon I'd built a controlling interest. But Metricom's business model was strategically flawed. The company tried to get too big too fast, in too many markets at once. As installation lagged behind manufacturing, piles of very expensive equipment filled our warehouses and drained our working capital. Given that Web browsing was still a novelty (our national subscription base peaked at around 51,000), a fast-tracked rollout was an act of hubris.

As Metricom's losses mounted, financing dried up. Telecom investors were among the first to hit bottom in the dot-com bust, and they had little left to invest. Meanwhile, mobile phone companies began to pour billions into their digital 2G wireless networks, with cell-based systems and cheaper chipsets.

Metricom filed for bankruptcy in July 2001. Just one year later, the BlackBerry smartphone would confirm my intuition that people were eager for mobile data. Five years after that, the iPhone would help establish a mass market for it. But consumers weren't quite ready for our product, and inept management was the coup de grâce. Metricom demonstrated the many pitfalls that lie between an idea's genesis and its execution.

ON AUGUST 9, 1995, Netscape doubled the opening share price for its initial public offering to $28 then watched the price soar to $75 by the end of the day. As the Internet continued to gain traction, I could see that it would soon swamp walled gardens like AOL. There could no longer be any doubt about the essential platform for the Wired World: It was going to be the Internet. By 1996, 36 million people were using the Web regularly, more than double the total from one year before.

For me, just one question remained. What pipe was best suited for bringing data streams into the home, to accommodate both the Web sites of the day and the more demanding content of the future? In 1995, twisted-pair phone lines ran analog networks at 28,800 bits per second (bps). DSL, which piggybacked on the copper lines, was rated at 128,000 bps. Satellite broadcast operators offered a broadband signal at a more competitive 12 million bps, but they were hamstrung by going predominantly one way, from operator to consumer, which made Internet service impractical.

That left cable TV, the poor-relation delivery system best

known for mediocre video quality, terrible service, and a lethargic monopoly mentality. Even so, it held the most promise for the long term—you could tell by the capacity of its pipes. Coaxial cable carried 10 million bits per second; optical fiber cable, the distribution backbone, 2.4 *billion*. A hybrid fiber-coaxial system, which some operators had begun to deploy, was hands down the fattest pipe around.

My excitement over cable had less to do with television service and more with the other things that could flow through it, from home shopping to streaming video. It seemed like the best bet for two-way, high-speed, affordable data, the most logical platform for Starwave and Ticketmaster and a thousand other applications. While not as ubiquitous as the telephone, cable was already in people's homes. By the end of the nineties, 65 million households would be subscribers. Just as the personal computer revolution had flowered with software applications like word processing and spreadsheets, cable was primed to become the interactive foundation of the Wired World.

Early on, I invested in companies that would prosper as high-speed data networks expanded, like Go2Net, a broadband Internet portal, and ZDTV (later TechTV), a network that covered the latest developments in technology. For greater impact, though, I thought I needed a pipe of my own. Cable was a big gamble. I'd have a smaller footprint than established powers like Time Warner and Comcast, and the price of admission was exorbitant. But I wanted to put my Wired World vision to a real-world test. And I felt sure that I could add value with innovative technologies and interactive content, key ingredients for the computing of the future.

As I hunted for a point of entry, a sequence of developments turned the industry upside down. The Telecommunications Act of 1996 opened cable-franchised areas to television service by satellite and phone companies. To stave off competition, cable operators responded with massive outlays to upgrade from analog to digital. They had a long and expensive way to go—by the end of 1997, only one in ten cable customers had access to digital TV. These pressures set off a furious wave of consolidations. Stronger companies swallowed weaker ones and swapped systems to concentrate their customer bases. The timing seemed perfect for someone with new ideas and lots of capital. But as *Fortune* observed in 2000, after I'd joined the cable fray: "As with any new technology wherein lots of players chase a limited pool of would-be subscribers, someone's bound to go down. Hard."

IN APRIL 1998. I paid $2.8 billion for Marcus Cable, a Texas-based operator with more than a million customers. That transaction, I told the press, culminated a long-standing dream: "Over twenty years ago, even before I helped to cofound Microsoft, I saw a connected future. I called that future the Wired World. By investing into Marcus Cable, I will finally have some wires for my Wired World."

My pivotal buying opportunity came three months later with Charter Communications, based in St. Louis. The tenth-largest MSO (multisystems operator) in the country, Charter had 1.2 million subscribers. It was the number-three cable provider in the balkanized Los Angeles market, which I saw as a potential anchor. Factoring in $1.9 billion of debt, Charter would cost me $4.5 billion, or fourteen times its projected operating cash flow. The *Los Angeles Times* called it "a rich price even by the standards of the merger-crazed cable industry."

Responding to that perception in a July 1998 e-mail, Bill Savoy optimistically advised:

> It is also important to note that Charter has the best performing cable properties in the industry, as measured by both growth and by cash flow per subscriber. So a 14x multiple is not outrageous, we paid almost 12x [actually 11.1x] for Marcus and AT&T paid 16x for TCI.

What Savoy failed to note was that I was buying at the top of the telecom boom in a notoriously cyclical industry. In three months, I'd spent more than $7 billion.

Scale and density are make-or-break factors in the cable business. I set a goal of 5 million customers—music to the ears of Jerry Kent, Charter's CEO, who loved making deals as much as Savoy. Over the next nineteen months, after merging Marcus with Charter, we acquired a dozen more cable businesses in a $23 billion spree. In 1999, to subsidize our rapid expansion and help upgrade our systems, Charter raised $3.7 billion in one of the largest IPOs in U.S. history.

It was a dizzying ride. None of us sufficiently scrutinized how well Charter's new pieces fit together operationally or, more important, whether the company could survive its mounds of debt if its growth curve were to flatten. Cable is a capital-intensive industry that borrows heavily to extend and upgrade infrastructure. During the boom of the late nineties, when bankers lent freely to operators, conservatively managed companies like Comcast and Cox were leveraging at around four times their operating cash flow (earnings before interest, taxes, depreciation, and amortization, or EBITDA). But within months of the Charter acquisition, our debt multiple stood at more than nine times EBITDA. We were wildly over-leveraged. (I can still hear Bill Savoy saying, "Jerry thinks nine times is what we should go with.") Our heavy debt service created negative cash flow, making us vulnerable to interest rate hikes, bumps in the economy, or corporate missteps. If all went well, our leverage would boost our stock price, but if something went wrong. . . .

That was my blind spot, and my first big mistake with Charter. My second: In deals to buy other systems with Charter stock, I guaranteed that the former owners could sell their shares back to me at a prenegotiated price. If cable values fell and the stock slumped, that price would be grossly inflated. The sellers were protecting their downside at my expense.

My third error was underestimating the importance of critical masses of customers. While other MSOs had been building out systems in major cities for years, Charter's acquisitions were mainly weighted in far-flung rural networks with relative handfuls of subscribers. Though we had substantial segments in St. Louis and in Fort Worth, Texas, along with a good share of Los Angeles, we never gained control of a top market. Our strategy to become the dominant operator in L.A. foundered when we were outbid for Adelphia and Century Communications.

What's more, our largest acquisitions were second- and third-rate assets. Most of Falcon's systems were in remote areas of Southern California and offered only thirty-five channels, barely a third of the industry's norm. It would take a huge capital investment for Charter to catch up, and a lot more to upgrade the company's infrastructure. Even after doing so, our returns would pale next to those of more urbanized operators.

In October 1999, hungering for a presence in New York and other major cities, I invested $1.6 billion in RCN, a high-end, fiber-optic "overbuilder" that tried to poach customers from entrenched cable franchises. The problem was that RCN couldn't get enough customers to justify the expense of building out its network. Plagued by steady losses and crushing debt, the company eventually filed under Chapter 11 in 2004. It emerged from bankruptcy with new management a few months later, but my investment was essentially wiped out.

As I pursued my cable vision into the new century, all the ingredients were in place for me to be in over my head: an over-leveraged company, stiff competition from satellite providers, a wheeler-dealer CEO, and my own lack of experience with the industry's financial variables. Then, in 2000, the tech bubble burst. Charter's plan for a secondary public offering, a much-needed capital infusion, had to be canceled. With Wall Street eyeing cable balance sheets skeptically, the company's valuation crumbled.

We were hanging by a string.

\*     \*     \*

IN A *CABLE WORLD* interview published in November 2000, Jerry Kent was asked, "What's it like to be the anchor of Paul Allen's Wired World?"

Kent replied, "When an individual entrusts a management team with a $7 billion investment . . . it means we have an awesome responsibility to execute and perform."

But while he said the right things in public, Kent behaved erratically behind closed doors. In the fall of 2001 (just after 9/11), in a decision that seemed impulsive and bizarre at the time, he announced his resignation.

One year later, Charter's subscription base peaked at 7 million customers. But as the tech slump became a crash, cable operators were hit hard. Adelphia collapsed into bankruptcy, leading Wall Street to downgrade its outlook on the whole industry. The value associated with each subscriber shrank by a third or more. Highly leveraged companies like Charter were valued at less than ten times operational cash flow, considerably under what I'd paid. The company's share price, as high as $25 a year earlier, tumbled by 80 percent.

That summer, I learned that Charter management was under federal investigation for accounting fraud, which led to the indictment of four top executives. With our reputation in tatters, the company's share price fluctuated wildly, sometimes dipping below a dollar. Charter's debt climbed to $17 billion. Jerry Kent's sudden resignation began to make sense to me. One could speculate that he saw serious problems heading Charter's way.

When I told David Geffen what was going on and described the guidance I'd been getting, he said, "You have been *so* poorly served." Then he wheeled into advice mode: "Here's your best chance to fix this. You've got to go to New York and find the best attorneys, the best restructuring guys—the people who really know their way around." I hired the New York law firm Skadden, Arps to guide Vulcan through our legal issues, and Miller Buckfire for strategic advice. Separately, Charter brought in Lazard Frères, a top advisory investment bank. In this dire situation, we finally had the right people on our side.

An outside financial analysis was both sobering and hopeful. Of Charter's $20 billion value, 85 percent was debt, a load that continued to gulp our cash flow and then some. But with most of our capital upgrade complete, the analyst concluded, the debt leverage should recede to more acceptable multiples by 2010. Some of my old optimism returned. Once we stabilized the financial operation, I felt confident that we could speed the innovations to lift the business.

But there was a catch, the analyst noted: "The challenge facing cable today is to learn how to effectively market its basic and advanced services in an increasingly competitive marketplace." As things turned out, the competition was even more intense than anticipated. And we failed to rise to the challenge.

JERRY KENT'S SUCCESSOR. Carl Vogel, worked hard to renegotiate our loan maturities and keep us afloat. The problem was that Charter was equally vulnerable on the operational front. A cable business must continually sweat all the details of customer service, from pricing tiers to just how many technician visits (or "truck rolls") it takes to get someone's service issues resolved. From where I sat, Carl wasn't up to that part of the job.

For years I'd been urging the cable industry to trump our satellite and telecom competition with faster deployment of digital video recorder set-top boxes and video on demand. I knew that consumers would want these features. I had them for years in my home-brewed multimedia system, and my visitors—several industry leaders among them—responded with enthusiasm. But as Cox and Cablevision began to roll out DVRs more aggressively (along with high-speed phone service, "triple-play" TV/phone/Internet packages, and, later, high-definition TV), Charter lacked the funding and focus to keep pace.

Smelling weakness, satellite providers targeted our areas with promotions and extra advertising. We lost subscribers by the bucketful, half a million during Vogel's four years at the helm. By 2003, Charter's debt load reached $20 billion. Much of it traded at less than half of face value, a dark forecast of the company's solvency. As the stock price plummeted, the people who'd sold us their cable systems redeemed their shares. I was forced to pay out another $2 billion in cash.

That fall it came time to drink "some castor oil," as I later told *Business Week*. I fired Bill Savoy and pared my investments to forty companies, with an eye to diversification and maximizing return—basic principles that I'd almost lost sight of in my headlong pursuit of the Wired World. (One of those shed was Asymetrix, my first solo business. After a subsequent merger, it is now called Sum-Total Systems and continues to be a leader in e-learning software.) The irony is that I was forced into retreat just as events affirmed my vision. Broadband data penetration rose from 0.3 percent of American households in 1998 to 7 percent in 2000 to 61 percent in 2005. The digital platform I'd imagined was fast becoming a reality.

In August 2005, Charter finally got the CEO it needed in Neil Smit, a former Navy Seal and an outstanding executive from Time Warner. Over the next three years, we fought our way back to stability by extending maturities on our debt load, keeping our creditors at bay and our bondholders paid.

Neil ran Charter's day-to-day operations with both expertise and a needed grind-away mentality. As he trimmed bureaucracy and got digital telephony running across our systems, fewer customers deserted us to satellite. Charter's cash flow was growing 10 percent annually, and would soon catch up to our interest payments. It looked like the company might have a future, after all.

But our progress could last only as long as the credit markets gave us space to breathe. On September 15, 2008, Lehman Brothers fell into bankruptcy. The credit markets seized up, and commercial lending ground to a halt. Our refinancing options disappeared overnight. Charter's debt load had swollen to $21 billion, with nearly $2 billion coming due in 2009, and the company lacked the cash flow to cover it.

In February 2009, after a decade of losses, we finally ran out of runway. Under the reorganization plan proposed by Lazard, Charter stockholders' equity—including my 52 percent share—would be virtually wiped out, a bitter pill. But with the company casting off $8 billion of debt, junior bondholders would invest $1.6 billion in new capital. Charter would reemerge stronger than before.

The wild card was how the company would pay off $12 billion of senior secured debt held by JPMorgan and other big banks. If the obligations were reinstated at their original, low-percentage interest rates, the restructuring could move forward. But if they were reissued at steeper current rates, the bump in annual debt service—hundreds of millions of dollars—would sink the whole plan. Without liquidity, the junior bondholders would lose all incentive to convert their bonds into equity. The company might lurch into "free-fall" bankruptcy, with uncertain implications for all concerned, including sixteen thousand employees.

To avoid a free fall and get the loans favorably reinstated, Charter had to show that the same interests would remain in control before and after the reorganization. The junior bondholders needed my cooperation (and my retention of a 35 percent voting stake) for the agreement to work. I wanted to help ensure a smooth transition. But it also seemed reasonable that I get some consideration for my role in the plan, which would save the company billions in interest payments. We arrived at a compromise, and Charter filed under Chapter 11 in March.

JPMorgan led the court challenge. On November 17, the U.S. Bankruptcy Court for the Southern District of New York ruled in our favor and affirmed the reorganization plan. A month later, Charter came out of bankruptcy. I resigned as board chairman, and later Neil Smit moved on to become Comcast's president of cable operations. We left behind a company with positive cash flow and a strong foundation, but the lessons I learned were among the most expensive ever. My net loss in the cable business was $8 billion.

WITH THE CLARITY of hindsight, I could say that I took the wrong people's advice in plunging into Charter. I needed savvier, more experienced executives to assess my risks and to run the company, and I didn't have them until it was too late. But the fact remains that the investment was mine, and I made serious miscalculations. Most of all, I failed to understand the downside of over-leveraging. My dreams of a Wired World empire finally sank under the weight of Charter's mountain of debt.

In placing the biggest bets of my life on cable, I focused on its potential to change the world, not the downside scenarios. After embracing SkyPix early on, I underestimated the challenge from satellite systems, with their reputation for superior service. I did the same with the phone companies' video and data offerings. And I failed to discern that the cable pipe couldn't galvanize change by itself, or at least not as quickly as I'd thought. Operators have reaped handsome profits from selling high-speed data, but they've yet to capture much added value with new products and services over the top of the data stream. Even today, the fat pipe remains by and large a "dumb" pipe.

At the same time, recent trends suggest that I was more right than wrong in my prediction of a broadband future. As TV channels' subscription fees squeeze profit margins, high-speed data is more vital than ever to cable's growth. People have a voracious appetite for faster information flow, and fiber-optic technology has made cable far and away the top provider of digital data into their homes. The fat pipe has helped bring Amazon, Google, Facebook, and YouTube into near-universal acceptance. It has changed the way we live.

As the industry embraced DVR boxes and other services I'd been early in urging, operators found that customers were willing to pay for them. Now they can plow the extra revenue into the next round of innovation, in a virtual cycle.

The Consumer Electronics Show in Las Vegas each year contains a cavalcade of ideas that once percolated within Interval Research and my vision for the Wired World, from wearable HD camcorders and holographic displays to fully functioning multimedia set-top boxes and TVs, Web browsers included. In some cases, I was just too early. In others, our execution failed for a slew of reasons.

But even if I'd had more luck in my timing, the cable industry was wrong for me. In consumer electronics, product cycles run as short as six months; in computer software, about every two years. But in cable, it takes five years or more to introduce something new across the customer footprint. Cable is like a mule train. It's moving as fast as it can but still takes forever to get anywhere. Case in point: When my company, Digeo, developed an Emmy-winning set-top box, it could not gain traction with Comcast and Time Warner, which were wedded to inferior boxes from their sub-servient legacy suppliers. Only recently have they begun to mandate Digeo-caliber boxes for future deployment.

Or consider that cable has yet to fully incorporate mobile phone service, a platform that now supersedes landlines, in a triple or quadruple play.

Consumers who came of age in the digital era are agnostic about delivery systems. A bit is a bit, regardless of how it reaches them. Though many of us have broken our picks in the pursuit of interactive television (including the ill-fated WebTV), there's no question that television and computer platforms are now converging. People might not choose to read long e-mails on their fifty-five-inch screens, but they'll use a tablet as a TV remote while scanning their Facebook page. Or they'll use Xbox to manage their photos and music.

An Internet port will soon be standard on higher-end television sets. If the cable industry doesn't move aggressively to integrate

Internet functionality with its TV offerings, providers like Apple TV and Google TV will fill the void with "over-the-top" services. If you can stream Amazon.com or Netflix films and videos to your television, with their tens of thousands of on-demand titles, how appealing is pay-per-view? More threatening still, broadband channels are moving to distribute "linear" network content as well: CBS, TNT, Comedy Central. Multichannel television could be gradually supplanted by streaming video, with only sports and political events left as obligatory real-time viewing.

The technology already exists. The consumers are up for grabs. The digital future will belong to those who seize it.

# CHAPTER 20

# SEARCHING

In the early 1990s, Carl Sagan met with me to pitch a cause he held dear. The federal government had been funding the SETI (Search for Extra-Terrestrial Intelligence) Institute through NASA, in what was supposed to be a ten-year plan to observe neighboring stars. But Congress balked, with one senator from Nevada calling the initiative "a great Martian chase," and the appropriation was canceled. The search for a signal from outside our solar system was about to be shut down.

"SETI's taking on one of the great scientific questions," Sagan said. "We need someone to step in and save it." He was delightfully sharp-witted and persuasive, and it didn't hurt that I'd watched every episode of *Cosmos*, his classic PBS documentary series on the universe and man's quest to understand it. Along with Gordon Moore, Bill Hewlett, and David Packard, I agreed to give $1 million to keep the SETI Institute running. It was just enough for the operation to pay for a bit of observation time on giant radio telescopes in Australia, West Virginia, and Puerto Rico. SETI was then looking at a mere 750 stars, a paltry number against the 200 billion in the Milky Way alone. To have even a ghost of a chance to succeed, it seemed clear that a dedicated telescope was needed.

Several years later, researchers figured out how to process data from "ganged" small-dish radio antennas, a big breakthrough for radio astronomy. The idea of creating the world's best SETI tele-scope—at a fraction of the cost of a single large dish—was enticing. I underwrote the creation of an installation at Hat Creek Observatory in the Lassen National Forest in northeastern California. Nathan Myhrvold, the former chief technology officer at Microsoft, chipped in for an electronics laboratory at the site. In 2007, after years of research and development, the Allen Telescope Array opened its "ears": a set of forty-two six-meter dishes combing the sky in a thorough, methodical hunt for a signal that might change everything.

The telescope array works on the principle that objects in space emit radio wave "signatures" that describe their size, shape, and chemistry. Much longer than optical waves, radio waves are less scattered by space dust and can get to us intact from the edges of our galaxy and beyond. When SETI uses the array to search for a signal, it can scan ten times more of the radio spectrum than any previous installation. Its detection beams can focus on six stars at once, or on three stars with two simultaneous beams apiece.

The array's other big advantage is its wide-angle, high-resolution view, which captures a field of sky as large as seven full moons across. (The thousand-foot-diameter Arecibo Telescope in Puerto Rico is far more sensitive, but it looks at a small area of space through the equivalent of a soda straw.) SETI has compiled a list of a quarter-million sunlike stars, the ones most likely to have livable planets within six hundred light-years of earth. In five years or so, after the galactic census satellite Gaia begins sending back its survey data, that catalog will swell to several million stars, a decent foundation for this type of search.

What's more, the array is a Moore's-law telescope; its digital signal processing will keep improving exponentially. It's already 100 trillion times more capable than the one that SETI founder Frank Drake used when he started signal hunting in 1960. The Institute's goal is to expand to 350 dishes, which would make the array one of the more powerful radio telescopes in the world.

Though there are no guarantees that SETI will turn up an alien communication, the history of astronomy suggests that its new-generation technology may lead to unexpected discoveries. With a portion of the array's observing time, the University of California–Berkeley's Radio Astronomy Lab is conducting investigations in more conventional astronomy: gamma ray bursts, black holes, stellar explosions. By mapping our galaxy's distribution of hydrogen gas, an essential ingredient in star formation, the Berkeley data should give us a clearer picture of the nature of dark matter, the galactic life cycle, and the structure of the cosmos itself.

WHENEVER THE ARRAY finds a SETI "candidate signal" that stands out from the background of garden-variety electromagnetic noise, a gauntlet of tests winnows out false positives. Computers quickly determine whether the candidate came from the scanned star or an orbiting satellite—or a stray cell-phone crackle. Once a signal successfully passes those tests, other radio telescopes will be contacted for independent confirmation. And if and when SETI actually verifies an engineered communication, a tweet across the cosmos, I'm told that I'll be the first person that director Jill Tarter calls outside her professional community.

My phone hasn't rung yet, and there's no way of knowing if it ever will. Frank Drake devised an equation that can theoretically calculate the number of communicating civilizations in the Milky Way. But because we can't determine the Drake equation's parameters (such as the life spans of civilizations that develop broadcast-capable technologies), it's hard to know what the real probabilities are. If those civilizations last only a few thousand years, the SETI Institute may be out of luck. If they last a few million years, our odds are far better.

When it comes to the existence of extraterrestrial life, there are strong arguments on both sides. In *Rare Earth: Why Complex Life Is Uncommon in the Universe*, Peter Ward and Donald Brownlee suggest that the specific conditions that produced animal life on earth—our distance from the sun, the amount of water in our atmosphere—add up to an unlikely accident. Yet recent research has shown that cellular organisms can exist at more extreme temperatures than we ever thought. Nearly five hundred exoplanets, those belonging to other stars, have already been discovered, and the Gaia probe should find tens of thousands more. In theory, any one of them could be the winning lottery ticket.

SETI is the longest of long shots, but I find its question gripping. Do we have company in the universe, even in our own galaxy? A yes would have implications we can only guess at. Any society with the ability to signal its existence would almost surely be older and wiser than we are, with technology that might offer huge benefits. But even if we never made contact (or followed Stephen Hawking's recent warning and declined to return the call), a confirmed signal by itself would permanently alter our perception of the universe.

IF SETI REPRESENTS our outward search for intelligence, a Vulcan initiative called Project Halo is helping to lead the inward search: to design software that can simulate certain aspects of human thinking. What we now refer to as artificial intelligence, or "AI," dates back at least to 1921, when a Czech science fiction play called *R.U.R.* coined the term "robot." When I was young, HAL-9000 (in Kubrick's *2001*) and Colossus (from the novel and movie of the same name) embodied nightmare scenarios in which super-intelligent computers turned on their human masters. Machines that behaved like people, even people gone mad, were all the rage back then.

But for me, even more compelling was the sci-fi theme of a dying or threatened civilization that saves itself by finding a trove of knowledge. Tagging along with my father to his library job, I spent hours amid acres of shelves that held what seemed like an infinite mass of information. The idea of gathering all the world's knowledge in one accessible repository—like the Final Encyclopedia in

Gordon R. Dickson's classic of that title—seemed both grandiose and seductive, with untold benefits for humankind.

With the development of the World Wide Web in the nineties, there were glimmers of hope that this repository might be under construction online. In reality, though, the "knowledge explosion" left us with mounds of sources but no direct way to get a quick and concise answer. It became too easy to get lost in a tangle of text and hyperlinks. And while modern search engines have proven to be invaluable in presenting lists of pages with specified keywords, they still fall far short of the ultimate goal of software that *understands*.

Aristotle, the Greek scientist and philosopher, was literally a know-it-all. He mastered the knowledge of his day on every topic that mattered, from history and political science to medicine and physics. Even more impressively, he could explain what he knew to his students. But in today's world, where scientific knowledge may be doubling by the year, it's impossible for any one person to absorb more than a small fraction of it.

Over the last decade, I began to think about a "Digital Aristotle," an easy-to-use, all-encompassing knowledge storehouse. I wasn't aiming to solve the mystery of human consciousness. I simply wanted to advance the field of artificial intelligence so that computers could do what they do best (organize and analyze information) to help people do what *they* do best, those inspired leaps of intuition that fuel original ideas and breakthroughs.

That's why we began Project Halo, a research program that is trying to create a Digital Aristotle. One near-term goal is Halobook, an electronic textbook that can answer typed-in questions with expert-level accuracy. Running on a laptop or tablet, Halobook could serve as a research aide for working scientists or as a tutor for college and high school students, like a personal digital teaching assistant.

In the inaugural Halobook, targeted for release in 2015, we'll have encoded most of the Advanced Placement biology syllabus, something no one else has yet attempted. After that, we may reach into biochemistry or move to a whole new area, like civil engineering. We might even take on economics or U.S. government. The humanities—philosophy, religion, history, classics—would be much, much tougher. As subject matter shifts from how things work to the values and language that define the human condition (fairness, morality, love), software systems quickly move out of their depth. I recognized this roadblock as early as 1977, in my interview with *Microcomputer Interface:*

> *In order to be truly intelligent, computers must* understand— *that is probably the critical word. It is one thing to feed* The Tale of Two Cities *into a computer. It's another to have the computer understand what's being said. You can't ask it a question about the theme of a book or why a character does something and get a coherent answer. We haven't yet reached that level with intelligent computers.*

And we still haven't today, but we're getting closer. (For a further explanation of Project Halo, see the appendix.)

Ultimately, a Digital Aristotle should make us more inventive and creative. With its steady progress in attacking classic problems like learning, language, and reasoning, I can foresee a time when artificial intelligence could greatly speed our ability to ferret out cures for diseases or help us preserve the environment. As Douglas Engelbart wrote in 1962 in *Augmenting Human Intellect: A Conceptual Framework:*

> *Man's population and gross product are increasing at a considerable rate, but the complexity of his problems grows still faster, and the urgency with which solutions must be found becomes steadily greater. . . . By "augmenting human intellect" we mean increasing the capability of a man to approach*

*a complex problem situation, to gain comprehension to suit his particular needs, and to derive solutions to problems. . . .*

*One of the tools that shows the greatest immediate promise is the computer, when it can be harnessed for direct online assistance, integrated with new concepts and methods.*

As computing grows increasingly cheaper and more powerful, it is now conceivable that virtually all the world's data will soon be found online. Organizing it coherently and logically will take a Herculean effort. Given the ever-accelerating expansion of human knowledge, not to mention its breadth and complexity, a final encyclopedia is an elusive goal. But it just might be closer than you think.

IN HIS ESSAY "The Law of Accelerating Returns," the futurist Ray Kurzweil predicted that the increase in computer processing power will soon lead to a "singularity" of technological change "so rapid and profound it represents a rupture in the fabric of human history." Kurzweil foresees the imminent arrival of "strong AI," machines as smart as human beings, the first step in an accelerating progression of smarter and smarter machines—to the point that we'll be able to download our personalities and self-awareness into computers and gain a sort of digital immortality.

Though I won't say that a singularity is impossible, I believe that it is centuries away at best. Although Kurzweil credits Moore's law as an inspiration, Gordon Moore agrees with me, noting that human development "involves a lot more than just the intellectual capability," and doubting that machines "could overcome that overall gap. . . ." The sheer complexity of human brain function is daunting in the extreme. It took forty years to develop a computer chess program that could consistently beat the best human players, even though grandmaster-level chess can be achieved with simple sequential logic and brute-force processing. To get a computer to read and understand human language is incomparably harder.

We can't replicate the brain because we've barely begun to understand how it works.

There are two basic approaches to artificial intelligence, both of them journeys of thousands of small steps. You can take the Halo approach, in which we're inventing software to emulate some of the things the brain can do. Or you can try to reverse-engineer the physical brain itself to see how it really functions, which is the story of an institute I founded in Seattle.

# CHAPTER 21

# MAPPING THE BRAIN

The brain is a never-ending source of fascination for me. It's the organ that unites us as a species and distinguishes us from one another. It keeps us breathing and upright, makes us elated or anxious, and, not least, harbors our creativity. Here is a truly astonishing piece of evolutionary engineering, one that does so many things so much better than the most advanced computer, and yet we're just scratching its surface.

The 1990s saw an explosion of new theories in genomics, informatics (the conversion of data into usable information), and molecular neurobiology. In February 2001, eleven years after it began, the Human Genome Project released a first draft of the roughly 3 billion base pairs that comprise our genes. The HGP confirmed that fewer than twenty-five thousand human genes were needed to create the brain's 100 billion multifaceted nerve cells, all linked in intricate networks totaling a quadrillion neural connections. How could such a small genome serve as the blueprint for such a complex organ? And how might the HGP's achievement be used to advance neuroscience?

I was meeting around that time with experts in early learning and linguistics, and their research was engaging, but I felt a pull to get inside the human brain, the ultimate machine. To think it through, I met with Jim Watson, the director of the Cold Spring

Harbor Laboratory and codiscoverer of the double-helix structure of DNA. Then in his seventies, Watson was a confirmed iconoclast, always ready to venture off the beaten path. He proposed that I found a behavioral research center to focus on gene expression in the brain, the phenomenon of different genes "switching on" in different cells. The cell's "expressed" genes direct the production of particular mixes of proteins, which in turn differentiate heart cells from skin cells (or tumor cells) and control how they function.

I also met with Steve Friend, the founder of a cutting-edge Seattle genome-analysis company. He, too, thought the time was ripe for a facility at the crossroads of human psychology, genomics, behavioral genetics, and brain biology. Advances in data storage and retrieval would enable us to compile and analyze the masses of new information we gathered.

"The more I read about the brain the more fascinated and interested I am," I wrote in a December 2000 e-mail that included my first mention of a brain institute. "I am especially interested in how the genetic 'blueprint' for building the brain works."

MOST NEUROSCIENCE RESEARCHERS are highly specialized, pursuing their questions in discrete areas of the brain as though they're drilling into an orange with a needle. I wanted to cover the entire rind and help scientists locate the most promising spots to drill, to get them probing faster and deeper that much sooner. In March 2002, I invited twenty-one scientists, including four Nobel laureates, to join me at a three-day brainstorming session, or *charrette*. The scientists assembled at a dock in Nassau in the Bahamas and ferried over to our conference center for the weekend, my yacht, *Tatoosh*, a serene setting for an intensive discussion.

In addition to Watson and Friend, the guests included Richard Axel, the Nobel Prize–winning neuroscientist who'd advanced the understanding of our sense of smell; Steven Pinker, the Harvard psychologist and bestselling author of books on linguistics; Marc Tessier-Lavigne, who did pioneering work on the assembly of the embryonic and fetal brain; Lee Hartwell, who won his Nobel for discovering the genes that control cell division; and David Anderson, a Cal Tech neurobiologist who'd play an instrumental role in defining our mission.

I came to the *charrette* with a rough vision of an institute on the frontier of brain science. One expert suggested that I establish a top-tier research facility, on par with the Rockefeller Institute, to recruit the best and brightest researchers from around the world. The price tag: $1 billion, half to start up and half to endow.

Money aside, I was wary of the traditional academic model for research institutes. Scientists of stature pursue whatever they find most interesting and are not easily steered. I had seen the downside of a loosely defined organizational mission at Interval Research, which Vulcan had closed two years earlier, and I wasn't eager to repeat it. The alternative was to concentrate on a single large-scale endeavor that might transform the field, a neuroscience equivalent to the Human Genome Project. We'd have concrete milestones en route to tangible results within a few years. I wanted a facility run on an industrial scale, with biotech urgency but without the profit motive.

My guests debated what exactly our institute should address. The discussions were lively, wide-ranging, and often competitive; great scientists are adept at putting forward their proposals. (It's what they do to get their funding grants renewed.) All sorts of ideas were floated. Was there an underlying genetic basis for happiness, or for love? How could we improve brain-imaging technology? What single disease might be most usefully explored?

By the second day, the conversation kept circling back to the idea that had first surfaced in my talks with Watson and Friend. What neuroscience needed more than anything else, I kept hearing, was something very basic: a better map of the brain.

In existing maps relating to gene expression, the anatomic resolution was too coarse to be of much help in deciphering how the organ really worked. The National Institutes of Health had recently funded a Brain Molecular Anatomy Project, but the work was too fragmented for consistent quality control, and there was only enough funding to look at six hundred genes per year. At that rate, a complete atlas might take half a century. Brain mapping was stuck in a cottage-industry stage, like the one that hobbled genome sequencing before the HGP and Craig Venter's Celera Genomics made the effort systematic.

By our closing session, the scientists were unanimous. A brain atlas was "an appropriate inaugural project for the Allen Institute because of the incalculable contribution the Atlas can make towards solving basic molecular and genetic questions about human behavior." The atlas would link genetics and anatomy, with maps of switched-on genes overlying the brain's three-dimensional structure. It would open new avenues of research into neurological and psychiatric disorders, as well as fundamental questions of brain science. Our initial effort, the scientists agreed, should map the adult mouse brain and focus on healthy specimens. (Most studies were then looking at embryonic brains, and NIH research emphasized diseases.)

A brain atlas of gene expression fit my main criterion, to go where important work lay undone. It was "big science" with obvious real-world utility. From Alzheimer's and Parkinson's to schizophrenia, brain disorders afflicted tens of millions of Americans. Once we mapped a normal "reference" brain, we'd be able to isolate the active genes that triggered these ailments. Scientists could begin to find ways to target them therapeutically. The potential was staggering.

And far down the path, I thought, our work might even help uncover the essence of memory, desire, compassion—of what makes us human.

I LOVE TO travel with close friends and family. My mother liked Tahiti and Japan, though she was less fond of Africa after a hippopotamus broke into the compound she was staying in and had to be rope-lifted out of the swimming pool. Her favorite trip was a plantation tour on the Mississippi, where she paused on people's porches to share iced tea and listen to their stories, just as she'd once lingered with her neighbors on her way home from school in Anadarko. She was still the best listener I'd ever known.

Over the years, I had bought up land around my home on Mercer Island, adding houses for my mother and sister. My mom thrived there amid her fifteen thousand neatly shelved books, most of them bought for a quarter or less at a thrift store. Nothing gave her more pleasure than perusing her stacks, meticulously organized by authors' last names, and finding an old friend.

My mother used to lead a book club for faculty wives from UW, choosing works by African authors one year, Eastern European novels the next. She took almost as much joy in selecting as in discussing. When she set out to compile a list of 100 favorites for me, she wound up with 165—as she'd often say, "What's better than a good book?" But her days as a reader were numbered. In a late-night e-mail journal entry on January 21, 2003, I wrote, "My mother is struggling right now with an Alzheimer's-like condition. (She was diagnosed in the last two weeks.) I'm sick at heart about this."

Her dementia was subtle at first. One minute she'd finish a crossword puzzle with ease, and the next she'd forget what she'd told me minutes before. She was angry about her memory loss; she'd reached that wrenching phase in which she knew she was slipping but felt powerless to stop it. Then came a long, slow twilight with gathering darkness. I saw the horrors of Alzheimer's up close, and I was devastated. If there was anything I could do to spare others a similar fate, I was determined to try.

I turned fifty the day I wrote that entry, the point in life where many of us begin to consider what we'll be leaving behind. In September 2003, I launched the Allen Institute for Brain Science with a $100 million contribution. Its charter was ambitious: "We believe this is a historic opportunity to unite the genome and the brain, and use the data and technology to tackle the challenges of neurodevelopmental, neurodegenerative and psychiatric disease."

We found a facility in Fremont, a peaceful Seattle neighborhood perched above a ship canal. There was space for our whole staff under one roof: process engineering, molecular biology, anatomy, software development, database creation. As president and chairman of the board, my sister would once again oversee my brainchild. A blue-ribbon group of scientists, including several strong voices from our *charrette,* would serve on an advisory board.

The highest hurdle for a brain atlas was the sheer amount of data to be collected and organized. Where the HGP's data consisted of sequences of letters, ours would be high-resolution images, which needed far more storage space. The initial mouse brain atlas would involve 85 million images on 250,000 slides—600 terabytes of data (600,000 gigabytes, or 600 trillion bytes), or more than half as much as the total content of the Internet when we began.

Early on, we confronted a pivotal issue. Should we charge for access to our database? Revenue from users and royalties from commercial work could help expand our operation. On the other hand, the institute's success had to be measured by the discoveries it sparked. The more widely the atlas was used, the greater the chance of a breakthrough. Charging for access might limit use to elite universities and the largest pharmaceutical firms, while shutting out some talented researcher in Johannesburg or Seoul who couldn't come up with the fee. We decided to place our data in the public domain, with free Internet access and a powerful, user-friendly interface. No registration would be required.

POSTMORTEM HUMAN BRAINS are all very different. The donors vary in age, genetic backgrounds, and upbringing, all variables that shape the organ's form and function. And so, like countless human-oriented studies before us, we opted to start with the ideal laboratory mammal, the mouse. The mouse brain is no larger than an almond, no heavier than a teaspoon of sugar. But it's a terrific template for mapping. It closely resembles our own brain in both form and content, with 90 percent of a mouse's genes having a human counterpart. Inbreeding would give us close-to-identical subjects at a uniform age of eight weeks, a near-perfect experimental system.

We chose a state-of-the-art hybridization technique developed at the Max Planck Institute in Germany and later implemented at Baylor College of Medicine. The mouse brains would be sliced north-to-south into hundreds of sections, then dunked into an RNA solution to probe for a specific active gene—one gene per slice, five or six genes per brain. All neurons expressing that gene would be revealed.

The scope of an all-gene atlas demanded an intensively choreographed, high-throughput approach to convert hundreds of thousands of slides into digital data. Modeling our work after Baylor's, we organized laboratory robots in assembly-line fashion, staining slides around the clock (up to four thousand per week), photographing the sections under microscopes, and channeling the images to our database.

A year after we launched, I promoted Allan Jones, who had overseen the collaboration with Baylor and recruited much of our staff, to run the project. It was a big promotion, but Allan quickly proved up to the task. In December 2004, we released the first installment of the Allen Brain Atlas: visual data from nearly two thousand genes. David Anderson, the advisory board member who first proposed the atlas project, calculated that we'd accomplished over fourteen months what might have taken a solitary scientist seventy-seven years.

A database is only as good as its interactive search functions. If people can't find and download what they're looking for, it's like a vast library with no call numbers. In structuring the mouse brain atlas database, we created software that answers both the "where is" and "what is" questions. Say, for example, you are looking at a gene that increases sensitivity to painkillers like morphine, and want to know just where it is switched on. First you'll be taken to the high-resolution, two-dimensional data for that gene at the cellular level. Then a viewing application, the 3-D Brain Explorer, will show how the gene is distributed across the "consensus" brain of all mice used in the study. Or, if you prefer, you can type in *amygdala* (the region of the brain that governs fear and anticipation) and see which color-coded genes are active in that area. Either way, for the very first time, you will have access to gene-expression data at the cellular level.

The neuroscience community initially greeted our tool with some skepticism. The Allen Institute was the new kid on the block, funded by a technologist with no track record in the field. Our industrial-scale approach was unorthodox, and it took a while for people to believe that the data was really free, no strings attached.

Less than two years after our launch, in September 2006, the full set of data for the mouse brain atlas was released on schedule, three years after we'd begun. With our first database complete, we made public these findings:

*The brain contains more genetic activity than we had thought.* Scientists had previously estimated that two thirds of the genome was expressed somewhere in the brain. The Allen Brain Atlas shows that the proportion is closer to 80 percent, which helps explain why drug therapies designed for other organs often have side effects.

*Genes are expressed in distinct areas.* Most of them are switched on in very specific subsets of cells or particular regions of the brain. This discovery has unveiled how biochemistry varies in different parts of the brain and how it relates to their specialized functions. By understanding these variations, scientists will be better equipped to modulate biochemical activity in diseased brain structures.

*Previous brain maps were sometimes inaccurate or incomplete, even on a gross anatomical level.* As they defined gene expression patterns, our scientists came across previously unnoticed structural subdivisions. These findings have refined the understanding of how the brain is partitioned, a key to better diagnoses and therapies.

After announcing the completion of the mouse brain atlas in Washington, D.C., I met Francis Collins, the former head of the Human Genome Project and now director of the National Institutes of Health. Early on, we'd felt a certain tension radiating from his agency; some at the NIH may have viewed our institute as a competitor. But Collins congratulated me wholeheartedly that day, and our institutional relationship has grown ever since. (In 2009, the Allen Institute won a GO Grant through the NIH as part of President Obama's stimulus package.)

Over time, any resistance to our work has dissolved. Susumu Tonegawa, a Nobel laureate and director of MIT's Picower Center for Learning and Memory, called the mouse brain atlas "a breakthrough in neuroscience. It's a new, extremely powerful approach to try to understand the brain. I would say it's revolutionary." *Time* said it was "a go-to source for researchers studying everything from multiple sclerosis to brain tumors." In 2007, after Allan Jones coauthored a paper on the atlas in *Nature,* user hits on the Web site rose to record levels and are now up to a thousand visitors a day.

WHEN I TRAVEL to scientific institutions, I'm delighted to hear stories of how our atlas has helped the field. "We use it every day," a Stanford neurology professor told the Associated Press after a brief Web site glitch sent worried graduate students pouring into his office. "We can't imagine life without this tool anymore." Like the genome sequence, the brain atlas can save grad students and postdocs years of grind-it-out preliminaries. Researchers can track expression patterns for their gene of interest from our database, and that becomes their starting point. It's like handing prospectors a map of a region's diamond reserves. They can concentrate on the digging, knowing they've been directed toward something of value.

One of the livelier topics at our *charrette* was breadth versus depth. Should we map the entire brain or focus on a single region? The wisdom of a whole-brain atlas is now clear. A Harvard researcher found a receptor gene expressed in the hypothalamus, in one of the few neurons in the brain linked to obesity; the atlas has accelerated his quest for a safe and effective drug therapy for appetite control. At the Seattle Swedish Neuroscience Institute at Swedish Medical Center, another researcher uses our data to zero in on genes with abnormal activity levels in glioblastomas, a lethal form of cerebral tumor. We've heard similar stories from researchers on Alzheimer's, epilepsy, Down syndrome, and just about any other process or disease associated with the brain.

I'm especially excited about the institute's role in what may be a landmark study on the origins of autism, the spectrum of brain disorders that impairs a person's ability to communicate, express emotion, and form social bonds. The project began in 2008, when Autism Speaks funded an effort led by Eric Courchesne of the Autism Center of Excellence at the University of California–San Diego. Courchesne had already established that autism was characterized by excessive brain growth in infants and toddlers, notably in the cerebellum and frontal lobes, but his studies had been limited by low-resolution imaging. Meanwhile, other studies had identified dozens of suspect genes but couldn't tell where they were located or what they might be doing. Courchesne wanted to pinpoint both the genes and their locations to understand what might be setting off the disorder on a molecular level. Fortunately, he had rare postmortem brain tissue from both autistic and normal children. (Previous autism studies had mostly used adult brains, a major drawback for work on a developmental disorder.)

That was where we came in. Our high-resolution techniques enabled us to look more deeply into cellular structure, and to focus in particular on genes that are normally expressed in cells in specific cortical layers. We could then tell if those cells were in the right places in autistic children or not. In essence, we could trace autism's fingerprint.

We began by sectioning brain tissue from both the autistic and control cases. In each, we explored a part of the frontal lobe tied to attention, working memory, and "theory of mind"—the ability to understand that other people have their own perspectives on the surrounding environment. Our goal was to find out whether this area of the brain was organized differently in autistic children.

Using our catalog from the mouse brain atlas and the narrower Allen Human Cortex Study, alongside data from two normal control brains, we identified about twenty genes that were strongly and consistently expressed in the target area. Of those twenty, five had already been implicated in autism. We then studied more than two thousand slides to compare those genes' expression in the autistic and normal brains. We expected to find abnormalities throughout the subregion, and we did. But we were surprised by the form they took: small, self-contained areas that were unusually dense with neurons yet showed a sharp *decrease* in the expression of most of the target genes. These pathological patches, as our scientists called them, existed in all of the autistic subjects. The brain tissue surrounding them appeared completely normal.

Here was powerful evidence that autism might be a *focal* disorder in self-contained local areas in the brain. Most of the pathological patches were measured in millimeters and were easy to overlook in the tight mesh of neurons unless you examined one layer of cortex at a time. Decades of experiments with lower-resolution MRIs had failed to detect them.

The UCSD–Allen Institute study represents a new and powerful way of doing large-scale neuropathological research at the molecular level. Beyond confirming that vaccines cannot possibly cause autism, it reveals clues that may clarify the disorder's developmental origins and help explain why children vary across its spectrum. By understanding the cellular basis for autism, scientists may be able to devise new interventions, from early diagnostic testing to drug and other therapies. It now even seems possible that we might establish the root causes of autism, along with schizophrenia and other diseases, within our lifetimes.

OUR AMBITIONS HAVE continued to grow. The Allen Human Brain Atlas, a four-year project scheduled for completion in 2012, represents a leap in scale and complexity. (The human brain is two thousand times as large as its mouse counterpart; flatten out the human cortex, and it's the size of a seventeen-inch pizza.) The challenges begin with finding suitable tissue. We need brains from "normal" adults between twenty and sixty-eight years old, with no local injuries, drug addictions, or history of neurological or psychiatric disease. (Suicides are ruled out by definition.) And because brain tissue deteriorates within twenty-four hours of death, it can be challenging to get it in time. Thanks to the institute's relationships with NIH-funded brain tissue repositories on both coasts, we have received three brains so far and hope to get ten to complete the initial atlas. That might seem like a small sample for building a reference brain map, but only a small percentage of human genes vary in their pattern of expression across individuals.

Given the amount of staining and scanning involved, it would be impractical to submit the entire human brain to analysis. Following the recommendation of our advisory council, we compromised. As a first step, we're building a comprehensive 3-D atlas that will cover all expressed genes in all areas and offer something for every specialty. Because this first 3-D cut can't get down to the cellular level, we'll also provide a finer-resolution database for up to five hundred genes of especially high value to researchers in each of the major brain structures. Together, these two approaches will furnish unparalleled information about the normal human brain.

Our second game-changing project is the Allen Mouse Brain Connectivity Atlas. At our *charrette,* Richard Axel pointed out that human behavior is primarily controlled not just by the expression of individual genes, but even more so by the physical and bio-chemical pathways that excite or inhibit billions of interdependent neurons. Most current research in this area is limited to efforts to define cell-to-cell or region-to-region connections. Our goal is to tackle the brain as a whole and to illustrate in detail how neurons are wired throughout.

A comprehensive brain circuit map demands new techniques for tracing connections, and the complete data set could run as large as several quadrillions of bytes. But if we succeed, this kind of diagram could dramatically expand our knowledge of how nerve cell communications are altered by disease and how new therapies might most effectively intervene.

DURING MY FIRST flush of excitement over the mouse brain atlas, I met Eric Kandel, the Columbia University neuroscientist who won the Nobel Prize in Physiology or Medicine for his work on memory storage in neurons. I told him, "We're going to know so much more about the brain in the next ten years."

Dr. Kandel gently applied the brakes. "I've been working in this field for fifty years," he said, "and not in my lifetime—and probably not in yours—will we understand the brain."

I was reminded of a question I'd put to the assembled luminaries at our *charrette:* "How many Nobel Prizes will need to be won in neuroscience before we really know how the brain works?" Their responses ranged between twenty-five and fifty.

That's a long, long way from here. In the meantime, I'm confident that our atlases will help those future laureates and speed them on their way.

# CHAPTER 22

# ADVENTURE

I wasn't raised as an adventurer. As a child, I traveled through books, the way my mother did. The piles of *National Geographic* in our basement depicted the larger world out there, but I didn't envision myself as a globetrotter. Then, as a young man at Microsoft, I simply lacked the time to explore. All that changed when I became ill at twenty-nine. I started scuba diving in Hawaii; I came to love France and its culture and cuisine, so different from what I'd known. Still, the last thing I thought I'd ever own was a yacht. Here was my image of boating: a society of snobs who drank Scotch and smoked cigars and wore double-breasted blazers and captain's hats. I wanted nothing to do with it.

But friends kept telling me about the great trips they'd had to Alaska, and that the only way to do it was to charter a boat. In 1992, I rented an eighty-five-footer and took my family up the Inside Passage. We saw a whale swim underneath us, and many others spouting. We dined on fresh spot prawns bought from passing fishermen. In Anan Bay, we watched bears gorge on salmon swimming upstream, so numerous that (as the Indian saying went) you could have walked across the water on their backs.

I had the time of my life. A boat seemed like the best possible way to share my budding passion for exploration, not to mention a terrific platform for my newfound passion for scuba diving. The following year, I was able to buy *Charade,* 150 feet long and five hundred tons, with a crew of ten. It had five staterooms and a Jacuzzi up top. I thought, *My gosh, I'm buying more boat than I'll need.*

Fast forward to a few years later, when my captain said, "What's your ultimate boat, Paul?" I told him that I'd been absorbed by the undersea world ever since my parents took me to see Jacques Cousteau's *The Silent World,* one of the first documentaries with underwater color cinematography, including shots from a two-man submarine. I said that I'd love to have my own sub to take my explorations literally down to the next level. While I wasn't after size for its own sake, a bigger boat could accommodate more of my friends on our far-flung journeys. I also wanted to upgrade my onboard recording studio with a full digital console. Dave Stewart had an idea for a shipboard concert stage, with audience seating on the aft deck.

That's how *Octopus* was born, in the spirit of Cousteau's underwater adventures. I went to Espen Øino, the naval architects based in Monaco, and they created a two-foot model that looked reasonable. Then the work started. It took a full year for more than a hundred draftspeople to design *Octopus,* and three years more for two companies to construct it. Midway through the process, the prime contractor invited me to their shipyard in Kiel, Germany, to show me how they built submarines for the German and Turkish navies. One of them had a torpedo, which piqued my interest. At the end of the tour, I asked them, deadpan, "Could I add a torpedo tube to my yacht?"

The two engineers looked at each other, and you could see the deutsche mark signs going off in their heads. One of them said, "*Ja, ja,* we can add the tube, it's possible to add the tube, *ja.*"

I let the image hang in the air for a few moments before telling them I was joking. And the guy nodded his head and said, "*Ja,* we could have added the tube, but getting the license for the torpedoes, that would have been difficult."

I've owned a couple of other yachts, *Meduse* and *Tatoosh*, but I was stunned by the sheer size of *Octopus* when it was delivered in 2003. At 414 feet, it was a third longer than a football field, more than twenty yards wide, seven stories high. At the time, it was the fourth largest yacht in the world, with the top three built for heads of state. (As the yacht industry continues to extend the realm of the possible, *Octopus* has dropped in the rankings and is now ninth largest overall.) It had a full-time crew of more than fifty and the most advanced nautical technology. When I first stood on the bridge, I felt as though I was on a spaceship.

It took me six months to get used to owning something of that scale. But over the years since, *Octopus* has realized every mission I had in mind for her. All my passions come together in one moveable feast: a basketball court, a movie theater, a swimming pool. The recording studio has ocean views in all directions and is painstakingly soundproofed from engine noise and vibration; it's about as good musically as any in the world. Dave Stewart has recorded there, and so has Mick Jagger. U2 once previewed their latest album on board and played it so loud that they burned out the speakers. We've had too many phenomenal jams in that space to count. Each year we host a shipboard party during the Cannes Film Festival, and the studio becomes a bandstand.

But while *Octopus* is ideal for get-togethers, musical and otherwise, my very favorite spot on the boat might be the most intimate one, a little aerie that seats a few people in total quiet at the very top. I've looked out over the Venice rooftops from there, and the factories and naval yards along the Huangpu River in Shanghai. With a top speed of twenty knots, *Octopus* has the range for long-haul explorations in the tradition of Cousteau's *Calypso,* the minesweeper that carried the oceanographer's crew of scientists and adventurers. It's less a Bentley than a Range Rover.

There's a glass-bottomed room where you can watch the stingrays and jellyfish swim by when you're at anchor, and a remote-controlled robot vehicle with a high-definition camera that can descend to three thousand meters. But no video can capture the immediacy of deep-sea exploring in a submarine twelve hundred feet below the surface. The sub holds eight people and launches from an internal lagoon, like a yellow underwater bus. For some reason, Pink Floyd sets an ideal mood as the surface recedes and the dark envelops us. For the next half hour, we're going down.

Our most memorable dive was onto the hangar deck of the USS *Saratoga*, the aircraft carrier that was sunk in the Bikini Atoll nuclear bomb tests in 1946. Another time we explored an ancient Roman wreck in the Tyrrhenian Sea. The wooden hull had long since rotted away, exposing its cargo of hundreds of graceful, long-necked amphorae, ceramic vases two thousand years old. They were just outside my porthole, close enough to touch.

*Octopus* has a reinforced steel nose to push aside small pieces of ice, and in February 2007 we traveled to the Antarctic. We had a rough crossing; the big boat doesn't roll, thanks to stabilizing wings, but it can pitch in a head sea when the wind is on your bow. As we went south from Ushuaia, Argentina, toward the Antarctic Circle, the iceberg traffic got heavier. Our captain ceded control to a specialist in polar navigation, the ice master. He sat on the bridge with binoculars, in a seeming Zen state, and calmly intoned, "Bring the ship to 273, please. . . . Now bring the ship to 142." He knew how to estimate the size and shape of the ice masses beneath the water, which were eight or nine times larger than what we could see above it.

It was near the end of summer, with the days still tolerably warm (often in the forties) and an endless twilight fading to a night about four hours long. Antarctica is a monstrously beautiful landscape, dead quiet whenever the wind stops blowing. It's a vast white canvas on which nothing has been written, except for chunks of ice a vivid blue where glacial pressure has squeezed out the air bubbles. You can helicopter to a mountaintop, seven thousand feet above sea level, and see fifty miles in every direction—with no sign of a living soul.

We had some unforgettable encounters there: a forty-foot humpback whale circling our tender, with its apple-size eye gazing at us in open curiosity; a bulbous gray leopard seal lazily basking on an iceberg barely large enough to hold it; thousands of squeaking penguins, as tame as puppies. I tried scuba diving in water one or two degrees above freezing, using a canister of argon gas to fill the suit and help keep me warm. The exposed part of my face went instantly numb, and my fingertips stayed blue for an hour after I got out.

SUB-SAHARAN AFRICA is the opposite of the alien Antarctic—hot, rolling landscapes, deep green after the rains come, with the clean smell of wild sage in the air. Strangely, it feels somehow familiar; some think it's our ancestral memory of this cradle of humanity. From the first time I set foot there, it became one of the most special places in the world to me.

I love to venture into Africa's sprawling animal preserves, most of all to see my favorite animals, the elephants. They are smart and curious, and even seem to have a sense of communal responsibility. There's an elephant orphanage in Nairobi for animals up to four years old whose mothers were poached by hunters. The young ones are fed with milk four times a day from the world's largest baby bottles. If a juvenile runs off into the bush before he's ready, wild elephants have been known to escort him back to his keepers.

We met a couple in Botswana who adopted three elephants when they were two and three years old, and that was twenty years ago. If you take a morning walk with one of them, you may find a trunk lightly touching your shoulder, like a friend placing his arm around you. (It's called *beaking*.) In the wild, though, they are a force to be reckoned with, as we discovered on our first trip to that country, in 2006. It was winter there, when male elephants are often in musth, a hormonal condition that's equivalent to a female going into heat. They secrete a pungent discharge from the sides of their heads and are unusually aggressive. When our Land

Rover was a mile or so from camp, we spotted an enormous bull elephant fifty yards away, chomping his way through the grass. Our driver said, "I'm going to drive right past him." And I'd never done this before, but I said, "No, he looks upset, let's stop and let him eat." There was something about the bull's body language that bothered me.

The elephant kept eating till it was almost past us, and then our driver got restless and put the Land Rover in gear. The bull promptly wheeled and charged at full speed from thirty yards. It must have weighed twelve thousand pounds, twice as much as our vehicle. In a collision, we would come out second best.

Everyone's head swiveled toward me, as though I'd know what to do next. But I was a rookie, too, and I had no idea. As the elephant closed to ten yards, a veteran guide named Sandor Carter sprang into action. He jumped up, threw his arms over his head, and shouted, "Knock it off!" The elephant pulled up and stopped and went back to eating. He had charged to let us know we were invading his space. By "getting big," our guide had made it clear that we would assert ourselves, leading the bull to doubt the wisdom of doing battle.

The most memorable part of our trip came in Kenya's enormous Rift Valley, where we stayed by the Maasai Mara game reserve. From a helicopter or hot air balloon, there are zebras and gazelles and wildebeests as far as you can see. They move in concert like a living lawn mower, up from the Serengeti and back down again in a circular path. Prides of lions lie at rest, waiting for the dark and a tasty wildebeest dinner.

The Maasai are a nomadic people who cling to tradition even as they've begun to use cell phones. As part of an animal conservancy that we've supported, they have agreed to let more wild animals return to the tribe's grazing lands in exchange for a share of government tourist fees, which in turn help build schools and basic infrastructure. One night, in a barren salt plain close to the Tanzania border, we celebrated a new dam that we'd funded to bring water to the Maasai and their livestock. (Cattle are their primary asset, and also a source of protein in their milk-and-cow's-blood tonics.) We set up a stage on the reddish, cracked-earth moonscape, with portable generators under an orange canopy. By late afternoon, we had a crowd of more than a thousand Maasai who'd walked dozens of miles to get there.

I was with my band and our special featured singer, Dan Aykroyd, a kindred spirit and true lover of the blues, whose absurdist humor never fails to crack me up. That night he sang and played harmonica, and danced as only Dan can. As we made our way through our set, the Maasai men answered by jumping in their red and orange and turquoise robes, spears in hand. Then a woman's clear voice sailed over the top of their layered chants. We were together in spirit but not always in tempo, and I felt the urge to create a song that would mix our two cultures, like Paul Simon's "Diamonds on the Soles of Her Shoes." But that's not something you can do on the spot, so we stuck with what we knew.

Halfway through Dan's rendition of "Messin' with the Kid," the Maasai suddenly switched from their regional chant to the staccato rhythms of our song. They even changed their dance to a stomp and a little stutter step, mimicking Dan. And they sang along with the chorus:

*What's this I hear, well there's a whole lot of talk,*
*People say they're trying to mess with the kid—hey hey*
*hey. . . .*

It was transcendent, sharing that Junior Wells song with the Maasai on the salt flats. A few bars later, they returned to their original rhythms, but we all felt that we'd connected. The sun set. As the stage lights came on, every six-legged flying thing within miles converged on us, and we called it a night. The Maasai seemed delighted. For most it was their first live encounter with the low frequencies of a bass guitar. As a chief told us afterward, "I liked your music because I could feel it in my stomach." I knew just what he meant. I'd felt the same way, the first time I heard rock live.

FOR VISITORS WHO'D known it mainly from stereotypical jungle movies, Africa is filled with an amazing variety of landscapes and peoples. One of my favorite places is the Okavango Delta in Botswana, where the river ends in an inland estuary and creates a verdant swampland. In the rainy season, when the floodwaters are high, the tops of hillocks become small islands. There are ebony and fig trees and an amazing profusion of predators and prey: hippos, giraffes, impalas, lions, leopards, African wild dogs. A few years ago, I leased Abu Camp. (It's named after its famous late resident, the bull elephant who costarred with Clint Eastwood in *White Hunter Black Heart*.) The camp stables train elephants who have been separated from their herds, and guides will take you through the lagoons in the golden light of the early morning or late afternoon.

I also love the Skeleton Coast of Namibia, where storms from the Kalahari Desert keep pushing the Atlantic coastline westward. In the nineteenth century, untold numbers of New England whaling ships were wrecked there in the treacherous currents. From a helicopter you can see miles of masts and splintered wood, like weathered matchsticks by the brilliant cobalt blue water.

Namibia is a dry, stark, isolated place. It feels like the edge of the earth, and you meet some intriguing people who thrive there. One was a guide named Chris Bakkes, a wild-haired, red-bearded South African who fought in the war in Angola and is also a fine published author. During our first dinner together, there was talk about the monstrous river crocodiles we'd seen that lie in wait for the zebras crossing the water. Trying to make conversation, I asked Chris how close he'd ever come to a crocodile.

The burly guide stared at me, raised the stump of his left arm, and asked, "How close do you *think,* Mr. Allen?" He'd lost the rest of it to a pair of crocs as a young game ranger in Kruger National Park.

Chris sometimes lends his services to Flip Stander, the Cambridge-educated carnivore expert who founded the Desert Lion Conservation Project. Flip lives out of a ramshackle truck and goes everywhere barefoot. He darts lions to sedate and collar them, then tracks their wanderings over hundreds of miles of the Namib Desert. When a collared lion is flagged as it approaches civilization to prey on cattle, Skip rallies Chris and others to set up a Land Rover picket line. The light and noise deter the big cats from coming in and getting killed by the farmers.

On one darting expedition, Skip invited me to check out a sedated lion up close. The animal's forelegs were massive, its paws a foot across. It wasn't so hard to imagine it breaking a zebra's back with one blow.

Skip said, "You need to smell the paw." Ignoring every primal instinct, I knelt down and stuck my nose a few inches from those razor claws. The smell was surprisingly sweet, but I didn't push my luck and linger too long.

IN 2008 I returned to Africa to visit the Bwindi Impenetrable Forest in Uganda, the fertile habitat for half the world's endangered mountain gorilla population. With our guides using machetes to hack a path through the dense vegetation, our party of five trooped down into a sun-dappled ravine. Three hours in, we spotted a big silverback, the alpha male: eight hundred pounds of primate muscle, knuckle-walking up the slope. Whenever we got within twenty yards, he'd move on, not wanting to be bothered. Then I happened to look up. Directly overhead, a juvenile gorilla was sliding down a moss-covered tree. When he was eight feet off the ground, just a few yards away, our eyes made contact in one of the stranger moments of recognition I'll ever have. Then the gorilla grabbed a vine, swung into the brush, and was gone.

From there we had to climb farther down and then up the back side of another ravine. Drenched with sweat in the misty humidity, I felt unusually tired and had to cling to a staff member's pack to get up the last series of hills. I took it as a sign that I was out of shape. I didn't know that I'd soon face the most challenging period of my life.

Two days later, after our tour boat skimmed past colonies of crocodiles and stopped before a stunning waterfall, we cast our lines for some Nile perch. The next thing I knew, I had collapsed in the bottom of the boat. I immediately went back to Seattle, where I had a similar episode on a walk around Green Lake. I felt odd and sat down to have a drink, and then I couldn't get up. An emergency room EKG found an arrhythmia that called for an immediate heart valve replacement. That weekend I was in surgery.

I woke up fitted with some internal technology, my pacemaker. Then one problem led to another, as fluid built up in my left lung. In March 2009, I had the Bill Clinton surgery, in which they deflate the lung and peel off scar tissue. "It went great," the surgeon told me. "Everything's going to be fine." But during a trip to Jordan a few months later, I became so short of breath that I could hardly make it up a flight of stairs. After a buildup of fluid in my other lung, a chest biopsy revealed non-Hodgkin's lymphoma, the disease that had so terrified me when I was misdiagnosed as a young man. I had the most treatable variety, but the cancer was so aggressive that it had already reached stage IV, spreading beyond the lymph nodes.

I was feeling far worse than I had with Hodgkin's, and I thought my number was up—that the deadly threat I'd dodged twenty-five years earlier had finally caught up with me. My internist was optimistic, my oncologist more down the middle. The standard chemotherapy was a cocktail called R-CHOP, which included a monoclonal antibody to stimulate the body's immune system. With luck, it would eradicate the lymphoma, though the odds of a cure were less than 50 percent.

In November 2009, I began treatment: six rounds of chemo, with three weeks between each round. It takes about six hours to pump a dose of R-CHOP into you, and I stayed overnight in the hospital the first time to make sure I could tolerate the treatment. Aside from a mild allergic reaction that turned the top of my head bright red, everything else was normal. Chemotherapy makes your body a battleground, and the first cycle kills so many tumor cells that it stresses your kidneys. There wasn't any nausea, but the fatigue was intense and lasted for days each time.

Early on, I thought I could hunker down and handle everything myself, but it was a bad idea to be alone. Nights were the worst. Jody was terrifically supportive and came over each evening to watch movies. I appreciated the company, though her choice of programming left something to be desired. She recommended a BBC miniseries of a Dickens novel, and at least one or two characters died of tuberculosis in each episode.

"Boy, this is really bleak," I complained.

"What do you expect?" Jody said. "It's *Bleak House.*"

Throughout this difficult period, one of my most regular visitors was Bill Gates. He was everything you'd want from a friend, caring and concerned. I was reminded of the complexity of our relationship and how we always rooted for each other, even when we were barely speaking. It seemed that we'd be stuck with one another for as long as we lasted.

I'd begun working in earnest on this book, and there were days when I feared that I'd never see it in print. It was only after the second round of chemo, when my scans came back nearly clean, that I had any confidence that I might actually pull through. In late April, after my sixth and final round, I nervously awaited the results of another pair of scans. That phone call was euphoric. I was officially in remission.

I wasn't totally back to normal, however. The tips of my fingers were slightly numb for a while from the treatments, which didn't improve my guitar playing. It takes months after the end of chemo before you feel completely normal again.

My illness didn't turn my head around the way Hodgkin's had, but it has left its mark. I want more than ever to cram as much as

I can into life. Shortly before my last treatment, I traveled to Tahiti for my first scuba dive in three years. It went fine, though my pacemaker limited me to a 50-foot descent. (I might go back for an upgrade to a model rated for 220 feet.) A week after my last report, I went white-water rafting in Utah's Cataract Canyon. I love the red-rock canyon lands, and the one-day outing sounded harmless enough. Failing to check the fine print, I hadn't realized that I'd have to splash through twenty-nine separate rapids over a two-hour span or that we'd get battered by the storm of the year, with horizontal rain and forty-mile-an-hour winds. That trip wasn't the smartest thing I'd ever done, and it left me with a touch of pneumonia. But it also affirmed that I was very much alive.

RECENTLY I RETURNED from my annual trip to the Oregon Shakespeare Festival in Ashland, a magical mountain town with some of the best theater on the West Coast. I took in a play called *American Night,* about a young Mexican immigrant who learns about U.S. history in unexpected ways while preparing to take his citizenship test. It was highly satisfying theater, even more so because our foundation's funding helped make it a reality.

I find regional and local philanthropy truly gratifying because you can see how one well-placed grant can make a difference. My first major effort was to help preserve endangered old-growth forestlands in the North Cascades, which circled back to my father's passion for green things and his love of the outdoors. (When you grow up in the Northwest, the impulse to safeguard the environment seeps into your consciousness.) Partnering with the Trust for Public Lands and other conservation groups, we purchased privately owned tracts, reconnected wildlife corridors, and repaired vital ecosystems that lend our region its health and natural beauty.

Of the billion dollars or so that I've given to date, the greater part has supported the work of nonprofits in the five states of the Pacific Northwest, my roots. Now in its twentieth year under Jody's leadership, the Paul G. Allen Family Foundation has five areas of focus that reflect my long-held personal interests: medicine and technology, community development, safety-net social programs, education reform, and arts and culture. In response to the Gates-Buffett challenge, I recently announced my long-held plan to leave most of my estate to these efforts.

In particular, I haven't forgotten my weekly childhood jaunts to the Seattle Public Library and what they meant to my development as a thinker. We've contributed $22.5 million to build an endowment for collection acquisitions and to help construct a children's center in the new downtown facility.

Outside the foundation, much of my giving is channeled into scientific research. I like to inaugurate small investigative programs with breakthrough potential or resuscitate worthy efforts that have stalled for lack of funds. We're also active in support of learning institutions and museums that celebrate some aspect of our common history, like the EMP—or the Flying Heritage Collection in Everett, Washington. Inspired by my father's service in the European theater, I've assembled fourteen vintage warplanes from the main combatants in World War II aviation: the United States, Great Britain, the Soviet Union, Germany, and Japan. They've been painstakingly restored inside and out with period materials, and most of them take to the air on "fly days." Some are the only models of their kind in existence, and all are living relics of sacrifice and bravery. Seeing them takes me back to my boyhood plastic kit model warplanes, which I'd glue together and paint with just the right camouflage markings.

Whenever I visit Flying Heritage, I feel uplifted by the beauty of those machines and their watershed technology. Two days before the museum's formal opening in 2008, I arrived for an emotional moment. Bud Tordoff, an eighty-five-year-old veteran, climbed into the cockpit of the actual P-51D Mustang fighter that he'd flown more than a dozen times over Germany. Bud recounted a 1944 mission on which he'd shot down two enemy planes to protect some B-17s, an event we've been able to document with gun-camera footage. (When the media asked him if he was tempted to fly the plane again, Bud reminded us all of the passing of time. "My wife won't even let me drive," he said.)

While I remain committed to our region, I also want to help Africa, where we're making some small headway at the Abu Camp and my other holdings in Kenya and Zambia. We're supporting vermiculture (worm composting) as part of a project to encourage sustainable farming, along with community development initiatives, micro-enterprise funding, and school subsidies. Recently Jody and I donated $26 million to Washington State University, the largest private grant ever given there, to finish construction of the Paul G. Allen School for Global Animal Health. An important part of the school's mission is to build up Africa's capabilities to respond to animal-based diseases. Research will focus on improving detection, blocking animal-to-human transmission, and discovering new vaccines to protect livestock and all the livelihoods that depend on it.

In years to come, I hope to find new ways to supply electric power and clean water in Africa, and to conserve threatened animal populations in the wild. If we do these things right, we'll create a better future while still guarding and respecting the past.

# IN SUM

When *Saturday Night Live* celebrated its twenty-fifth anniversary in 1999 in New York, Dan Aykroyd took me underneath the stage and flashed back to how it all started for him. "I was mainly a writer," he said, "but then they asked me to do one of the first skits," playing a home security technician who breaks into a home to show a terrified couple—John Belushi and Gilda Radner—that they need his service. Dan admitted he was nervous, "but the skit went great. When I came off the stage, I knew that I'd found what I wanted to do."

I know that feeling. I found my own path when I helped create Altair BASIC in that two-month rush of creativity back in 1975. Later, when the IBM PC shipped with our operating system at its core, it struck me that the code I had helped to write would fundamentally change the way people worked, played, and communicated. Having that kind of impact forever changes your sense of purpose in life. It's a feeling you'll always want to find again.

When I became gravely ill in my twenties, I found myself regretting that my life was so narrowly focused. But after I recovered and traveled the world, I soon became restless. I discovered that what I missed most was *creating* things. And so I went back to work.

If there's any irony to my life, it's that my time with Microsoft was atypically one-dimensional. When I was younger, I immersed myself in rockets, robots, music, and chemistry. An omnivorous reader, I thrilled to the exploits of pilots and explorers. I was inspired by Thomas Edison and Alexander Graham Bell. My curiosity was boundless.

I went on to spend eight driven years with the single purpose of making Microsoft the leader of the personal computer revolution. And it happened, far beyond what I could have hoped or expected. But my old passions still tugged at me, deferred but not forgotten. They were squeezed into playing along with Hendrix at three in the morning or stealing a weekend from coding to watch a momentous spaceflight.

After I left Microsoft, the wealth that I'd helped create there—and then the company's explosive growth—freed me to pick up where I had left off. At times I cast my net too widely. But my choice of ventures wasn't arbitrary. Most of them were seeded long ago, in my youth. Over the last twenty-seven years, I've been able to do things I once only imagined.

I have now lived half my life post-Microsoft. What we achieved there will always be a source of pride. But my second act, in all its range and variety, is truer to my nature.

SOME PEOPLE ARE motivated by a need for recognition, some by money, and some by a broad social goal. I start from a different place, from the love of ideas and the urge to put them into motion and see where they might lead. The creative path is rocky, with the risk of failure ever present and no guarantees. But even with its detours and blind alleys, it's the only road that I find fulfilling.

From early on in the Microsoft era, I was looked at as the source of seminal ideas. These days, my role is often to listen to smart people and recognize when something special has emerged. Then I try to place the thought into a new context or extend it into something more powerful, as we did in our neuroscience *charrette*. The idea of a genetic brain map had been batted about in many private meetings, but it crystallized when a dozen top scientists came together and engaged in a free flow of ideas. The Allen Brain Atlas, a product of their consensus, emerged as the most persuasive way to move the field forward.

Few things worth doing can be done alone. To get past the conceptual stage, ideas need to become crusades; you've got to convince people to join you. I was lucky right off the bat to find Bill Gates, whose passion for business matched mine for tracking technology. Later I'd be fortunate to meet Bert Rutan en route to SpaceShipOne and to find Allan Jones to lead our brain work.

I've also seen what can happen when the right team isn't in place, how the best ideas can founder. I made more mistakes in pursuing the Wired World than I can count, but the first and worst was this: I often failed to find the right people to help me execute my vision. My own history probably swayed me to take a flier on some with slim track records and to entrust them with too much too soon. Since then I have learned to be more careful. Talent is indeed essential, but seasoning and maturity are not to be underestimated.

Above all, I've learned the pitfalls of getting so locked in to looking ahead that you miss the pothole that makes you stumble, or the iceberg that sinks you. Still, any crusade requires optimism and the ambition to aim high. For as long as I can remember, I've wanted to find my own challenges, see them through to fruition, and—if everything breaks right—change the world for the better.

PEOPLE ASK HOW wealth has changed me. It's a question I find difficult to answer. There are times when I feel unaffected, and then I wonder if I'm kidding myself. The manifestations of wealth—homes, boats, planes—have clearly altered how I live and get around. More important, though, are the doors of possibility thrown open to me, the opportunities I've enjoyed.

Yet for all these evident changes, the people I've known longest tell me that I'm much the same in the ways that matter. I still try to take people as I meet them. And I'm still a dreamer more intrigued by what might be doable than by what has already been done.

My recent illness made me more impatient and patient, simultaneously. It was a harsh reminder that there is no time to waste, and it's made me more urgent and demanding of myself and those who work with me. Still, it's humbling to await the results of a PET scan and know that you can't make the clock wind faster. I've come to realize that many things happen at their own pace, beyond your control, from the development of a young point guard to the trial of a potential Alzheimer's therapy. I'm learning to be less harried in anticipation and more accepting of each necessary, incremental step.

I do my best to keep up with science, technology, and current affairs, and most of my reading now takes place online. I want to keep stretching the boundaries of the possible; I want my thinking to stay forward-looking and unconstrained. *What is next?* That's a question that will never get old for me. I'll always be on the hunt for the next Big Idea.

And there's one more thing that hasn't changed. I'm still fascinated by the inner workings of machines of all sorts; I still love to delve into their intricacies. At a minute level of detail, I'm doing it with the Allen Institute's journey to understand the human brain, the most complex mechanism in the history of the planet. At the other end of the spectrum, I'm just now considering a new initiative with that magical contraption I never wearied of sketching as a boy: the rocket ship.

Someone, after all, is going to have to get behind SpaceShipThree.

# ACKNOWLEDGMENTS

The creation of this memoir has followed much the same path as the ideas that compose its subject matter. Inspiration may begin with an individual, but I learned long ago that it does not reach its full fruition without collaborative development. The more ambitious and challenging the project, the more intensive and inclusive that collaboration needs to be.

*Idea Man* was highly challenging and, at least for me, extremely ambitious; it was one of the hardest things I've ever done. And so I have many people to thank. If anyone is omitted here, it reflects the limits of my memory and not of my gratitude.

From start to end, I received vital guidance from what became an in-house editorial board: Richard Hutton, Bert Kolde, Jonathan Lazarus, and David Postman. They put in untold hours reviewing countless drafts and were invaluable as honest critics. I am genuinely in their debt.

For their detailed review and keen-eyed comments on all or parts of the manuscript, I'd like to thank Rich Alderson, Dan Aykroyd, Lea Carpenter, Paul Ghaffari, Allen Israel, Rob Glaser, Mark Greaves, Allan Jones, Tod Leiweke, David Marquardt, Bill McGrath, Larry Miller, Dave Moore, Rosalyn Nguyen, Christina Orr-Cahall, Nancy Peretsman, Pat Peyser, Albert Rich, Alessandra

Rubelli, Doug Shane, Mike Slade, Dave Stewart, William Turner, Jann Wenner, and Mark Zbikowski.

I am grateful to all of those who contributed their recollections of the eventful times we shared—and who helped me to retrieve many memories that enrich this book. From my pre-Microsoft years: Bob Barnett, John Black, Craig Buhl, Monte Davidoff, Mike Flood, Bruce Flory, Doug Fullmer, Paul Gilbert, Tom Grubbs, Guela Johnson, Chris Larson, Marc McDonald, Rita Schenck, Dee Simpson-Snyder, and Jeff Wedgwood.

From the Microsoft period: Richard Brodie, David Bunnell, Don Burtis, Eddie Currie, Pamela Duran, Bob Greenberg, Dottie Hall, Mike Hunter, Gordon Letwin, Kazuhiko Nishi, Bob O'Rear, Tim Patterson, Chris Peters, Vern Raburn, Gary Runyan, Charles Simonyi, Tandy Trower, and Steve Wood.

And from my life after Microsoft: David Anderson, Jim Billmaier, Jim Boyden, Bucky Buckwalter, Sue Coliton, Lance Conn, Terry Davison, Ralph Derrickson, Glenn Edens, Marwan Fawaz, Rob Glaser, Harry Glickman, Mike Holmgren, David Liddle, Mike Melvill, Geoff Petrie, Tom Phillips, Kevin Pritchard, Geoff Reiss, Robbie Robertson, Burt Rutan, Bill Savoy, Neil Smit, Jill Tarter, Jennifer Todd, Nathan Troutman, Larry Wangberg, and Nick Wechsler.

I am also thankful to those who provided more general or logistical assistance for this demanding project: Marilyn Valentine, Jane Repass, Dave Dysart, Anson Fatland, Bill Gates, Steve Hall, Miles Harris, Adrian Hunt, Elaine Jones, Ferina Keshavjee, Ian King, Betty Mayfield, Keith Perez, Allen Range, Nick Saggese, Will Stewart, Andrea Weatherhead, and Nathan Mumm, and the executive support group. And I'd like particularly to thank Erik Davidson, who helped with the jacket design and other graphics.

Jill Jackson, my archivist, helped me locate contemporaneous documents that made this memoir more immediate. I also appreciate the help of Amy Stevenson, her counterpart at Microsoft.

I didn't fully realize it at the time, but the genesis of this book was an oral history project that I initiated in 2000 to preserve first-hand accounts from my school days through the early Microsoft years. My gratitude to Faye Gardner Allen, Chuck Bower, David Dekker, Roger Fisher, Stu Goldberg, Dick Hamlet, Andrea Lewis, Bob McCaw, Rudy Miller, Forrest Mims, Harvey Motulsky, Bud Pembroke, Steve Russell, Paul van Baalen, Nelson Winkless, Bill Weiher, Fred Wright, Marla Wood, Carl Young, and Robert Zaller.

And to those who participated in the oral history project but are no longer with us: Miriam Lubow, Aaron Reynolds, Ed Roberts, Bob Wallace, and Ric Weiland.

I'd like to thank my editors at Portfolio, Adrian Zackheim and David Moldawer, and their talented team: Emily Angell, Katherine Griggs, Jaime Putorti, and Gary Stimeling. And my literary agent, Esther Newberg at ICM, who brought me to them.

I must acknowledge Dr. Brad Harris and Dr. Hank Kaplan for getting me through not one but two lifesaving recoveries, spaced nearly thirty years apart. They made it physically possible for me to finish this book.

I am especially grateful to Valentina Turri, for her extraordinary support throughout this process. And to Jeff Coplon, who helped me to realize the book I had envisioned.

My sister, Jody Allen, has played an indispensable role in my life as my business partner, sounding board, and the adviser who knows me best. As with so many of my initiatives, I couldn't possibly have taken on this project without her encouragement and support.

# APPENDIX: ARTIFICIAL INTELLIGENCE, THE DIGITAL ARISTOTLE, AND PROJECT HALO

Over the past thirty years, researchers have made real progress engineering artificial intelligence (AI) into commercial systems. Automatic translation, speech understanding, reasoning with constraints, logic, game playing, image recognition, and industrial robotics are all well on their way to being mastered. But one benchmark problem still exposes some of AI's deepest remaining challenges: reproducing the simple act of reading a textbook, understanding the material inside, and answering questions about it.

Why is this so difficult for computers? After all, learning new things, working though their implications, and answering questions are all second nature to us—we do them so easily that we rarely stop to consider the mechanisms involved. And computers certainly have enough raw power to do the job; modern search engines can sift through the Web in less than a second and deliver pages that match our search terms, ranked in order of usefulness. Nevertheless, getting a computer to answer ordinary questions of the sort commonly found on high school exams and answered by millions of students is extremely challenging to replicate.

The problem has to do with the nature of human knowledge itself. Knowledge is often thought of as a large collection of facts, like multiplication tables or lists of chemical properties. Indeed, existing artificial intelligence technologies can answer questions that depend only on simple facts. ("How many chromosomes does a blue jay have?"). But the most important elements of human knowledge involve much more sophisticated constructions. Even cut-and-dried knowledge includes rough statements of causality ("Too little sunlight can lead to stunted plants"), generality ("Most birds can fly"), metaphor ("DNA is like a blueprint"), counterfactuals ("If Earth's gravity were halved, trees could be twice as tall"), rule knowledge ("If a cell dies, its cell membrane disintegrates"), and prediction ("Mutations should increase in the presence of radioactivity").

The goal of the Digital Aristotle project is to find ways for computers to grapple with all types of human knowledge, and to manage and manipulate their full range and richness. In order to succeed, it will need to acquire knowledge intelligently, reason through it effectively, and find appropriate answers on a truly massive scale.

Our Project Halo research program is designed to build the systems that can ultimately lead to a functional Digital Aristotle. We began Project Halo several years ago by targeting biology at the level of a high school Advanced Placement course. This subject area served our purpose because it has significant (but not overwhelming) scale, features a set curriculum with accepted tests for competence, and exhibits many of the more challenging types of knowledge. Thus far, we have analyzed standard biology textbooks line by line in order to categorize each type of knowledge they contain. Now we are working on ways to encode these types of knowledge into Project Halo's computers, merge them with the knowledge that is already there, and keep everything in a form that will allow our various reasoning systems to respond with the correct answer to a user's questions.

The basic challenge in all this work is its pervasive brittleness. Many tough problems in computer knowledge encoding and reasoning have been successfully addressed at a small scale in a laboratory. But when these efforts scale up—even to the amount of knowledge in a single biology textbook—they break. Furthermore, the individual approaches are often incompatible with one another, and so current AI systems can't match people's fluid shifts between different ways of using their knowledge.

The international Project Halo team has made considerable progress in our research. We believe that by 2015 we'll be able to build a system that includes most of the knowledge required to answer Advanced Placement–level biology questions. This system, in the form of a tabletlike Halobook, will constitute an important step in our pursuit of the Digital Aristotle. Nevertheless, difficult challenges remain; the ultimate solution will require many more breakthroughs. Here are ten areas of knowledge representation that are currently formidable for machines to handle and are of interest to Project Halo, grouped into three tiers of difficulty:

## I. DIFFICULTY TIER 1: PROMISING APPROACHES STILL HALFWAY AT MOST TO A ROBUST SOLUTION

- *Human language is powerful and complex.* There are many ways of saying the same thing, and many different things communicated in every sentence. For a machine to process the full range of human language, it must "understand" and react appropriately to a huge variety of potential expression. Many promising techniques are being developed using both manual and automated analysis of language, including statistical studies of massive data sets drawn from the Web. The intersection of language and knowledge is an area that we have great interest in and are actively pursuing in Project Halo, dealing with the full range of linguistic expression.

- *Visual/spatial learning and reasoning.* Can seventeen suitcases fit inside the trunk of a typical car? What about an open umbrella? Can a jetliner land on a sidewalk? What information is represented in a diagram? How does DNA uncoil? Humans perform rough-and-ready spatial and visual reasoning tasks and visual simulations with ease. While the computational geometry that is needed for navigation, manufacturing, and architecture exists and is commercially available, progress has been much slower in dealing with the kind of intuitive geometry that we routinely use every day. Project Halo does not currently focus in this area but welcomes new ideas.

- *Knowledge about actions, causality, and simulation.* If a cup is on a table in a room, and a person enters the room, the cup is unaffected; it will still be on the table. But other things do change as a result of this action: the person will no longer be outside the room; the person's body and clothes will be in the room; the room will no longer be empty, and so on. Humans effortlessly perform mental simulations in their heads, both in a "forward" direction to predict how events might play out, and in a "backward" direction to identify likely causes. Computationally, however, this is a difficult and long-standing problem for AI. Reasoning about actions, change, and causality is extremely complex, especially when an action's effects are uncertain and have indirect consequences. The best current solutions are found in business processes, automatic planning, and robotics, but they tend to be highly customized and difficult to apply to new areas. Project Halo has made substantial progress in general reasoning about processes and actions.

- *Handling pervasive uncertainty and vagueness.* Much of our knowledge is uncertain, vague, and approximate, yet we have a remarkable ability to draw conclusions and act. After listening to the weather forecast, a person who knows that it *might* rain can make contingency plans. People can read vague statements ("John is fairly tall"), approximations

("The human genome contains about 23,000 genes"), or statements with exceptions ("All birds can fly") and still draw useful conclusions despite the imprecision. Classic techniques of statistics can already address these issues in selected domains, and may yet work in general, but progress has been slow. Project Halo has made some advances in this area, which remains an important focus of our research.

## II. DIFFICULTY TIER 2: RESEARCH THAT IS STILL PRELIMINARY AND EXPERIMENTAL

- *Unstated and implicit knowledge in language.* Human language is full of ambiguity and gaps in knowledge that a reader or listener must interpret correctly. Take, for example, the statement "A teaspoon of salt is dissolved in water." Is it the teaspoon or the salt that is dissolved? Is the teaspoon made of salt? Humans use knowledge to instantly resolve such ambiguities, while machines struggle. If we read that "acids can cause some dyes to change color," we immediately assume that the acid and dye must be in contact, although it's not explicitly stated. To accurately understand statements like these, our brains make use of a rich interplay between textual and background knowledge. For a computer to have full language understanding, it needs to overcome this critical problem.

- *Evolving knowledge.* Acquiring new knowledge is not simply a matter of memorization. New knowledge always needs to be "fitted in" with existing knowledge in a way that is coherent. For example, if you learn a simple model of how cells divide, and then come across a more complex description, you recognize that you need to align the two, which modifies your original understanding. Perhaps what you originally thought of as a single process now needs to be revised and conceptualized as two linked ones. This process of maintaining, revising, and expanding existing knowledge is critical for large-scale systems like the Digital Aristotle. Simple, specialized techniques for doing this exist, but a fully automated solution seems decades away.

- *Contradictions, fragility, and handling messy knowledge.* While knowledge bases for small- and medium-scale artificial intelligence systems can be fully debugged, knowledge bases above a certain size inevitably become "messy" with errors, inconsistencies, gaps, and contradictions. As the volume of available data and knowledge grows, AI systems need to both effectively debug artifacts and to continue to reason in a robust, sensible way. This challenge becomes particularly significant in Web-scale systems, where sources of knowledge and data may be geographically, culturally, and temporally diverse. A variety of new techniques exist here, from fancy new logics to systems inspired by Web search technology, but they are still experimental. Project Halo is actively working on reasoning techniques that will handle several specific kinds of conflict and contradiction, but general solutions have been elusive.

- *Commonsense reasoning.* A vast amount of our understanding draws on general, commonsense knowledge and rules of thumb. For example, if you are told that "carbon dioxide is a raw material for photosynthesis," you readily infer that carbon dioxide is used in photosynthesis, that it is required and also consumed. You can draw these inferences because you understand these general notions ("raw material," "require," "consume") and the relationships between them. Commonsense knowledge provides great flexibility in human question-answering and reasoning, but correctly applying it in machines is a major challenge. A range of systems now exist, from those that attempt to use the Web to systems like Cyc (www.cyc.com), which are mostly human-authored. But while computers can demonstrate examples of commonsense reasoning, their ability to reliably acquire and use this type of knowledge at the scale required for a Digital Aristotle remains unproven. Project Halo is working to find solutions.

## III. DIFFICULTY TIER 3: SOME OF THE TOUGHEST REMAINING CHALLENGES IN AI

- *Applying knowledge in new contexts.* Humans apply their knowledge in new contexts, constructing innovative and often novel ideas. For example, when a high school student designs an experiment to validate a chemical principle, she is capable of managing her existing knowledge about actions and objects to assemble it into a suitable sequence. We do the same thing when we imagine fictional situations, using what we know in new ways and applying it to new contexts. This ability to manipulate existing knowledge in complex and original ways remains a major challenge for computers. Very little exists in this area beyond preliminary research.

- *Metaphor and analogy.* When confronted with something new, people frequently draw on and adapt what they already know. For example, one biology text states, "Microtubules in the cell are like miniature springs." The analogy prompts a reader to draw on existing knowledge to understand how microtubules expand and contract, yet avoid the conclusion that microtubules are likely made of metal. This skill requires identifying, mapping, and selectively adapting existing mental models to new tasks for which the model was never intended. Such a process remains almost impossible to automate. Very little exists in this area beyond preliminary research.

For each of these types of knowledge representation (and several more), Project Halo is actively seeking solutions worldwide. If you have serious technical ideas in these areas, please contact us at ideas@projecthalo.com.

# INDEX